# MANAGING HUMAN
# RESOURCES AND
# INDUSTRIAL RELATIONS

# MANAGING WORK AND ORGANIZATIONS SERIES

Edited by Graeme Salaman, Reader in Sociology in the Faculty of Social Sciences and the Open Business School, the Open University

Current and forthcoming titles include:

Peter Anthony: *Managing Culture*
Michael Armstrong: *Managing Reward Systems*
David Casey: *Managing Learning in Organizations*
Rohan Collier and Susanne Hickmott: *Sexual Harassment in the Workplace*
Patricia Findlay: *Managing Company Employment Policy*
Paul Iles: *Managing Assessment Processes*
Ian McLoughlin and Stephen Gourlay: *Enterprise Without Unions*
John Storey and Keith Sisson: *Managing Human Resources and Industrial Relations*

# MANAGING HUMAN RESOURCES AND INDUSTRIAL RELATIONS

## John Storey and Keith Sisson

Open University Press
Buckingham · Philadelphia

Open University Press
Celtic Court
22 Ballmoor
Buckingham
MK18 1XW

and
1900 Frost Road, Suite 101
Bristol, PA 19007, USA

First Published 1993
Reprinted 1994, 1995

A catalogue record of this book is available from the British Library

ISBN 0 335 15655 X (pb)        0 335 15656 8 (hb)

*Library of Congress Cataloging-in-Publication Data*
Storey, John
    Managing human resources and industrial relations/John Storey
and Keith Sisson.
        p.  cm. – (Managing work and organizations series)
    Includes bibliographical references and index.
    ISBN 0–335–15656–8  ISBN 0–335–15655–X (pbk.)
    1. Personnel management.  2. Industrial relations.  I. Sisson,
Keith.  II. Title.  III. Series.
HF5549.S878    1993
658.3 – dc20
                                                        93–10116
                                                        CIP

Typeset by Type Study, Scarborough
Printed and bound in Great Britain by
Biddles Ltd, Guildford and King's Lynn

*This book is dedicated to*
*Anne, Jan, Rebecca and David*

# CONTENTS

# PREFACE

This book has been written with two main audiences in mind: practising managers and students of business and management. With regard to the needs of the first, we have tried to attend to their concerns and their agenda but in an academically rigorous fashion. Hence, the book brings the results of research to bear upon issues of the day. It eschews the breathless style associated with so many recent management books which purport to offer easy solutions. We do not believe there are any quick fixes. However, there have been many fascinating developments – most of these only now in the process of unfolding – and there is a pressing need to make an assessment of them.

The managers whom we seek to address are just as likely to be line, general and project managers as they are to be specialist practitioners in personnel management or industrial relations. A crucial feature of the new developments in human resource management has been the way in which vital new initiatives have been driven, as well as delivered, by managers from outside the specialist personnel function. The adage that every manager needs to be his or her own people manager has rarely been as relevant as it is now.

The issues discussed in this book are all of critical contemporary importance. Performance-related reward, quality, training and development, performance management and other themes associated with managing in a highly competitive environment constitute the heart of the analysis. While this is designed to be an introductory text it does not seek to locate these issues within the full historical and theoretical contexts in the way a conventional full-length textbook would aspire to achieve. There are plenty of these latter works which can be consulted for the wider picture. Here we seek to home in on the vital contemporary issues. This treatment should meet the needs of most practising managers who want to be briefed on the main themes. For this segment of our audience the book can be used either for private reading or as part of a short course programme.

The second audience whose needs we have tried to meet will be found among the student population. Here we have in mind MBA students and undergraduates. The latter group of readers is likely to be from a wide range of courses – business, engineering and many more. The common element is the need for a concise, up-to-date analysis of themes and topics relevant to the management of human resources today. With the trend towards modularization there are increasing numbers of students who are exposed to just one main course (or 'module') on the management of the human resource. Conventional texts are not geared to the needs of these students. It is intended that this one will be. To meet their needs the content is up-to-date and relevant to contemporary organizational management practice. The style is intended to be approachable and to the point. The material is arranged into chapters, each of which could appropriately constitute the required reading for a week-by-week programme extending over ten weeks (an increasingly standard 'module' in higher education).

The book is distinctive in two other key regards. The central underlying theme which threads through the analysis is the tension between 'individualistic' versus 'collectivistic' solutions to employment problems. An increasing number of texts make reference to 'individualism and collectivism' as being an important emerging issue. None, so far, has given it any extended treatment. We seek to correct for that. Most books are either 'about' industrial relations or 'about' personnel management. In real situations, problems of motivation, communication, discipline and the wage–effort bargain are suffused with collective and individual aspects. That is how we treat them.

There is a further central rationale to this book. The great bulk of material on personnel management falls into one of two categories. On the one hand, much of it is highly prescriptive. It consists of statements asserting how managers 'should' devise a training programme, evaluate training, conduct appraisal and so on. In some versions this is followed or substituted by 'cookbook' checklists. The problem with this genre is not that advice is proffered (on the contrary, this is a laudable objective). Rather, the problem lies in the lack of contextualization of the prescriptions normally on offer. This is compounded typically by a failure to base the prescriptions upon any adequate body of research.

There is also, however, another genre and this is the descriptive, analytical, context-painting review. Books of this nature trace historical developments and painstakingly weigh the complex forces which shape behaviour. There is sensitivity to process and context. But the problem here is the typical failure to draw-out implications for practice.

In this book we aim to set ourselves demanding objectives – i.e. to analyse the complexities of process and context; to take close note of empirical research findings about actual practice; and in addition, we aim to identify what it all means for the practitioner.

# LIST OF ABBREVIATIONS

| | |
|---|---|
| ACAS | Advisory Conciliation and Arbitration Service |
| AEEU | Amalgamated Electrical and Engineering Union |
| APL | Accreditation of Prior Learning |
| BIFU | Bank, Insurance and Finance Union |
| BT | British Telecom |
| BTEC | Business and Technical Education Council |
| CBI | Confederation of British Industry |
| CEGB | Central Electricity Generating Board |
| CIR | Commission on Industrial Relations |
| COAB | Company Advisory Council |
| DES | Department of Education and Science |
| DPAs | departmental purpose analyses |
| EDAP | Employee Development and Assistance Programme |
| EI | employee involvement |
| GDP | gross domestic product |
| GMB | General, Municipal and Boilermakers Union |
| GNVQ | General National Vocational Qualifications |
| HR | human resources |
| HRD | human resource development |
| HRM | human resource management |
| HRP | human resource planning |
| IDS | Incomes Data Services |

# List of abbreviations

| | |
|---|---|
| IIP | Investors in People |
| IPA | Involvement and Participation Association |
| IPM | Institute of Personnel Management |
| IR | industrial relations |
| IRRR | Industrial Relations Review and Report |
| IRRU | Industrial Relations Research Unit |
| ITBs | Industrial Training Boards |
| JIT | just in time |
| MIT | Massachusetts Institute of Technology |
| MRPII | manufacturing resources planning |
| MSC | Manpower Services Commission |
| NBPI | National Board for Prices and Incomes |
| NCVQ | National Council for Vocational Qualifications |
| NHS | National Health Service |
| NIESR | National Institute of Economic and Social Research |
| NJICs | National Joint Industrial Councils |
| NVQ | National Vocational Qualifications |
| OD | organizational development |
| OECD | Organisation for Economic Cooperation and Development |
| PBR | payment by results |
| PMS | performance management system |
| PRP | performance related pay |
| RDR | Recruitment and Development Report |
| RMT | Rail, Maritime and Transport Union |
| SBU | Strategic Business Unit |
| TECs | Training and Enterprise Councils |
| TQM | total quality management |
| TVEI | Technical and Vocational Education Initiative |
| UCW | Union of Communication Workers |
| USDAW | Union of Shop, Distributive and Allied Workers |
| WIRS | Workplace Industrial Relations Survey |
| YTS | Youth Training Scheme |

# HUMAN RESOURCES AND INDUSTRIAL RELATIONS: THE CHOICE OF RECIPES

---

Just about every book on the subject of managing human resources and many a company chairman's statement, make the same point: it is people that make the difference. The workforce is the most vital asset. Technology and capital can be acquired on varying terms by a wide range of players around the world: the real, sustainable, competitive advantage, or edge, has to come ultimately therefore from the way capable and motivated teams put these resources to work.

Statements such as these are by now well accepted and understood. They largely constitute the conventional wisdom. The message has been repeated *ad nauseam* by whole ranks of management consultants such as Tom Peters and Robert Waterman. The real cause for surprise today therefore is not the message but the plain facts which show how little has been done to put it into effect!

Numerous signs of change are relatively easy to find. But many of these, when subject to close scrutiny, turn out to be fairly superficial in their nature and impact. Other changes which may seem relatively innocuous, such as the redistribution of responsibilities between different management functions, turn out to carry significant consequences. One of the key tasks we set ourselves in this book therefore is to separate the significant from the insignificant; the real change from the apparent; the important issues from the trivial.

In this chapter, to begin our fundamental analysis of the nature and size of the problem, we go back to basics and dissect the employment relationship into its elemental components. These are then synthesized in a series of interlinked frameworks and models.

The title of this book reflects, in itself, something of the change which has swept across the practice and study of people management in recent years. Originally, it was planned that this Open University Press series would have two separate titles to cover the issues discussed in this book. One was to have been entitled *Managing Human Resources*, the other, *Managing Industrial Relations*. However, the current title serves to highlight something of the contemporary blurring of the boundaries between these two subjects. An increasing number of managers now find themselves handling issues which do not fall neatly into either category. Modern strategies and tactics *vis-à-vis* the 'labour issue' frequently contain elements which, in former times, would have been viewed as part of industrial relations *or* personnel management. Essentially, personnel management could be traditionally understood as concerned with policies and practices directed towards the *individual* employee, whereas, industrial relations could be suitably regarded as concerned with *collective* labour issues. The former could be characterized as focused on matters relating to recruitment and selection, appraisal, reward and training. The latter was focused on trade unions, collective bargaining and the handling of collective grievances and disputes.

The interesting development is that this traditional divide between the two realms of practice is becoming less tenable. Managerial initiatives in the 1980s were targeted mainly in the individualistic sphere. Hence, there was extensive interest in new selection techniques such as psychometric testing which were driven by the desire to get the 'right' individuals on board. Likewise, internal direct communications were attended to as a major agenda item. Investments were made in cascade briefings, in a host of company newspapers, magazines and video initiatives. The aim was to speak directly to individual employees rather than indirectly through trade union representatives. Appraisal systems were launched in organizations which previously lacked them, re-launched in those organizations which had previously tried them and extended to new groups. Each individual employee was, through this device, set particular goals and targets. Their progress or lack of progress towards meeting these goals could also be individually monitored. Indeed, the appraisal device was recognized not only as a tool for managing by objectives, its potential for tracking conformance to pre-designated behavioural norms was also recognized. The spread of appraisal across the workforce at all levels expresses the trend towards *individualization* of the employment relationship in clear terms.

Meanwhile, during the period when these sorts of initiatives were proceeding apace, the management of industrial relations was de-emphasized. This has occurred in two ways: through the pushing of trade union affairs to the margins of managerial concern and second, through the constriction in the range of issues brought to, or allowed, within the sphere of collective bargaining. As the Employment Department's most recent survey reveals (Millward et al., 1992: 102) the recognition of trade unions for jointly determining pay 'registered a substantial decline over the decade'.

The consequence of these policies and practices was a *dualism* in human resource management and industrial relations which was of a different order to that which had previously existed. Formerly, the prime thrust in employer strategies with regard to the mass of the industrial workforce had centred on ways and means of dealing with trade unions. Personnel management, as distinct from industrial relations, had confined itself to administrative arrangements relating to recruitment and selection, wage administration, training, and the like. The 'new dualism' meant that initiatives were driven in spheres largely outside industrial relations and the latter was now maintained in ticking-over mode.

The signs are, however, that the mid to late 1990s are likely to witness a new agenda. This will involve a clearer articulation between the erstwhile largely separate categories of industrial relations and human resource management. The pressures for change derive from an altered configuration in political, economic and cultural forces. The consequence of these changes is that the handling of *both* collective and individual issues (in unison) is likely to be the essential management requirement during the forthcoming period. This theme is also the focal point of this book.

# Changing recipes

For much of the period following the ending of the Second World War in 1945, the conventional wisdom in labour relations was that 'good practice' equated with formalized procedures. To a large extent, government led the way. A characteristic constituent feature of all of the nationalization acts in the late 1940s was the inbuilt statutory requirement for managers of the new public corporations to negotiate and consult with recognized trade unions. Official encouragement was also given to private sector companies to follow this example of (the then) 'good practice'.

Continuation of, and indeed elaboration of this formula, could be seen clearly in the report of the Royal Commission on Trade Unions and Employers' Associations (Donovan, 1968). The analysis made by the commissioners was that the prevailing levels of industrial disruption were too high and that the source could be traced to inadequacies in the institutional arrangements which were supposed to regulate these things. The national or industry-level negotiating bodies such as the National Joint Industrial Councils (NJICs) were perceived as failing in this task. For a host of reasons, much of the activity in industrial relations had shifted to the level of the workplace.

Activity at this level was typically more difficult to control and regulate. Arrangements were fragmented and dispersed. The nature of the relations between, for example, plant managers and individual shop stewards were highly informal. Agreements were usually makeshift and unwritten. The Commission's classic recommendation was that the divide between the 'two systems' (the first of these being the formal national-level arrangements and the second being the informal local arrangements) should be closed by moving towards the *formalizing* of the latter. The solution can be seen as an elaboration of the received notion of good practice as it had been understood in Britain for some decades.

At first sight the incoming Conservative government took a more radical step and departed from the British tradition by copying large tracts of American labour law. The 1971 Industrial Relations Act installed a legislative framework for the control of industrial conflict. The tradition of voluntarism was breached in significant ways. Mechanisms for compulsory recognition of trade unions were put in place; a cooling-off period prior to the commencement of industrial action was drafted and legislative controls were placed on the conduct of strikes. Trade union opposition to the legislation was adamant. The gaoling and subsequent release of London dockers' leaders cast the new legislation into disrepute. The campaign of industrial opposition was a key contributor to the fall of this Heath-led administration in 1974. It is important to note, however, despite the significant legislative departure from the tradition of voluntarism which the 1971 Act entailed, a central plank of the statute marked a continuation of the basic official philosophy in Britain – this was the centrality of *collective bargaining* as the declared preferred path to the management of industrial relations. In that Act, the provisions for statutory recognition, for legal enforceability of collective agreements and even the emergency procedures for handling conflicts which did occur, could be viewed as essentially about trying to make collective procedures work.

This central plank remained in place during the subsequent period of Labour rule (1974–9). The 1971 Industrial Relations Act was repealed and the pre-existing arrangements with collective bargaining at the core were, for all intents and purposes, reinstated. The main point of distinction was that a framework of industrial labour law was put in place. Much of this was borrowed from modern European practice and entailed employment protection as guaranteed by a recourse to law through a newly created network of industrial tribunals. Part of the thinking behind this framework of employment rights was that there would be less need for a recourse to industrial action if redress for peremptory dismissal and similar felt injustices could be pursued through the courts.

Clearly reflecting this same recipe was the elaboration of *procedures* within individual companies for all manner of problems relating to discipline and grievance handling. 'Sophisticated companies' were, it was maintained, already pursuing these steps anyway. The need for the official spelling-out of these formal procedures was mainly to disseminate this modern good practice to the less enlightened. The Codes of Practice on discipline and grievance handling as promulgated by the Advisory Conciliation and Arbitration Service (ACAS) provide good examples of this approach. Notably, these codes were not in themselves legally mandatory in any direct sense. However, observance or breach of these formulations of recommended practice could be used in tribunals and courts as evidence of behaviour should a case be brought to law.

The fundamental point to note in this resumé of post-war industrial relations is the centrality of installing and following procedures as the *leitmotif* of acceptable practice. Granted, there were numerous layers of subtlety in the way seasoned practitioners (on either side) would have recourse to, and use, these procedures, but the critical factor was the necessity for proceduralizing as the very foundation stone for all of this.

This recipe was to be abruptly played down, if not entirely discarded, during the 1980s. At the beginning of that decade the talk was of 'macho management' and of retribution for the humiliations suffered by management at the hands of the unions during the preceding period. But a parallel theme and concern was the lack of direction in managerial thinking. What were managers going to do with their newly found, or newly rediscovered, power? Did they know what to do with it? These doubts found expression at the beginning of the 1980s. As the decade progressed, however, a veritable flood of initiatives, programmes and philosophies appeared to dispel all such worries.

Before analysing the nature of these developments any further, it is useful to remind ourselves that there are, in fact, many potential and actual approaches to managing a labour force. The most notable attempts to classify the various types have been made by Fox (1974), Purcell and Sisson (1983), Guest (1990) and Purcell and Ahlstrand (forthcoming). Fox (1974) forged the way with his codification of four 'styles': traditionalist; sophisticated paternalistic; sophisticated moderns; and standard moderns.

1 The *traditionalist* style is based on a firm belief in management's right to manage without interference. It is characterized by adamant hostility to trade unions and is associated therefore with a refusal to recognize unions – still less to negotiate with them.

2 The *sophisticated paternalistic* style is also marked by opposition to trade unionism but it differs from the former in the way in which the management of companies practising this style bring to bear an array of benefits and positive personnel devices to substitute for collective bargaining. These include above-average arrangements relating to pay, welfare and consultation.

3 *Sophisticated moderns* are sophisticated in a rather different way. They recognize that, at least in certain industries, it would be unrealistic to seek to defend absolute managerial prerogative. Workforce expectations of trade union representation are met with a set of measures which legitimate these expectations but which none the less seek to contain and channel the consequences. Thus joint procedures which can contain and institutionalize conflict are honed.

4 *Standard moderns* represent the pragmatic stance. This is perhaps the predominant style in Britain. It is reactive and opportunistic rather than principled. The approach adopted at any one time will depend primarily upon the nature of the pressures experienced.

The vital distinction between these various types can perhaps best be seen as resting upon whether trade unions are recognized or not. Fundamentally, this raises the issue as to whether the emphasis in the managerial approach will be upon the individual or the collective. Trade union recognition and all that flows from it may be regarded as either a 'given' or a decision to be made (or a combination of both). Wherever the balance may rest, the issue can be seen as a crucial one. Individualism and collectivism or individualism versus collectivism is the continuing thread running throughout this book. Whether consciously realizing it or

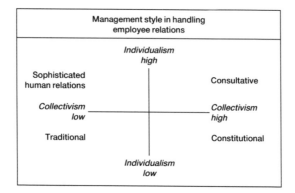

| Management style in handling employee relations | |
| --- | --- |
| | |

Individualism
high

Sophisticated human relations      Consultative

Collectivism
low      Collectivism
high

Traditional      Constitutional

Individualism
low

**Sophisticated human relations**
Employees (excluding short-term contract or subcontract labour) are viewed as the company's most valuable resource. Firms adopting this style often deliberately have above-average pay, and clear internal labour market structures with promotion ladders; periodic attitude surveys are used to harness employees' views. Emphasis is placed on flexible reward structures, employee appraisal systems linked to merit awards, internal grievance, disciplinary and consultative procedures and extensive networks and methods of communication. The aim is to inculcate employee loyalty, commitment and dependency. As a by-product these companies seek to make it unnecessary or unattractive for staff to unionize.

**Consultative**
Similar to the sophisticated human resource companies except that unions are recognized. The attempt is made to build 'constructive' relationships with the unions and incorporate them into the organizational fabric. Broad-ranging discussions are held and extensive information provided to the unions on a whole range of decisions and plans, including aspects of strategic management; the 'rights of last say', though, rests with management. Emphasis is also placed on techniques designed to enhance individual employee commitment to the firm and the need to accept change (share option schemes, profit-sharing, briefing or cascade information systems, joint working parties, quality or productivity circles/councils).

**Constitutional**
Somewhat similar to the traditionalists in basic value structures, especially for unskilled and semiskilled workers, but unions have been recognized for some time and accepted as inevitable. Employee relations policies centre on the need for stability, control and the institutionalization of conflict. Management prerogatives are defended through highly specific collective agreements, and careful attention is paid to the administration of agreements on the shopfloor. The importance of management control is emphasized with the aim of minimizing or neutralizing union constraints on both operational (line) and strategic (corporate) management.

**Traditional**
Labour is viewed as a factor of production, and employee subordination is assumed to be part of the 'natural order' of the employment relationship. There is often a fear of outside union interference. Unionization is opposed or unions kept at arm's length.

**Figure 1.1** Models of management style
*Source:* Sisson (1989: 10)

not managers are likely to be influenced in their actions by their presuppositions and their situation with regard to the union/non-union question.

Figure 1.1 summarizes the amendments which Purcell and Sisson (1983) have made to Fox's typology. It uses the individualism-collectivism dimensions to show that certain ideal-types of managerial approach to labour management can be best located by considering them in relation to the individualism-collectivism issue. As the figure shows, it is possible for managers to combine elements from both. Thus the top right quadrant contains the 'consultative' type. This label is used to signify those approaches where unions are recognized but, in addition, emphasis is also placed on the steps which can engage the commitment of individual employees.

In response to criticisms that the management styles matrix presents the approaches in a rather static way, Purcell and Ahlstrand (1993) have re-cast it to allow for movement from one type to another. Figure 1.2 illustrates this point.

For illustrative purposes just two forms of movement are picked-out for special notice. Arrow number 1 indicates those instances where employees are encouraged to sign new individual contracts, and union recognition for collective bargaining purposes is withdrawn. New forms of performance management are likely to be introduced along with greater attention to training and welfare measures. A number of the new National Health Service (NHS) Trusts attempted to move in this way. A second type of movement is indicated by arrow number 2 where bargained constitutionalism gives way to a 'sophisticated consultative' approach. Here, cooperative, consultative relations with trade unions are fostered using company councils while, at the same time, a new emphasis is given to policies which engender employee development.

Guest's (1990) typology is illuminating because it reveals sharply how human resources management (HRM) can be regarded as but one *sub*-category in a range of options or possibilities. The first category is labelled 'traditional/conservative'. Under this mode the emphasis is upon cost minimization. This is perceived to be attained through a hard-nosed approach to labour demands. The tradition may survive

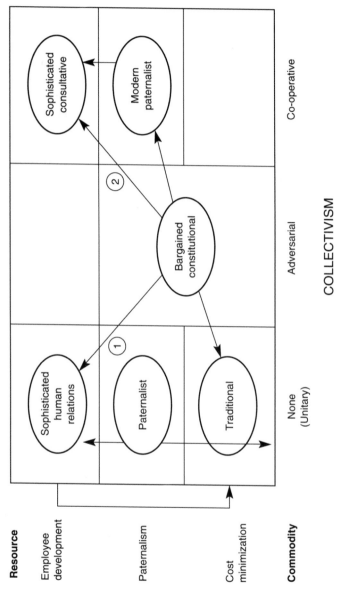

**Figure 1.2** Movements in management style in employee relations
*Source:* Adapted from Purcell and Ahlstrand (1993)

because of lack of imagination or knowledge about how things might be otherwise or because of a belief that this approach works sufficiently well and other approaches would carry too much risk. A second category is labelled 'radical/conservative'. This is characterized by a tough programme of redundancies and plant closures; a confrontation with and facing-down of the unions and a re-assertion of managerial prerogatives. Michael Edwardes' stint at British Leyland is the archetypal case in point. The third, 'pluralist/innovative', features such 'new' devices as quality of working life programmes and close cooperation/collaboration with the unions. This is the new industrial relations model. It has figured rather more in the United States than in Britain and has been associated, for example, with concession bargaining where trade unions cede certain terms and conditions including wage cuts in exchange for security of employment commitments.

The fourth category, 'unitarist/innovative' shares the innovatory characteristics with the previous one but is markedly different in that these new initiatives are entirely driven by management and often in circumstances where there is perceived to be no legitimate place for unionism. The approach contains two sub-categories: HRM and 'behavioural Taylorism'. HRM we have already discussed but behavioural Taylorism deserves some explanation and comment. It entails the use of sophisticated behavioural science techniques such as winning commitment to a team, interlaced with elements of Tayloristic work design principles such as clear task definition and circumscribed discretion in job performance. Disney theme parks, McDonald hamburger restaurants and Bodyshop stores seem to display many aspects of this approach.

Euro-Disney, located near Paris, illustrates 'Behavioural Taylorism' nicely. The recruitment of 12,000 employees in early 1992 has been described as 'West End musical meets McDonalds'. Recruits are not described as employees but 'cast members' and they are not allotted to jobs but 'cast for a role' following not selection but 'auditions'. Induction is intense. Cast members are imbued with the Disney ethos, history, standards and values. Communications, marketing and training become one. Publications, bulletins, orientation and training sessions inculcate and reinforce a consistent set of fundamental messages about quality and the priority of service to guests. The nature of the task and the way it should be performed day in and day out has already been preconceived by senior management. The vital element which remains for the management of employees therefore is to ensure understanding of the role and the acceptance of its consistent performance to a consistent standard. The aspects of Taylorism are plain. Conformance methods have, however, moved on – in addition to careful selection and training there is careful attention to fostering a willing acceptance of these norms.

It is evident from the above that there are *options* available among an array of different approaches to managing employees. This is very much in line with contingency theory in social science – that is, the choice of an appropriate stance is dependent upon the particular configuration of circumstances and there is no universal best way to manage. However, there has been an increasing volume of claims that trends are discernible in preferred approaches. This could imply that environmental circumstances have changed in such a way as to render certain traditional recipes less relevant and that other recipes are increasingly appropriate. An example of such a shift might be the widespread popularity of Rosabeth Moss Kanter's (1984) formula for responsive, adaptive organizational forms. This 'modern' model is very similar to Burns and Stalker's (1961) 'organic' form, one which they suggested was suited only to limited circumstances. Arguably, such circumstances have now become the norm and hence the notion has grown that this is an idea whose time has come.

Just such a general movement from 'mechanistic' to 'organic' form is reflected in the constellation of managerial and organizational responses to heightened international competition. The famous analysis of business strategy made by Michael Porter (1980; 1985) identifies one path to 'competitive edge' as deriving from a differentiation strategy based on innovation and another one based on quality enhancement. These forms of distinctive advantage (when regarded as pure types) can be seen as archetypal modern responses which have supplemented 'cost minimization' as favoured recipes. An aspiration to compete through innovation and quality suggests a need for human resource policies which are fitted to those business strategies.

The associated HRM formula reveals marked similarities with other associated summaries of change including, for example, those known as the 'flexible firms' model and 'Japanization'.

Each of these sets of analyses (adaptive/organic forms and differentiation strategies) posits a major shift in the rules of competitive advantage. Changing product market conditions collude with changing production technologies to render increasingly obsolete the standardization and cost minimization strategies associated with the mass production era. Taylorism and Fordism are seen to give way to a new order with a different set of rules. This new state of affairs involves adaptability, customized products and services and quality. In turn, these require a different set of *behavioural characteristics* in the workforce. In other words, the underlying expectation of what is needed from the workforce undergoes a shift. Under conditions of relative stability employees are expected to follow rules, perform efficiently, be compliant and work within known parameters. Under conditions of instability markedly different behaviour patterns are required: employees are expected to foresee opportunities and be adaptable, attend to quality and seek out continual improvements, be flexible, proactive and creative, and work comfortably within complex and ambiguous settings.

This depiction of changing priorities in required behavioural characteristics is reflected also in Schuler and Jackson's (1987) classification of 'needed role behaviours' which are at a premium under different business strategies. For example, when the corporate strategy hinges on innovation the required employee behaviours relate to creativity, a longer-term focus, risk taking and a high tolerance of ambiguity and unpredictability. A corporate strategy based on competitive advantage gained through quality enhancement places a premium on employee behaviour which displays a high commitment to the goals of the organization and which shows a great concern for process.

This discovery of the importance of the human side of enterprise lies at the heart of the best-selling packages marketed by gurus such as Philip Crosby, W. Edwards Deming, Tom Peters and Robert Waterman. The pivotal idea for each of these is the need for a way of managing which induces a competent, flexible and committed workforce. A workforce, that is, which does not

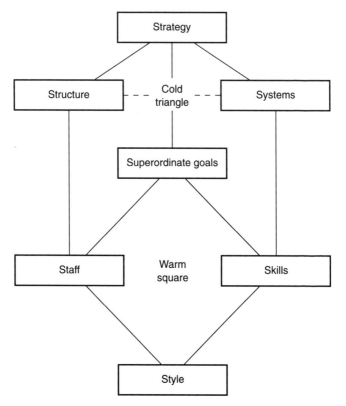

**Figure 1.3** The McKinsey 7S diagram

merely passively follow rules and directives but which produces ideas, seeks out continual improvements, and responds spontaneously to ever-changing customer requirements.

The shift in business education from the 1970s-style stress on business planning and quantification to a wider spectrum of factors which include also the 'softer' issues of culture and style, is well captured in the McKinsey '7S framework'. This draws attention to the perceived most important factors in effective management. Moreover, its originators maintain that all seven of these elements must be in harmony if the corporate strategy is to be successful. The increased emphasis given in recent years to the softer Ss is emphasized in the 'cold triangle' and 'warm square' version of the McKinsey 7S model. This is shown in Figure 1.3.

The four elements in the warm square: superordinate goals (i.e. overarching values), skills, management style and staff, are all evidently elements firmly within the realm of human resource management. The model is at once suggestive of the kind of end-state to be desired and of the factors which need shaping if that end-state is to be attained or approached. The framework is, however, not a theory. It does not set out an interrelated set of testable propositions. What it does do is point to factors which are perceived to be important. The human resource management idea has in a sense used this framework as a springboard. HRM as a *distinctive* approach to managing labour elaborates upon the original 7S framework.

## The coming of human resource management

Human resource management (HRM) began to emerge in Britain in the middle to late 1980s. As a set of ideas and practices it originated in the United States where, in turn, it can be seen as the Americanized version of 'Japanese' methods. Human resource management has proved to be a highly controversial concept. Controversy revolves around three aspects:

1 the meaning of the concept
2 evidence of take-up and implementation
3 consequences of implementation.

Each of these is worth attending to in turn.

### The meaning of human resource management

What are the constituent elements of HRM? One rather quick way to grasp the notion is to contrast HRM with the pragmatic style discussed above. It was suggested earlier that the pragmatic style has long been the predominantly practised mode. If it could be shown that there were signs of a shift along each of the identified dimensions from the pragmatic to HRM, then this

| | Dimension | Personnel and IR | HRM |
|---|---|---|---|
| | | Beliefs and assumptions | |
| 1 | Contract | Careful delineation of written contracts | Aim to go 'beyond contract' |
| 2 | Rules | Importance of devising clear rules/mutuality | 'Can do' outlook: impatience with 'rule' |
| 3 | Guide to management action | Procedures/consistency control | 'Business need'/ flexibility/commitment |
| 4 | Behaviour referent | Norms/custom and practice | Values/mission |
| 5 | Managerial task *vis-à-vis* labour | Monitoring | Nurturing |
| 6 | Nature of relations | Pluralist | Unitarist |
| 7 | Conflict | Institutionalized | De-emphasized |
| 8 | Standardization | High (e.g. 'parity' an issue) | Low (e.g. 'parity' not seen as relevant) |
| | | Strategic aspects | |
| 9 | Key relations | Labour-management | Business-customer |
| 10 | Initiatives | Piecemeal | Integrated |
| 11 | Corporate plan | Marginal to | Central to |
| 12 | Speed of decision | Slow | Fast |
| | | Line management | |
| 13 | Management role | Transactional | Transformational leadership |
| 14 | Key managers | Personnel/IR specialists | General/business/line managers |
| 15 | Prized management skills | Negotiation | Facilitation |
| | | Key levers | |
| 16 | Foci of attention for interventions | Personnel procedures | Wide-ranging cultural, structural and personnel strategies |
| 17 | Selection | Separate, marginal task | Integrated, key task |
| 18 | Pay | Job evaluation: multiple, fixed grades | Performance-related: few if any grades |
| 19 | Conditions | Separately negotiated | Harmonization |
| 20 | Labour-management | Collective bargaining contracts | Towards individual contracts |
| 21 | Thrust of relations with stewards | Regularized through facilities and training | Marginalized (with exception of some bargaining for change models) |
| 22 | Communication | Restricted flow/indirect | Increased flow/direct |
| 23 | Job design | Division of labour | Teamwork |
| 24 | Conflict handling | Reach temporary truces | Manage climate and culture |
| 25 | Training and development | Controlled access to courses | Learning companies |

**Figure 1.4** IR and HRM: the differences
*Source*: Storey (1992: 35)

would indicate a departure of some real significance. Figure 1.4 shows the contrasts in ideal-typical fashion.

The key variables are drawn from the literature and from practitioners' own accounts of their actions. The two resulting sets are mirror opposites of each other: each finds its identity in relation to the other.

We will turn in a moment to report on the findings from a recent study which used these 25 variables to track actual change in British employment methods. But before doing this it is necessary to attend to a crucial feature of Human Resource Management. As Storey (1987) pointed out, human resource management has its 'hard' and its 'soft' dimensions. The hard aspects place emphasis on the idea of resource – that is, something to be used dispassionately and in a calculative, formally rational manner. The soft usage lays emphasis on the term human, thus conjuring up echoes of the human relations movement and a stress on employee development, group relations and constructive supervision.

What is striking is that the same term is thus capable of signalling diametrically opposite sets of messages. Hence, some observers are found objecting to the term 'human resource management' because it smacks of an instrumental treatment of people, while conversely, other critics are inclined to dismiss it because it connotes a vapid, liberal approach to management.

In sum, the hard face of HRM emphasizes the 'quantitative, calculative, and business strategic aspects of managing the headcount resource in as "rational" a way as for any other economic factor' while the soft face emphasizes 'communication, motivation and leadership' (Storey, 1987: 6).

It is easy to see that the hard face of HRM will often place it in confrontation with trade unions – especially in those settings where unions still retain some strength. For example, London Underground's wide-ranging plan consists of a package of measures which include staff reductions, salary status for all employees, the abolition of premium pay for weekend working, a reduction in the number of separate grades of staff from 400 to 70, and the replacement of promotion based on seniority to one based on assessed merit. A central plank in its attempted reform of working practices is the tackling of 'split shifts' where drivers work the morning and evening rush hours, take the middle part of the day off but are paid for 12 hours. At the time of writing the Rail, Maritime and Transportation Union (RMT) is planning an indefinite strike in response to a breakdown in negotiations on this package.

But even the 'soft' aspects – increased communication with employees, team participation techniques, harmonization of terms and conditions, appraisal and reward – can lead to difficulties between management and unions. The basic reason for this is that whether the hard or soft aspects are being activated, HRM in broad terms represents, or is seen as, a departure from the 'joint procedure' formula. To this extent, Guest's (1989) summation would seem to be correct: HRM and trade unionism are incompatible.

But under competitive conditions some sort of *modus vivendi* between industrial relations and HRM (between collectivism and individualism) would appear to be necessary. In some situations managers may choose to take the route of trying to dispense with the unions and thus clear the way for human resource management methods without the need for compromise. Certain greenfield site start-ups and certain NHS Trusts have taken this path. But in the latter cases there are examples where the reality of continuing union membership and the lack of trust emanating from management's refusal to recognize trade unions has eventually led to a decision to recognize the union – albeit on terms relatively more favourable to management than hitherto.

The implication is that in the larger number of cases in the British context some degree of *balance* between individualism and collectivism will have to be struck. This will clearly involve compromises by both sides. The precise nature of that balance and the way it can be managed is currently something of an open question. This issue is at the cutting edge of contemporary practice in the management of human resources and industrial relations. In large measure it is the central theme traced throughout this book.

### Evidence of take-up and implementation

Using the 25 key HRM variables as a checklist of critical issues it becomes possible to measure the degree of movement from one approach to the other. This exercise was taken in relation to 15 mainstream companies (Storey, 1992). In summary form the pattern of results is revealed in Figure 1.5.

The way in which the data was derived is of crucial significance here. The ticks, crosses and black dots are not simply the usual record of respondents' replies to a survey. They are the researcher's own judgements based on multiple sources of information. Two particular problems in devising the figure should be noted. The first is the problem of continuity. In many of these cases there would be a particular period of time when one or more of the 25 features was clearly being given paramount attention. A year later the emphasis might well have shifted to a new initiative. For the purposes of this figure a tick is recorded where the criterion in question was, at some point during the research, being given clear emphasis. It does not mean that the particular item persisted necessarily for more than a few months as a key feature of the organization's employment management approach. The second difficulty in constructing such a simple summary of complex findings is the way in which, in practice, initiatives may be directed at only one part of the workforce and not another. This in fact was found to be quite a normal state of affairs. Certain levels or certain divisions might be included or excluded for all sorts of different reasons. In these instances a black dot is used to indicate an 'in part' score.

The figure can be read both horizontally and vertically. Horizontally one gets a picture of the take-up or neglect of the key HR dimensions. Reading vertically the figure reveals those organizations which had adopted, or experimented with, HRM-style practices with most vigour. The overall pattern, in itself, reveals some fascinating results. Notable first of all is the extensive take-up of HRM-style approaches in the British mainstream organizations. Two-thirds of the companies recorded a definite tick scoring on at least 11 of the dimensions. The level of managerial activity is indicated even more forcefully if one takes into account the 'in parts' scoring device as well as the definite tick. Such has been the apparent level of engagement with these new sets of beliefs, values and practices that the evidence points to a wholesale shift away from the proceduralist recipe in our major employing organizations.

| | Austin Rover | British Rail | Bradford Council | Eaton Ltd | Ford | ICI | Jaguar | Lucas | Massey Ferguson | NHS | Peugeot-Talbot | Plessey | Rolls-Royce | Smith & Nephew | Whitbread | |
|---|---|---|---|---|---|---|---|---|---|---|---|---|---|---|---|---|
| **Beliefs and assumptions** | | | | | | | | | | | | | | | | |
| 'Business need' is prime guide to action | ✓ | ✓ | ✓ | ● | ✓ | ✓ | ✓ | ✓ | ✓ | ● | ✓ | ✓ | ✓ | ✓ | ✓ | 13 |
| Aim to go 'beyond contract' | ✓ | ● | ✓ | ✓ | ✓ | ✓ | ✓ | ✓ | ● | ✓ | ✓ | ● | ● | ✓ | ✓ | 11 |
| Values/mission | ✓ | ● | ✓ | ✓ | ✓ | ✓ | ✓ | ✓ | ✓ | ✓ | ✓ | ● | ● | ✓ | ✓ | 11 |
| Impatience with rules | ✓ | ✓ | ✓ | ● | ● | ✓ | ✓ | ✓ | ● | ✓ | ● | ● | ● | ● | ✓ | 10 |
| Standardization/parity not emphasized | ✓ | ● | ✓ | ● | ● | ✓ | ● | ✓ | × | × | ✓ | × | × | ✓ | ● | 8 |
| Conflict de-emphasized rather than institutionalized | ✓ | ✓ | ● | ● | ● | ✓ | ● | ● | ● | ● | ✓ | × | ● | ✓ | ✓ | 5 |
| Unitarist relations | ● | ● | × | × | ● | ● | ● | ● | × | × | ✓ | × | × | × | ✓ | 2 |
| Nurturing orientation | ● | × | × | ● | ● | ● | ● | ● | ● | ● | ● | ● | ● | ● | ● | 0 |
| **Strategic aspects** | | | | | | | | | | | | | | | | |
| Customer-orientation to fore | ✓ | ✓ | × | ● | ● | ✓ | ● | ✓ | ✓ | ● | ✓ | ✓ | ✓ | ✓ | ✓ | 11 |
| Integrated initiatives | ✓ | × | × | ● | ● | ● | ● | ● | ● | ● | × | × | × | × | ✓ | 3 |
| Corporate plan central | ✓ | ● | × | ● | ● | ● | ● | ● | × | ● | × | ● | ● | ● | ✓ | 3 |
| Speedy decision-making | ✓ | × | × | ● | ● | ● | ● | ● | × | × | ● | × | × | × | ✓ | 2 |

Line managers

| | | | | | | | | | | | | | | | |
|---|---|---|---|---|---|---|---|---|---|---|---|---|---|---|---|
| General/business/line managers to fore | √ | √ | √ | √ | √ | √ | √ | √ | √ | √ | √ | √ | √ | √ | 15 |
| Facilitation is prized skill | √ | √ | √ | √ | √ | √ | √ | ● | √ | √ | × | ● | ● | √ | 9 |
| Transformational leadership | √ | × | ● | ● | ● | ● | ● | √ | ● | ● | ● | ● | ● | ● | 4 |

Key levers

| | | | | | | | | | | | | | | | |
|---|---|---|---|---|---|---|---|---|---|---|---|---|---|---|---|
| Increased flow of communication | √ | √ | √ | √ | √ | √ | √ | √ | √ | √ | √ | √ | √ | √ | 15 |
| Selection is integrated key task | √ | √ | √ | √ | √ | √ | √ | ● | √ | √ | √ | ● | × | √ | 12 |
| Wide-ranging cultural, structural and personnel strategies | √ | √ | ● | √ | √ | √ | √ | √ | √ | √ | ● | ● | √ | √ | 12 |
| Teamworking | ● | √ | √ | √ | √ | √ | √ | ● | √ | √ | ● | ● | √ | √ | 11 |
| Conflict reduction through culture change | √ | ● | √ | √ | √ | √ | √ | √ | √ | ● | ● | ● | √ | √ | 11 |
| Marginalization of stewards | √ | ● | ● | × | √ | √ | √ | √ | √ | ● | ● | ● | √ | √ | 8 |
| Learning companies/heavy emphasis on training | √ | ● | √ | ● | √ | √ | √ | √ | ● | √ | √ | ● | √ | ● | 6 |
| Move to individual contracts | ● | √ | ● | × | × | √ | ● | ● | √ | ● | ● | ● | × | √ | 3 |
| Performance-related pay, few grades | √ | ● | ● | × | × | × | ● | ● | × | ● | × | ● | ● | ● | 1 |
| Harmonization | √ | ● | ● | × | × | × | ● | × | × | √ | × | ● | × | ● | 1 |

Key: √ = yes (existed or were significant moves towards)  × = no  ● = in parts

**Figure 1.5** Key HRM characteristics
*Source:* Storey (1992: 82)

The first section of the table covers prevailing beliefs and assumptions. 'Business need' as a guide to action was the norm. Associated with this was the view that procedures, rules and contractual arrangements were impediments to effective performance. Notably, despite the emphasis given to the 'nurturing' orientation in the idealized portraits of HRM, none of the cases was judged to have unambiguously embraced this.

HRM is said to be fundamentally unitarist. This means that it supposedly has little tolerance for the multiple interest groups and the multiple expression of interests which trade unions and the proceduralist traditions make manifest. Yet the pattern of findings shown here reveals that despite extensive engagement with large parts of the HRM recipe, Britain's large mainstream organizations have placed little emphasis upon disengagement from their pluralist stance.

What was found to be happening on the industrial relations and trade union front was a duality of approach. Trade union recognition and the appurtenances of union relations, such as collective bargaining, were being maintained. But running quite separately from all of this were the new initiatives shown in the figures. In some of the cases this dual dealing was even conducted by separate departments or units and the communication between them was rudimentary and even hostile. To this extent, what can be said to have been revealed in British industrial relations is the coexistence of two traditions. Whether this dualism can survive long into the 1990s is an issue of some significance.

The second part of the figure covers strategic aspects. Interestingly, apart from an insistence on a customer orientation, most cases failed to show much in the way of an integrated approach to employment management, and still less was there evidence of strategic integration with the corporate plan. This finding lends some support to the view that the HRM model is itself not a coherent, integrated phenomenon. Many of the initiatives recorded in the case research, and indicated in summary form here, arose for diverse reasons, and in practice they shared little in common. The fragmentary application of the model could of course be attributed simply to imperfections in take-up and implementation.

Alternatively, the 'pick-and-mix' way in which these organizations were operating might indicate the true nature of the HRM phenomenon – i.e. that it is in reality a symbolic label behind which lurk multifarious practices, many of which are not mutually dependent upon each other. If this is so, it would further explain how these largely pragmatic and opportunistic organizations have found it so relatively easy to pick up diverse elements of these 'new' initiatives.

The third part of the table shows how the case studies uniformly revealed the impressive emergence of general 'business managers' and line managers as key players on employment issues. In all 15 cases there was evidence of these managers devising, driving and delivering new initiatives. The discussion as to whether personnel specialists should 'give human resource management away' will need to be reconsidered in the light of this finding. Are personnel managers in a position to make such a decision? The scoring with regard to 'key levers' produced other surprises. All of the initiatives on the list had been extensively talked about by the mid to late 1980s in Britain. However, as the figure reveals, there was wide disparity in actual take-up and implementation of these contemporary ideas.

Harmonization of terms and conditions, and performance-related pay are shown to have been only fractionally introduced at this time. However, continuing contact with most of these organizations up to the present time leads us to the view that, while harmonization continues to make extraordinarily slow progress, performance-related pay would record a much higher scoring today.

Perhaps less surprisingly, the emphasis given to direct communication with the workforce and the increased flow of this form of communication was observed in all cases. Rather more notable, arguably, was the extent to which line managers as well as personnel directors were intent on stressing their engagement with 'culture change' activities. Ten years ago this would have been an extraordinary state of affairs: now it is almost *de rigeur*.

Reading the table vertically, the take-up of these initiatives on a company-by-company basis is revealed. It is not part of the intent of this chapter to go into detail on the company comparisons. However, what is notable is the variation in the range of summary scores. Whitbread and Austin Rover score highest on this measure, Smith and Nephew scores lowest. Ironically, this last company, despite (or could it be because of?) its conservative stance in these regards, has consistently been a top performing company in financial terms.

Perhaps more surprising than the lack of close association between financial performance and the sheer number of human resource initiatives taken, is the similar low correlation between such a score and the quality of working life in these organizations. Employee commitment, trust and satisfaction in the case organizations were not found to be closely associated with scores on this checklist. The reason for this finding may reside in the fact that HRM has, it will be recalled, hard as well as soft dimensions. An emphasis on the former is likely to be associated with a calculative approach to the handling of the labour resource.

The crude scores also say little about the degree of coherence in each company's take-up of these initiatives. Whitbread recorded a high score, and the sense of coherence between the initiatives was also high among the different sites and the levels of the company. Conversely, while Austin Rover and Massey Ferguson also scored highly on the sheer number of initiatives undertaken, the perceived relationship between the various initiatives and the persistence in their application was found to be much lower.

British Rail had launched fewer initiatives, and even for these the degree of coherence and persistence was weak. Ford had, as expected, preserved a connection with its tried and tested constitutionalist approach. None the less, it had also launched a surprising number of initiatives of the modern kind. It played to the advantage of having comparable overseas sites in which to test ideas and applications.

Many factors were found to influence the differential pattern of take-up of initiatives between the case organizations: foreign ownership, the complexity of company structure and the variation from single-product focus to complex multi-product situations, for example.

It has to be recognized, of course, that summation of complex data against a checklist inevitably leads to a rather crude and simplistic representation of reality. The subtle interpretations can only be explored in the full version of the research report. None the less, there is a great value in standing back and taking a summary overview of the kind presented here, because from such a perspective one can capture a unique sense of the overall pattern.

What has really been happening to personnel management and industrial relations in Britain is, as was perhaps to be expected, a multi-faceted and complex affair. Typical practice in large organizations in Britain could still be interpreted as broadly in accord with Sisson's (1989) depiction of it as lacking in strategic integration and, moreover, falling far short of textbook prescription on practically all constituent measures.

However, what clearly emerges is that British managers have been extraordinarily active in relation to labour matters in the recent years. There is now evidence that the take-up by mainstream organizations of initiatives of a kind much discussed in connection with 'lead' organizations has been very extensive. It can even be said that there has been indeed a clear aim to go 'beyond contract'. However, what is less clear is the ability of the initiatives taken to deliver this, given the shortcomings in the way in which they have been applied.

### Consequences of implementation

The fundamental message arising from this review of models and recipes is that neither the collectivist/procedural nor the individualist/HRM 'solution' is adequate. There is a need to operate on both planes – as will be argued throughout the rest of this book. At this juncture it can be said that the paramount issue on the employment management agenda ought to be the attempt to marry together the individual and the collective approaches.

In hindsight, the unbridled enthusiasm for formalization of collective procedures as expressed in the Royal Commission on Trades Unions and Employers' Associations (Donovan Report, 1968) and in the classic work of Hugh Clegg (1970), Alan Flanders (1970a, b, c), and other authorities of that period, can be seen as very partial. There was almost a total disregard for issues of selection, recruitment, communications, motivation, and development. Likewise, the questions of competitiveness, quality and enterprise were significant in their absence.

Under current competitive circumstances it is now abundantly clear that the vital industrial issues are not the closed shop or procedural agreements. The central issues now are those of quality, training, change and responsiveness. Pragmatically, it seems unlikely that these sorts of processes can lend themselves easily to joint regulation. It is now the case that certain leading figures in the trade unions, such as John Edmonds of the General Municipal and Boilermakers Union (GMB), are expressing definite interest in getting involved in issues of training, quality and careers. In 1991 the GMB and the Union of Communication Workers (UCW) jointly launched an important policy document entitled *The New Agenda*. This was designed to steer trade unions towards these sorts of issues. In one passage the New Agenda document states:

> Unions have remained stuck in an historic posture of responding critically to all management initiatives. We have rarely looked beyond the next pay round. Trade unions should wish to work together with employers and government to create successful industry, a strong economy and a caring, sharing society in the 1990s.

Notwithstanding the fact that a main objective of the UCW's General Secretary was to manoeuvre the expected in-coming Labour government to adopt a system of coordinated bargaining, this sort of language was nevertheless novel. In an attempt to build on it, the Involvement and Participation Association (IPA) (1992) launched an initiative which brought leading employers and trade union general secretaries together to see if these ideas could be developed. Following a series of meetings, a joint declaration was issued in September 1992 which recorded a joint commitment to the success of economic enterprise, a recognition of the legitimacy of each party, a commitment to strive towards security of employment through the means of job flexibility, training and development, gainsharing and an acceptance of the right of employees to be 'informed, consulted and represented in matters of concern to them' (p. 3). This joint declaration was signed by such notable figures as David Sainsbury, deputy Chairman of J Sainsbury plc, Hugh Stirk, UK Personnel Manager of Unilever, Sir John Harvey Jones, Dennis Cassidy, Chairman of the Boddington Group, and by prominent trade union figures such as Bill

Jordan, President of the Amalgamated Electrical and Engineering Union (AEEU), John Edmonds, General Secretary of GMB, Garfield Davies, General Secretary of the Union of Shop, Distributive and Allied Workers (USDAW) and Leif Mills, General Secretary of Bank, Insurance and Finance Union (BIFU).

Even with this unusual level of cooperation it seems unlikely that joint regulation on this wider set of employment issues is seriously in prospect. But without some such symmetry between human resource strategy objectives and the prevailing industrial relations approaches it is difficult to see how the laudable and much declaimed new visions noted earlier in this book can be attained. The unbridled enthusiasm for individualism in recent years is in itself an incomplete and deficient response. There are still some nine million trade union members and most large employers still seek to maintain relations with trade union representatives. The lack of clarity about how industrial relations fits with the new initiatives will sooner or later have to be addressed. Then there is the question of how individualism squares with the requirements of fair administration. Excessive inconsistencies in treatment between different employees will not be conducive to the grander aims of 'winning commitment'. Already, many of the upbeat messages of 1980s-style individualism such as 'celebrating successes' in change-management programmes are breeding deep cynicism. As a part reflection of all of this, the Advisory, Conciliation and Arbitration Service reports an increase in individual grievances (ACAS, 1992). How are these to be handled and what does this trend tell us about the level of satisfaction among the 'vital human resource'?

Evidently, neither individualism nor collectivism is an adequate recipe for managing human resources (HR) and industrial relations (IR). There is a need for both. Future strategies will have to demonstrate an *integration* of individualism and collectivism. The Germans, Italians and French already have arrangements which cater for both these aspects in a way which is seen as more acceptable than the current tension in the British system. If British managers are to move forward with a balanced regard for these aspects of employment policies there will be a need for a more thoughtful and strategic approach to managing IR and HR than we have typically seen so far. The current offerings from the literature and from most management consultants offer little guidance here. Most of these sources of advice are still wedded to, if not indeed fully besotted with, one partial recipe or another. We see the rationale for this book as the opening up of this new agenda.

## The plan of the book

The rest of the book picks up the themes raised in this introductory chapter and examines each of them in greater detail. Chapter 2 provides concrete examples of the extent and nature of the types of change described in conceptual terms in this first chapter. Chapter 3 tackles the question of strategic action in HR/IR: an analysis is made of what strategic HR/IR would entail and an explanation is advanced as to why, so far, it has been found so difficult to achieve in the British context. Chapter 4 explores one of the major strands of strategic action – the way in which work is organized and the structuring of organizations. If an integrated and strategic approach is to have any chance at all then the Human Resource Planning process must be an essential feature: this is the subject of Chapter 5. Then, in Chapter 6, the lynchpin role of 'performance management' is explored. This is shown to be a crucial means to bring individualism and collectivism into alignment. Chapter 7 examines the place of training and development (vital elements it will be recalled in the 'New Agenda'). Chapter 8 brings the recently popular topics of vision, mission and culture management under the spotlight and Chapter 9 examines the key decisions which managers have to make with regard to trade unions. Chapter 10 is the concluding chapter. Therein, we bring together the main issues involved in managing human resources and industrial relations – i.e. in balancing individualism and collectivism – and we use this assessment as the basis on which to point a way ahead.

# 2

# MANAGING HUMAN RESOURCES AND INDUSTRIAL RELATIONS: THE STORY SO FAR

A great deal has been said and written about the need (given that human resources are so vital) for a *strategic* approach to their management. A parallel message has emerged in the reports from other countries of 'transformation' in the management of the employment relationship. But, the central issue to be faced in this book is that while there have undoubtedly been some important changes in British management (Storey, 1992 describes the nature and extent of these) there is still a long way to go.

There is no room for complacency. Superficially, the employee relations' problem in Britain has been solved. The governmer ζ's White Paper, *Industrial Relations in the 1990s* (Employment Department, 1991: 1–3) in effect claims as much. A whole new framework of labour law has been introduced. Strike statistics are at their lowest for 65 years. Flying pickets and secondary industrial action have virtually disappeared. Restrictive practices are now rarely reported to be a problem. And yet. . .and yet. . .

The central point is that while most of the management literatures (and practically 100 per cent of the training videos) are upbeat and supportive of the message that the key to managing human resources and industrial relations has now been found, the reality is somewhat different. Many initiatives have been taken, programmes launched and changes undoubtedly wrought. None the less, the fundamental issues of planning and resourcing for people, training and developing staff, managing performance, finding appropriate structural arrangements for organizations and for work, and, perhaps most telling, devising appropriate strategic approaches, remain highly problematical in most British employing organizations – public and private.

On an international comparative basis Britain still has a long way to go. In the following section we undertake a wide-ranging review of the state of play to date with regard to work organization and flexibility, training and development, performance management and the strategic management of HR and IR. In particular we assess the extent of transformation in employment management. The overall picture tends to point towards a low productivity, low investment and low pay economy.

## HR/IR in Britain

Views about what has been happening to IR/HR in the UK in recent years turn on two related judgements. One is the choice of cases. It is perfectly possible, for example, to focus on a number of 'greenfield' workplaces such as those owned by Continental Can, Nissan, Sony and others and come to the conclusion that IR/HR in the UK is being 'transformed' (see, for example, Bassett, 1986). Or the focus can be on the 'brownfield' workplaces of mainstream companies and public sector organizations; in which case a much more cautious conclusion is appropriate (see, for example, Storey, 1992). The second judgement is whether to put the emphasis on change or continuity. Here a range of positions is possible. One commentator (MacInnes, 1987), for example, has argued that very little has changed in IR/HR in the UK, which cannot be explained in terms of an economic and political climate exceptionally hostile to trade unions.

In the circumstances, it is proper at the outset that the authors make their own opinions known about these matters. They are,

**Table 2.1** Growth of productivity (GDP per person in employment) (annual average growth rates in percentages)

| Years | Australia | Canada | France | Germany | Italy | Japan | Spain | Sweden | UK | USA |
|---|---|---|---|---|---|---|---|---|---|---|
| 1960–68 | 2.4 | 2.3 | 4.9 | 4.1 | 6.2 | 8.5 | 6.9 | 4.0 | 2.7 | 2.6 |
| 1968–73 | 2.6 | 2.4 | 4.3 | 4.3 | 4.9 | 7.7 | 5.7 | 3.0 | 3.1 | 0.7 |
| 1973–75 | 0.9 | 0.5 | 1.5 | 1.5 | 0.0 | 1.4 | 3.3 | 0.6 | −0.9 | −1.3 |
| 1975–79 | 2.2 | 1.8 | 3.0 | 3.0 | 4.1 | 3.6 | 3.2 | 0.5 | 2.5 | 0.7 |
| 1979–83 | 0.7 | 0.4 | 1.7 | 1.7 | 1.3 | 2.1 | 3.2 | 0.8 | 2.2 | 0.2 |
| 1983–89 | 1.0 | 1.3 | 2.4 | 2.4 | 2.7 | 3.4 | 2.2 | 1.7 | 1.3 | 1.3 |

*Note:* Aggregates computed on the bases of 1987 GNP/GDP weights expressed in 1987 US dollars.
*Source:* OECD *Employment Outlook*, July, 1991.

first, that the focus should be on mainstream rather than the 'state of the art' workplaces and, second, that the emphasis should be on change *and* continuity rather than one or the other. The reason for the first is that, while 'state of the art' workplaces are important in formulating hypotheses about possible future directions, in the UK a very false impression would be gained from concentrating on them. The reason for the second will be clear from the conclusion of a recent report from the Industrial Relations Research Unit at the University of Warwick:

> During the 1980s they [industrial relations] altered dramatically, while retaining many features from the past. The fact that change has been complex and uneven reflects one key aspect of continuity, namely, that neither employers nor unions, nor for that matter the state have been able to press through a coherent strategy of renewal and rationalization. All parties still labour under a legacy of the past. (Edwards et al., 1992: 61)

An appropriate place to begin the analysis is with the comparative statistics on productivity. The claimed British 'economic miracle' of the 1980s needs to be put into context and be grounded in reality. As Table 2.1 shows, the growth of productivity in Britain between 1983–9 was actually lower than in the two previous periods. It was also among the lowest, apart from Australia, of the other Organisation for Economic Cooperation and Development (OECD) countries. In addition, the annual real growth in gross domestic product (GDP) across 12 industrial countries is compared in Table 2.2.

In the light of these basic statistics we review the overall pattern of HR/IR practices in the UK. The discussion which follows is organized under the following four headings: work organization, training and development, performance management and the strategic management of the corporation.

### Work organization

The absence of a framework of law and collective bargaining defining the rights and obligations of the parties is especially

**Table 2.2**   Annual real growth in GDP

| Year | Australia | Canada | Denmark | France | Germany | Italy | Japan | Norway | Spain | Sweden | UK | USA |
|---|---|---|---|---|---|---|---|---|---|---|---|---|
| 1962 | 6.76 | 7.08 | 5.45 | 6.68 | 4.58 | 6.20 | 8.79 | 2.81 | 9.30 | 3.86 | 0.81 | 5.31 |
| 1963 | 6.63 | 5.19 | 0.64 | 5.32 | 2.75 | 5.61 | 8.36 | 3.79 | 8.76 | 5.75 | 4.48 | 4.11 |
| 1964 | 5.99 | 6.66 | 8.97 | 6.52 | 6.56 | 2.80 | 11.35 | 5.01 | 6.18 | 7.01 | 5.34 | 5.34 |
| 1965 | 5.91 | 6.60 | 4.83 | 4.78 | 5.25 | 3.27 | 5.83 | 5.28 | 6.33 | 3.80 | 2.19 | 5.79 |
| 1966 | 2.77 | 6.79 | 2.22 | 5.21 | 2.85 | 5.98 | 10.48 | 3.79 | 7.05 | 2.20 | 2.03 | 5.79 |
| 1967 | 6.13 | 2.93 | 3.69 | 4.69 | -0.24 | 7.18 | 10.91 | 6.26 | 4.32 | 3.42 | 2.74 | 2.85 |
| 1968 | 6.82 | 5.35 | 3.80 | 4.27 | 5.74 | 6.54 | 12.12 | 2.26 | 6.77 | 3.55 | 4.23 | 4.15 |
| 1969 | 7.40 | 5.36 | 6.53 | 6.98 | 7.49 | 6.10 | 12.09 | 4.21 | 8.94 | 5.03 | 1.33 | 2.43 |
| 1970 | 5.21 | 2.59 | 2.27 | 5.73 | 5.01 | 5.31 | 10.35 | 2.29 | 4.08 | 6.57 | 2.79 | -0.29 |
| 1971 | 5.00 | 5.76 | 2.45 | 4.79 | 3.05 | 0.03 | 4.37 | 4.58 | 4.95 | 0.94 | 2.76 | 2.84 |
| 1972 | 3.40 | 5.73 | 5.45 | 4.43 | 4.34 | 4.31 | 8.28 | 5.17 | 8.14 | 2.29 | 2.37 | 4.98 |
| 1973 | 5.60 | 7.71 | 3.81 | 5.44 | 4.84 | 7.11 | 7.70 | 4.11 | 7.86 | 3.97 | 7.68 | 5.19 |
| 1974 | 1.87 | 4.40 | -0.93 | 3.11 | 0.05 | 5.43 | -0.76 | 5.19 | 5.72 | 3.20 | -1.01 | -0.54 |
| 1975 | 1.83 | 2.60 | -0.65 | -0.28 | -1.27 | -2.65 | 2.92 | 4.17 | 1.10 | 2.55 | -0.68 | -1.26 |
| 1976 | 4.05 | 6.16 | 6.46 | 4.24 | 5.54 | 6.25 | 4.23 | 6.81 | 3.01 | 1.06 | 3.65 | 4.89 |
| 1977 | 0.89 | 3.61 | 1.63 | 3.22 | 2.55 | 3.69 | 4.76 | 3.58 | 3.30 | -1.60 | 1.04 | 4.67 |
| 1978 | 3.54 | 4.58 | 1.47 | 3.35 | 3.45 | 3.68 | 4.96 | 4.54 | 1.79 | 1.75 | 3.85 | 5.23 |
| 1979 | 3.60 | 3.87 | 3.53 | 3.24 | 4.03 | 5.99 | 5.56 | -12.38 | 0.19 | 3.84 | 2.34 | 2.53 |
| 1980 | 2.31 | 1.49 | -0.44 | 1.63 | 1.04 | 5.28 | 3.48 | -7.20 | 1.54 | 1.67 | -1.94 | -0.16 |
| 1981 | 3.68 | 3.67 | -0.89 | 1.17 | 0.11 | 0.55 | 3.41 | 0.88 | -0.25 | -0.99 | -1.08 | 1.93 |
| 1982 | -0.14 | -3.22 | 3.03 | 2.55 | -1.11 | 0.21 | 3.43 | 0.33 | 1.22 | 1.14 | 1.32 | -2.55 |
| 1983 | 0.59 | 3.29 | 2.52 | 0.69 | 1.85 | 0.97 | 2.81 | 3.87 | 1.80 | 2.83 | 3.66 | 3.57 |
| 1984 | 7.39 | 6.18 | 4.39 | 1.32 | 3.07 | 2.69 | 4.31 | 3.83 | 1.80 | 3.99 | 1.80 | 6.64 |
| 1985 | 4.83 | 4.77 | 4.29 | 1.88 | 1.81 | 2.60 | 5.12 | 8.13 | 2.31 | 2.22 | 4.06 | 3.48 |
| 1986 | 2.38 | 3.32 | 3.64 | 2.53 | 2.17 | 2.92 | 2.69 | 4.18 | 3.28 | 2.19 | 3.95 | 2.85 |
| 1987 | 4.33 | 4.05 | -0.60 | 2.19 | 1.49 | 3.14 | 4.28 | 1.99 | 5.58 | 2.45 | 4.64 | 3.36 |
| 1988 | 3.48 | 4.39 | -0.16 | 3.82 | 3.65 | 4.07 | 6.31 | -0.51 | 5.23 | 2.90 | 3.88 | 4.42 |
| 1989 | 4.49 | 2.99 | | 3.73 | 3.80 | 3.03 | 4.67 | 0.37 | 4.82 | 1.96 | 1.91 | 2.51 |
| 1990 | 1.17 | 0.90 | | 2.81 | 4.49 | 1.95 | 5.66 | | 3.66 | 0.54 | 0.74 | 0.96 |

*Source: International Financial Statistics Yearbook*, International Monetary Fund, 1991.

important in understanding the 'traditional' pattern of work organization in the UK. In the words of Edwards et al. (1992),

> The rules of employment were settled on a day-to-day basis within the workplace. A major source of authority was 'custom and practice': the unwritten norms and understandings which established in a particular workplace the rules of work. Workplaces developed their own sets of custom and practice rules, which naturally had some family resemblance with each other but which stemmed from negotiation at the point of production and not from any higher level authority.

In the case of task or functional flexibility, surveys and case studies suggest there have been considerable changes in work organization due to new technologies and altered competitive strategies. These will be discussed further in Chapter 7; changes include the 'combination' of jobs – with elimination of differences within and between crafts; team-working involving interchangeability and flexibility between jobs; 'balanced labour force' techniques designed to deal with surpluses and shortages; the ending of 'trade supervision under which craftsmen would accept instructions only from a first-line manager who had completed an apprenticeship in the same trade; and the breaking down of the distinction between manual and non-manual jobs (NEDO, 1986; ACAS, 1988d; Cross, 1988). In the case of time flexibility, there have been considerable developments in hours of work including the adoption of annual hours systems which guarantee annual salaries in return for the freedom to vary the number of hours worked each week (IRRR, 1991b).

Three points need to be made about these changes. First, there is a great deal of continuity with earlier phases of productivity bargaining in the 1960s (see, for example, the argument in Marsden and Thompson, 1990; Elger, 1991) and with what has been described as the 'reconstruction' of workplace industrial relations (Purcell and Sisson, 1983) in the 1970s. Significantly, the team working which has received so much attention in America is very much the exception rather than the rule; survey evidence suggests only a fraction of workplaces (Millward and Stevens, 1986; ACAS, 1988d: 15; Marginson et al., 1988) have autonomous working groups. Second, it is a moot point whether these changes have gone as far as they at first appear. For example, the much heralded changes in task flexibility turn out to be not what they seem (Cross, 1988); major alterations in job content have been rare as has the amalgamation of production and mainten-ance jobs. Third, the main preoccupation, as with earlier at-tempts, seems to have been 'financially-driven cost reductions' (Jones, 1991: 245). Even team working appears to have more to do with the implications of the de-layering of management than with a commitment to new theories of working arrangements (Geary, 1993).

There have been two sets of developments in involvement and participation which parallel the changes in work organization. One is the growth in face-to-face communications systems such as team briefing. The survey evidence suggests that these are widespread and affect as many as two-thirds of large companies with over 1,000 employees (Marginson et al., 1988). The other is the introduction of problem-solving groups such as quality circles (Collard and Dale, 1989). Although the number of companies with quality circles is much smaller – probably no more than one-fifth of large companies have them (Marginson et al., 1988) – the number is up from a handful in the late 1970s to perhaps as many as 700 to 800 by 1988 (Storey and Sisson, 1989: 170).

By comparison, as will be discussed in more detail below, there have been few initiatives in arrangements for collective involve-ment and participation. Thus, although unions have been involved in negotiations over changes in working practices, their role in the introduction of new technologies which frequently pave the way for these changes has at best been consultative. As with much else, management's approach to the introduction of new technology has been essentially opportunistic, consulting with unions where it felt constrained to do so, but not otherwise. Unions, for their part, appear to have been most concerned to negotiate over the impact on pay and employment rather than the design of or the wider implications of new technology (Daniel, 1987).

In terms of outcomes, there was certainly some increase in productivity in manufacturing in the 1980s – both in labour productivity and total factor productivity. But much of this simply reflected the shake-out in employment (see the discussion of OECD statistics in Nolan, 1989). Significantly, there was no major improvement in the reduction of unit costs (Ray, 1990). There are two explanations for this: first, earnings in the UK rose faster than competitor countries and, second, there was no substantial investment in new technology – capital spending per employee between 1980 and 1989 was considerably less than in other competitor economies (see, for example, the calculation based on OECD data by the Confederation of British Industry (CBI, 1991)).

### Training and development

The distinctive features of the British training scene are am- bivalence at company level and an unconvincing vocational education and training system at national level. There has been a failure to evolve and maintain a coherent institutional framework in the UK. If, once again, one starts out with the statistics it is easy to see why there is cause for concern under this heading. Table 2.3 reveals a low level of provision in this country for each of the three types of education and training for young workers.

**Table 2.3**  Education and training of young workers

|  | % of youth in vocational education | % Post secondary | % University[a] |
|---|---|---|---|
| United States | 30% | 57% | 36% |
| West Germany | 70% | 30% | 26% |
| England | 18% | 21% | 8% |
| France[b] | na | 50%[c] | 27% |
| Sweden | 50% | 37% | 26% |
| Japan | 28% | 30% | 24% |

Notes:  [a] First year enrolment in schools conferring baccalaureate degrees or higher.
[b] French data is from Training and Employment: French Dimensions, CEREQ, Spring 1991.
[c] This number has risen to 50% in 1990 from 30% in 1975.
Source: Training Strategies: Preparing Noncollege Youth for Employment in the US and Foreign Countries, US General Accounting Office, 1990, p. 12.

**Table 2.4**  Enterprise related training (1990) – per cent of individuals receiving training

| Country | |
|---|---|
| United States | 11.8% of all workers (current population survey, formal training) |
| Canada* (1985) | 6.7% all workers (formal training) |
| West Germany | 12.7% all workers |
| | 76% 15–19 year old |
| Great Britain | 14.4% all workers |
| France | 4.6% all workers |
| | 43% 15–19 year old |
| | 26.6% employees in firms 10+ |
| Norway | 33.1% workers in firms > 2 employees |
| Sweden | 25.4% all workers |
| Japan | 36.7% (within last two years) |
| Australia | 34.9 % (in-house) |
| Spain | 2.4% all workers |

*Note*:  * Canadian data is from the 1985 Adult Training Survey, Statistics Canada, 1986.
*Source*: *Employment Outlook*, OECD, July, 1991.

It might be thought that the lack of external, state provision is compensated for by increased in-company training. But, as Table 2.4 shows, this is not unfortunately the case.

The measure of the competition is perhaps best revealed in the detail. A recent study of investment in the human resource in the motor industries of different countries revealed how much greater care the Japanese devoted to training their workforce. For example, new hire assembly workers in the car industry in Japan were given 310 hours of training per person, Japanese transplants gave their new hire workers 280 hours of training, but American car companies only provided 48 hours (Krafcik, 1990). There are no comparative data for Britain in this study but it is known that British practice is much closer to that in America.

The antecedents of this dismal record have been traced by Keep (1989) to two sources: first, the fact that vocational training has often been virtually synonymous with a distinct form of exclusive craft apprenticeship and second, the 'voluntarist' bias towards training provision in this country. The traditional apprenticeship system which catered for some 240,000 apprentices in manufacturing in 1964 was, in effect, the near totality of the vocational educational system at that time. It is hardly surprising therefore that its rapid decline (there were only 63,700 by 1986) has caused much anguish. Yet the system was in any case itself flawed. Entrance into the scheme was severely restricted by management–union agreements and in practice was confined to a limited proportion of males of school leaving age. The training experience was itself defective with its heavy emphasis upon serving time on the job for four to five years with little regard given to efficient learning or tests of achievement. Apprenticeships were also bound-up with traditional craft demarcation lines so there were in-built barriers to expanding learning and competency horizons for the apprentices themselves and even more so for the unskilled and semi-skilled who were outside the system.

Education, training and development in the UK, like so many other aspects of IR/HR, can also be seen as having been massively influenced by the 'voluntaristic' tradition. Responsibility for education has long been highly decentralized in the hands of a 'multiplicity of local education authorities, often at odds with central government and a profusion of examining and validating bodies' (Keep, 1989: 189). Until recently, for example, there was no national curriculum in schools. Vocational education and training were assumed to be the responsibility of individual employers and employees and, for practical purposes, vocational training was synonymous with a distinctive form of exclusive craft apprenticeship system.

Concerns about the effects of these arrangements, which date back to the last century, have intensified in recent years. In the case of compulsory education, there has been increasing debate about declining standards. In the case of post-compulsory education, it was the relatively low staying-on rate which has been subject to comment (OECD, 1990) and the generally low levels of attainment achieved in comparison with other countries (for a compendium of the reports of the National Institute for Economic and Social Research on this matter, see Prais, 1990). Other influential reports complained about the relatively low priority given to training and development at work (Coopers and Lybrand Associates, 1985; MSC/NEDO, 1987).

Attempts were made, as in 1964 with the passing of the Industrial Training Act, to attend to the evident inadequacies of training provision. This Act established Industrial Training Boards (ITBs) in the main industrial sectors and these were invested with authority to operate a levy upon employers and to administer grants to those carrying out appropriate levels of training. The system acted as a catalyst and new groups including technicians were given improved access to training. Training departments were established and the level of consciousness and awareness about training was raised.

The ITB system was subject, however, to employer criticism and the incoming Conservative government abolished the majority of ITBs. The new policy was predicated upon a preference for a 'system' in which employers, not government, took the lead. A White Paper entitled 'The New Training Initiative' extolled the virtues of wider opportunities and a flexible trained, adaptable workforce fitted to market needs. The Manpower Services Commission (MSC) was charged with operational-izing the objectives and it established two bodies to assist it in its task: the National Council for Vocational Qualifications (NCVQ) and the Training and Enterprise Councils (TECs). The NCVQ was to direct its attention to standards and accreditation; the TECs were to attend to training by enhancing and monitoring training provision. There have been myriad other training initiatives including Investors in People (IIP) and Accreditation of Prior Learning (APL). Typically, these are embraced within, and supportive of, the main thrusts as represented by NVQs and the TECs. These two elements of the new training initiative therefore deserve further comment.

The NCVQ has sought to rationalize standards across the vast array of vocational qualifications. The Council does not itself act as an awarding body, rather it seeks to establish National Vocational Qualifications (NVQs) as a common standard of achieved competence using already available qualifications. A key objective is to devise universal standards which can aid transferability.

The launch of the NCVQ and the TECs signalled a new training policy in Britain. But progress to date suggests that this is highly problematical and that headway will still have to be made mainly at the organizational level. The content of training in Britain even under the new system will fail to be wide enough and to be demanding enough (Lane, 1990).

TECs are the second major leg of the recent training initiatives. TECs operate locally and are intended to act as foci for debate, design and policy formulation. They are supposed to get involved in the identification of training needs and the organization of training provision in their designated areas. There are currently 81 of them. They offer training advice to small- and medium-sized businesses as well as having responsibility for Youth Training Scheme (YTS) and Employment Training. TECs have had a controversial short life. Their role is broad and currently rather ill-defined. Different TECs are focusing their attention on different issues and different groups. A particular bone of contention has been underfunding. In fact there have been many reports of cuts in funding to TECs at a time when their responsibility for unemployment training has been expanding.

On the optimistic side, the New Training Initiative promised greater clarity of skill levels attained. NVQs should assist employers in understanding what skills potential employees have. Employees should be able to continue training despite moving between jobs and encouragingly, NVQs are reported to enjoy the support of personnel managers. TECs promise to open up training opportunities to groups previously left out of the system and to companies which formerly perceived training as too expensive.

These points do need to be placed in the context of Britain's relatively poor record in the sphere of industrial training. Finegold and Soskice (1988) refer to Britain as in a 'low skills equilibrium' with the majority of companies staffed with poorly trained managers and workers producing low quality goods and services.

While NVQC and TECs represent the main elements of the state-level new training initiative they are not, however, the only ones. Another important programme is the Technical and Vocational Education Initiative (TVEI). This is designed to effect a shift in the secondary education curriculum by offering a vocational education provision which is of equal status to the academic for the whole ability range. The ten-year programme, to be managed from within the Department of Employment rather than the Department of Education and Science (DES), was announced in the mid-1980s. As part of the vocational aspect, secondary school pupils have direct contact with local employers through short work placements, 'shadowing' and visits to places of employment. Assessments of the impact of TVEI have been cautious. Students participating in the scheme report that they had received useful work preparation. But there is lack of reliable information from employers and uncertainty about the actual ability range of students attracted into the scheme (Helsby, 1989; Training Agency, 1989).

Measured in terms of absolute participation rates in further and higher education, Britain's record has typically not looked very good when compared with other industrialized economies. In recent years, however, participation rates in post-16 year-old education have risen steadily. Seventy-five per cent of 16 year olds now attend full-time at school or college. Part of the explanation probably can be found, however, in higher unemployment levels for young people and the withdrawal of benefit entitlement for 16–18 year olds. For an increasing proportion of those 'staying on' there have been moves to give vocational qualifications a higher profile and status. Business and school partnerships are growing with local employers providing work experience, training and sometimes jobs at the end.

Establishing a highly regarded vocational education route has proved to be difficult but the search continues. The NCVQ, with backing from government, employers and trade unions has just launched a new framework and a new set of awards known as General National Vocational Qualifications (GNVQs). The Business and Technical Education Council (BTEC) who will be the first to offer these awards claim they offer 'a genuine alternative to the purely academic route' and that these vocational qualifications will be 'recognized throughout the country as respected as GCSEs and A levels' (BTEC statement, November, 1992). The problem of course is that it is not possible simply to proclaim 'recognition' in order to make it happen. In fact, the history of previous attempts suggests that those seeking to establish these courses and qualifications will face an uphill struggle.

**Table 2.5**  Hourly compensation costs for production workers in national currency (index US = 100; all manufacturing)

| Year | Australia | Canada | Denmark | France | Germany | Italy | Japan | Norway | Spain | Sweden | UK |
|------|-----------|--------|---------|--------|---------|-------|-------|--------|-------|--------|----|
| 1980 | 86 | 85 | 110 | 91 | 125 | 81 | 57 | 118 | 60 | 127 | 75 |
| 1981 | 90 | 85 | 87 | 74 | 97 | 68 | 57 | 102 | 52 | 109 | 66 |
| 1982 | 85 | 86 | 76 | 67 | 89 | 63 | 49 | 93 | 46 | 86 | 58 |
| 1983 | 76 | 89 | 72 | 64 | 85 | 63 | 50 | 87 | 39 | 73 | 53 |
| 1984 | 78 | 88 | 64 | 58 | 75 | 58 | 51 | 82 | 36 | 73 | 47 |
| 1985 | 63 | 83 | 62 | 58 | 74 | 57 | 49 | 81 | 37 | 74 | 48 |
| 1986 | 64 | 83 | 84 | 78 | 101 | 76 | 70 | 102 | 41 | 94 | 57 |
| 1987 | 70 | 88 | 108 | 91 | 126 | 91 | 80 | 128 | 58 | 112 | 66 |
| 1988 | 81 | 97 | 109 | 93 | 131 | 94 | 92 | 136 | 63 | 121 | 75 |
| 1989 | 86 | 103 | 101 | 88 | 124 | 95 | 88 | 131 | 64 | 122 | 73 |
| 1990 | 88 | 108 | 121 | 103 | 146 | 111 | 86 | 148 | 79 | 142 | 84 |

*Source:* US Department of Labor, Bureau of Labor Statistics, November, 1991.

There are some signs that managements themselves have begun to take training and development more seriously. In a number of industries, including chemicals and engineering there has been a radical overhaul of the apprenticeship system involving standards-based training. Provision for adult training has also increased – the number of workers benefiting from job-related training was reported to be up from around 9 per cent in 1984 to 15 per cent in 1990 (Employment Department, 1991). A number of companies, including BP and Shell in chemicals, have introduced payment for skills. There has also been a big increase in management education. The output of MBA programmes, for example, has more than quadrupled from fewer than 2,000 to over 8,000 per year. Expenditure on training has also increased, according to the Confederation of British Industry (CBI) (1991).

Many commentators remain unconvinced, however, that UK companies are devoting anything like the necessary time and resources to training and development – despite recent attempts by the government and the CBI to claim to the contrary. Here the link with business strategies is seen to be especially critical. In the words of Keep (1992),

> the UK's training problems do not simply stem from difficulties with the supply of training and skills. They also reflect the fact that, because of their product market strategies, demand for skills from many employers is weak. The lack of a sufficiently strong demand for skills in the economy limits not only the efficiency of the training supply system, but also the incentives available to individuals to get trained.

The whole issue of training and development is obviously crucial to the theme of managing human resources and we focus centrally upon it in Chapter 7. There, in line with the overall orientation of this book, we concentrate discussion on managerial policies, practices and options at the organizational level.

### Performance management

Again let us begin with the facts. Hourly compensation costs for production workers across a range of leading industrial economies are shown in Table 2.5.

These data confirm the point we made earlier, that to a considerable degree Britain can be fairly described as a low wage economy. In a very real sense, labour as a cheap resource actually presents a problem. While it may attract a certain amount of inward investment the resulting jobs tend to be low skilled and low value-added.

Let us dig a little deeper. Compensation is very much a status issue in the UK. A typical manual worker has been paid each week in cash for a standard number of hours plus overtime, whereas the typical non-manual worker has been paid a salary each month, without payment for overtime, by bank transfer. The manual worker would more likely have had a proportion of pay related to results; the non-manual would more likely have received annual increments. Appraisal and individual performance pay were largely restricted to management grades; the same goes for profit sharing and share ownership. The status divide was also reflected in non-pay items; there were significant differences in holidays, sick pay, occupational pensions supplementary to the state system, and so on (for further details, Price, 1989).

In recent years the status divide has closed. There has been some harmonization of terms and conditions such as sick pay and pensions (Price, 1989). Many of the developments discussed later in the book, such as the extension of profit sharing and share ownership, are also now commonplace. Even so, single status arrangements covering a company's entire labour force remain rare – it has been estimated, for example, that only one in eight organizations have 'integrated' job evaluation schemes involving most groups of workers (ACAS, 1988b: 7). Equally rare though much discussed, are 'single table' bargaining arrangements involving manual and non-manual workers (Marginson and Sisson, 1990).

In the case of payment systems, there have been two major changes. One is the growth in individual performance pay. In the case of manual workers, although the 'rate for the job' remains dominant, there is evidence of the extension of appraisal and merit pay. The Institute of Personnel Management, for example, found a phenomenal increase in the appraisal of skilled manual workers – up from 2 per cent in 1976 to 26 per cent ten years later

(Long, 1986). In the case of non-manual workers, appraisal and merit pay are increasingly widespread in both the public and the private sector (ACAS, 1988a; IDS, 1991). In financial services, for example, they are increasingly replacing automatic annual pay increases and increments (for further details, see Blissett and Sisson, 1989). Significant groups of managers, notably in the public services and the recently privatized public enterprises, have been taken out of collective bargaining and put on individual performance-related contracts.

The second major change is the growth in the coverage of group performance-related systems. These include work group schemes, plant and enterprise schemes, and profit sharing. In its survey of 667 workplaces in 1988, for example, ACAS found that the number covered by such arrangements were 30 per cent, 13 per cent and 37 per cent respectively. The WIRS3 survey (Millward et al., 1992: 261) shows there was a substantial increase in profit sharing arrangements between 1984–90. The proportion of workplaces covered by such schemes rose from 18 to 43 per cent during this period.

A key structural change has been the further decentralization of pay determination. In the private sector, the shift from multi-employer to single-employer bargaining has been accompanied by moves from multi-establishment to single-establishment bargaining. Bargaining units are increasingly being aligned with business units (IRRR, 1989c; 1990). In the public sector, the state has promoted similar developments. The Post Office, for example, has been split into a number of 'businesses' each with its own bargaining unit. National bargaining is also likely to go in the civil service with the hiving off of 'executive' agencies. The same may happen with the introduction of semi-independent 'trust' hospitals in the National Health Service and the provisions for the opting-out of schools from local authority control in education.

In terms of general trends in pay, three main conclusions suggest themselves. First, earnings rose faster than prices throughout the decade, despite high levels of unemployment. Average earnings in manufacturing rose annually by more than 7.5 per cent (New Earnings Survey, quoted in IRRR, 1991b). Second, there was a considerable widening of the distribution –

managers in particular did very much better than the rest (Remuneration Economics/British Institute of Management Survey, quoted in IRRR, 1991b). Third, notwithstanding these developments, the UK remained a relatively low pay economy; not only did pay remain low so too did non-pay labour costs (Ray, 1987 and 1990) – which helps to explain the attraction of the UK in the 1980s to inward investors.

## Strategic management of the corporation

A continuing theme of public policy throughout the post-Second World War period is that British management has not taken IR/HR matters seriously enough (see, for example, Donovan Report, 1968; CIR, 1974; MSC and NEDO, 1987). One measure that has often been quoted is the lack of board level IR/HR appointments. Probably no more than one-third of companies with 1,000 or more employees have a specialist IR/HR director (Marginson et al., 1988). Another is the importance that is given to IR/HR matters. Even large companies, it seems, do not have a clear cut strategy or approach to IR/HR and IR/HR issues do not rank very high in business decisions (Marginson et al., 1988).

Evidence to suggest that this state of affairs is changing is available. One recent survey carried out by communications consultants Smythe Dorward Lambert (1991) involving 46 chief executives of major companies in the UK concluded that:

1 A substantial proportion of large UK companies was aware of the ideas associated with 'HRM', i.e. focusing more on employees; orientating the companies towards achievement; placing more reliance on trust, respect and mutual communication than on rules and procedures; and fostering a sense of shared purpose.

2 Two-thirds claimed to have embarked on culture change programmes in recent years; the most popular techniques used to manage change were the use of internal communications, changes to structure, and management development; a large number had replied that they had mission statements and that such statements outlining the organizations' goals and objectives helped staff understand how their job fitted in and helped to motivate them.

3 The reasons cited for taking such ideas more seriously were the effect of changing market conditions, including the globalization of business, increased competition, new technology, the growth of decentralized control of the company and increased social awareness and corporate responsibility.

Among the organizations in the survey were BP, Cable and Wireless, ICI, Ford and several US-owned computer companies as well as the large conglomerates BET and BTR.

A major problem with this type of survey, however, is that they simply report the views of chief executives. It is difficult to establish if the companies are doing the things they say they are or whether they are paying lip-service to what they think they should be doing. Certainly research in IRRU and elsewhere suggests grounds for caution. For example, often even very senior managers regard total quality management (TQM) as something they have to take on board. Significantly, there is very rarely a change in the management appraisal system to reflect supposedly changing priorities.

Another problem is the interpretation which is to be put on some of these developments. It is a moot point for example whether the widespread adoption of the multi-divisional pattern of organization is designed to give 'strategic business' managers greater 'ownership' or whether it is primarily designed to give senior managers greater control. The autonomy that Strategic Business Unit (SBU) managers have, both the case study and survey evidence suggests, is severely qualified. Even in apparently highly decentralized organizations, a very tight framework of budgetary and financial controls is laid down from divisional or corporate headquarters. Similarly, it emerges, many of the policies in force in the workplace are the result of 'guidelines' that 'SBU' managers have received from headquarters (for further details, see, Kinnie, 1985a and b; Goold and Campbell, 1987; Marginson et al., 1988).

There have been very few signs of attempts on the part of British managements in the 1980s to re-structure their relationships with trade unions. In the second half of the 1980s considerable attention focused on what the Advisory Conciliation and Arbitration Service has termed 'new style' agreements

(ACAS, 1987). The precise package varied but typically involved the exclusive recognition of a single union; flexibility of working; single status; a joint consultative council; 'no strike' provisions which ruled out industrial action even as a last resort; and pendulum (final offer) arbitration (for further details, see Bassett, 1986; Wickens, 1987; see also Trevor, 1988). Such agreements remain very rare, however. Latest estimates put the number at no more than about 70 (IRRR, 1992). They have also been concentrated on green-field sites, are extensively but not exclusively found on foreign-owned sites, and affect relatively small numbers of workers.

More generally, there is evidence that, even though managements have not withdrawn recognition from trade unions on the scale they have done in the USA, they have taken advantage of the economic and political situation to limit the role of trade unions. Few have been prepared to concede recognition on new sites, particularly in private services where employment growth has been strongest. A number of managerial groups have been taken out of collective bargaining and put on individual contracts. Meanwhile, some of the developments in higher level joint consultation which were initiated in the 1970s, such as those involving the extension of joint consultation to business planning and investment at ICI and Cadbury-Schweppes, have been put on hold or abandoned.

Few companies have managed to synchronize their initiatives towards individual employees with their approach to trade unions. Very often HR and IR are even the responsibility of two separate departments. There is also case study evidence of attempts to switch the emphasis from joint regulation to joint consultation and communications. Meetings with shop stewards that in the 1970s involved the joint regulation of an issue have been turned into consultative or in some cases straightforward communication exercises (Terry, 1988).

The implications of the widespread decentralization of collective bargaining in the large multi-establishment companies are also potentially far-reaching. For managements, decentralized negotiations may have resulted in greater control within the company. There has been a price, however: the inability to coordinate pay bargaining in the way that managements do in a number of other EC countries (for further details, see IRRR, 1990).

In summary, there have been major changes in British HR and IR in recent years. Management has responded to pressures from the marketplace and the opportunities presented by new technology to introduce practices which would have been unthinkable a decade or two ago. As Storey (1992: 28), observed after a detailed study of 15 mainstream organizations, there has been a 'remarkable take-up by large British companies of initiatives which are in the style of the "human resource management" model'.

Fundamental though the changes have been, there has not yet, however, been a transformation of UK IR/HR. Indeed, there are good reasons for suggesting that UK industrial relations have been characterized by continuity as much as change. Many organizations remain more or less untouched by these changes; the number with quality circles, for example, as we noted earlier, is very small and the number with autonomous working groups even smaller. There must also be question marks about the depth and the permanency of many of the changes; some revised working arrangements turn out, on close inspection, to be relatively superficial; some practices, such as team briefings, have fallen into disuse in organizations which had previously been enthusiastic users. The initiatives associated with 'HRM', where they are practised, rarely seem to add up to an integrated approach. There are also major inconsistencies such as the determination to have individual performance-related pay arrangements despite a desire to install teamworking. And different forms of participation and involvement are too often seen as alternatives rather than as complementary.

What has been happening is best seen as essentially *ad hoc* or piecemeal reactions by UK managements to the economic and political context. Sir John Cassels, formerly secretary of the Donovan Commission and recently retired as Director-General of the National Economic Development Organization, offers a fitting overall conclusion to this discussion. In commenting upon managerial plans to deal with the implications of the demographic dip, he observed:

49

The disappointing results . . . indicate that we are in for a bout of 'muddling through', British-style . . . many companies are chucking money at the problem and assuming that will do the trick. Given that level of complacency, can hysteria be far behind? The unfortunate truth is that, at any rate in personnel matters (because labour is so cheap?), most employers live hand-to-mouth and the idea of taking a strategic view and of doing so at board level is quite alien. (Cassels, 1989: 6)

Finally, it is important to note that a great deal of the HRM discourse is curiously decontextualized from the real world. All the talk of 'winning commitment', encouraging flexible working and gaining trust can appear rather glib in economies where unemployment is high (it is already at the level of 9.3 per cent in the European Community, and projected to rise to 11 per cent); where workforce reductions are announced virtually daily; and where pressure from the Treasury results in reductions in public-funded training budgets rather than increases.

## Conclusions

Superficially, given the reduction in overt industrial conflict and the apparent increase in attention to human resource matters by general and line managers as well as personnel specialists, the industrial relations and HR problem might seem to be close to a solution. However, the overview in this chapter of the basic data on the management of human resources and industrial relations in Britain makes clear that such an assessment would be a long way from the truth. Despite the ubiquitous references to the importance of the 'human resource' there is demonstrably a massive gap between rhetoric and reality. In the light of the rhetoric one would expect to find impressive evidence of an upturn in the amount of training and development, in the utilization of appropriate performance management techniques, in the integration of human resource practices and business strategy, and, not least, in the economic performance outcomes of British industry. However, as the data presented in this chapter reveals, on an international comparative basis, Britain

still has a long way to go. Senior managers are either not practising what they espouse or they are installing new initiatives in
an incompetent and ineffective way.

As we said at the beginning of this chapter, there is little room
for complacency. On the contrary, far from the human resource
and industrial relations issue having been 'solved' the overall
picture points uncomfortably to a drift towards a low investment,
low pay and low productivity economy. And yet, as the overview
also makes evident, there have undoubtedly been *some* important
changes which have been made. Handled in the right way, these
could contain the seeds of a way forward befitting the new
competitive environment which most managers now face. The
more detailed analysis carried out in each of the subsequent
chapters will draw-out the lines of development, the obstacles to
further progress, and the policy options for practitioners.

# 3

# MANAGING STRATEGICALLY

Central to the very idea of HRM is the notion that it entails a more *strategic* approach to the management of people than do traditional personnel management or industrial relations models. An ever-increasing number of books and articles now proclaim this feature (Beer et al., 1985; Fombrun et al., 1984; Armstrong 1992a, b).

The assumption underlying virtually all of this material is that to move from *ad hoc*, pragmatic management to strategic management is relatively straightforward. The principles appear very simple and the process apparently merely entails a series of logical steps. To move up to managing strategically therefore seems only to require the appropriate degree of will on the part of the managers concerned. In this chapter we will seek to demonstrate that these assumptions are ill-founded. We suggest that strategic HRM is problematical both at a conceptual and a practical level.

The chapter is organized into three sections. The first of these evaluates the purported 'best practice' models which are on offer to managers seeking to act strategically. Most notably, the models put forward by the teams at Harvard Business School and at the Massachusetts Institute of Technology (MIT) are critically appraised. We contend that while both of these offer seductive frameworks, managers attracted to either camp need to realize that they will be entering a minefield. In section two we emphasize that even when the manager has chosen a particular path, there are further problems to be faced. There are, we suggest, certain difficulties associated with the very concept of 'strategic HRM' whichever type of approach may be preferred – in particular, the common assumption that managers can exercise a free choice across a range of strategies is closely questioned. In the third section we seek to explain why strategic HR/IR is so difficult to achieve in the British context. The chapter concludes with a summary statement of its central messages.

## Best practice models of strategic HRM

The influential idea of 'strategic HRM' came to prominence in the early to middle 1980s in the United States. One of the most popular formulations of the idea has been the Harvard model (Beer et al., 1984). This model appears to suggest that there is, in effect, one preferred and superior set of HR 'policy choices'. The details of how these might be concocted in any specific situation are, not unnaturally, left to be filled-in for each concrete situation, but the main features of the prescribed strategy are made clear enough. Figure 3.1 shows the suggested elements and their interconnections.

In essence, the thesis advanced is that HRM policy choices will be influenced by a set of 'stakeholders' (shareholders, government, trade unions, etc.) and by the particular set of situational factors which will surround any particular case (such as product market conditions, the production technology and so on). Management's strategic task is to make certain fundamental policy choices in the light of these factors. Four clusters of choices are seen as especially important: these relate to the degree and nature of influence which employees will have; decisions about resourcing, throughflow and outflow of personnel; reward systems and the organization of work.

Here we reach the crux of the matter, for Beer and colleagues suggest that if appropriate choices are made across these clusters of decisions then beneficial 'HR outcomes' will follow. These

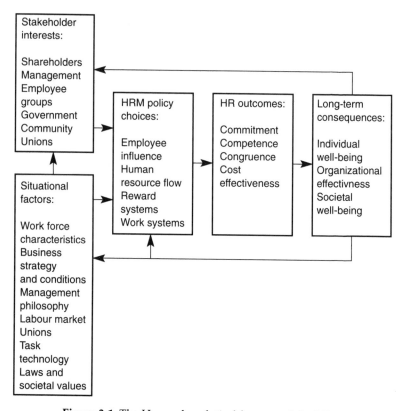

**Figure 3.1** The Harvard analytical framework for HRM
*Source*: Beer et al. (1984: 16)

include a committed workforce, a competent workforce, a balanced fit between HR interventions, and cost-effective operations. Thus, although ostensibly the Harvard model allows for considerable variation and appears to contrast itself with situational determinism, in fact the model posits what Guest (1987: 510) has termed an 'implicit theory'. In other words, the analysis of strategic choice contained herein has a strong prescriptive overtone. The specified desirable outcomes of commitment, competence and the like can be seen as the elevation of one particular strategic approach over all others.

Guest (1987) has taken this approach a logical step further. He clarifies the 'implicit model' and elaborates the underlying interconnections between a particular set of policy choices and a desired set of goals such as commitment, adaptability and quality. He has been criticized for this approach (Keenoy, 1990; Boxall, 1992). But the critics seem to miss the point that he is setting out in an explicit way *one type* of strategic choice which is then open for scrutiny alongside other strategic options.

The manager interested in developing a strategic approach to HR and IR is not, however, simply confronted with just one best practice model. The industrial relations specialists at MIT in Boston (Kochan et al., 1986) have constructed a persuasive alternative to the Harvard model. At first sight the MIT model (Kochan et al., 1986) might appear to be simply a descriptive account of transformative change in certain leading American companies. But in fact what is on offer is an implicit set of pointers to a new strategic approach. It becomes apparent that the 'transformed' approach as it is described is also the *recommended* strategy for the future.

The first key element to note in the MIT model is that it is clearly predicated on the concept of 'strategic choice'. Kochan et al. (1986: 5) state:

> the ultimate purpose is not simply to describe and interpret current developments. Instead, we wish to develop a more *strategic* perspective on US industrial relations and thereby demonstrate that future patterns are not unalterably pre-determined by economic, technological or some other forces . . . our central argument is that industrial relations practices and outcomes are shaped by the interaction of environmental forces *along with* the strategic choices and values of American managers, union leaders, workers and public policy makers.

A central element in the new framework is the idea that *choice* has a vital impact on the emergent IR system. Here Kochan et al. are clearly contrasting their own approach with the previously prevailing model of Dunlop (1958) which largely interpreted industrial relations systems as outcomes of determining contextual variables. Running alongside the idea of strategic choice is a three-tier institutional structure within which choice is exercised. This is shown in Table 3.1.

**Table 3.1** Three levels of industrial relations activity

| Level | Employers | Unions | Government |
|---|---|---|---|
| Long-term strategy and policy making | Business strategies<br>Investment strategies<br>Human resource strategies | Political strategies<br>Representation strategies<br>Organizing strategies | Macroeconomic and social policies |
| Collective bargaining and personnel policy | Personnel policies<br>Negotiations strategies | Collective bargaining strategies | Labor law and administration |
| Workplace and individual/ organization relationships | Supervisory style<br>Worker participation<br>Job design and work organization | Contract administration<br>Worker participation<br>Job design and work organization | Labor standards<br>Worker participation<br>Individual rights |

*Source:* Kochan et al. (1986: 17).

The top tier is the strategic decision making level, the middle one is a functional tier of collective bargaining and personnel policy making, and the lowest tier is concerned with day to day workplace activities. Running laterally across the figure are the three main 'actors': employers, unions, and government. Their roles and activities, when cross-cut with the three levels described above, give rise to the nine cells which depict the different types of IR behaviour.

The MIT team use this framework to track the fundamental changes in American industrial relations over a 50-year period. The main contrast they draw is between the new system and the orthodoxy which settled upon the American system from the 1930s onwards as a result of the political settlement between government, labour and employers. This 'New Deal' as it was known in the United States was formalized by the passage of the National Labor Relations Act in 1935. A new stamp was now put on public policy: a more pluralistic model of the employment relationship of a kind favoured by 'institutional' labour economists in place of the free market model favoured by the classical economists.

The key features of the fundamental change from the New Deal model to the 'New IR' are shown in Table 3.2.

**Table 3.2** Models of US industrial relations

| Levels of activity | 'New Deal' model | 'Non-union' model | 'New industrial relations' model |
| --- | --- | --- | --- |
| Business strategy and policy-making | Management prerogative | Management prerogative | Joint consultation |
| Collective bargaining and personnel | Comprehensive contracts | Comprehensive HRM policies | (Enabling agreements) |
| Workplace | Job control | Individual commitment | Cooperation and flexibility |

*Source*: Kochan et al. (1986).

The crux of the system was the middle level – collective bargaining. Here American IR practice moved towards serious negotiations aimed at producing comprehensive collective contracts which were legally binding. At the corporate level, in contrast, IR made little impact and business strategy was seen as the preserve of managerial decision. At the workplace level, 'job control' unionism entailed quasi-judicial grievance procedures to resolve disputes during the term of the formal collective contracts. These disputes over 'rights' were linked to notions of highly delineated and demarcated jobs. Seniority rights determined career progression and lay-offs were regulated by sets of joint rules. This is the system at the workplace level which Kochan and colleagues refer to as 'job control unionism'.

Moving across to the far right-hand side of the figure we come to the 'new industrial-relations model' which the MIT team see as having displaced the traditional framework. This is the transformed state to which their book title refers. The first notable feature here is the involvement of unions at the business strategy level. This is indicated in the figure by the term 'joint consultation' but in fact the process described in the book carries rather more significance than would be inferred from conventional British practice in joint consultation. In this cell of the figure the MIT team denote nothing less than 'union engagement', by senior union figures, in strategic business decisions. They refer here to decisions such as new investment, new technology, workforce adjustment strategies and new forms of work organization. Seeking a new role in such areas calls not only for a new mental set for management but also 'an equally fundamental shift on the part of union leaders' values and strategic thinking' (Kochan et al., 1986: 179–80). It will involve a 'great deal of internal union political debate and conflict; some union leaders argue that getting involved with management breaks with revered traditions and threatens to erode the independence that historically gave unions bargaining power' (p. 180).

So, new attitudes were required by both unions and management. These came about, argue Kochan and colleagues, because of the experience of deep crisis and the associated severe pressures to try a new direction. Traditional attitudes are changing, they suggest, and both sides are wanting to experiment.

These new attitudes also find reflection at the two lower levels. The middle tier experiences a move away from tightly constraining comprehensive contracts to 'enabling agreements' which set out general principles. The workplace level moves towards experimentation with flexible working and management-worker cooperation across a range of operational issues.

Two features, for us, are especially significant about this account of transformative change by these influential analysts of the American scene. First, the shifts they describe in management-union cooperation evidently go far beyond what has so far happened in Britain. Second, the analysis is not purely descriptive. The new model is evidently the preferred route for the authors. The traditional model is castigated because it proved 'inadequate in meeting the contemporary needs of employers for efficiency, flexibility and adaptability and of unions for organising and representing workers' (Kochan et al., 1986: 224). But the new HR is on its own insufficient as a substitute – 'instead what is needed is a blending of traditional representation and newer participatory processes along with perhaps additional, more individualised forms of voice and representation' (p. 225).

Before we leave this approach it is worth emphasizing that it is this mix between description, prediction and prescription that makes much of the human resource strategy writing so messy – and for some so attractive (see Guest's, 1992, analysis of the *In Search of Excellence* phenomenon).

## Contingency models of strategic HRM

The discussion so far is perhaps complicated enough, but there is yet another level of complexity to be confronted. The manager persuaded of the need to act strategically in HR and IR will soon discover that there are not only a range of prescriptive 'best practice' models on offer but additionally there are models which suggest the need to 'manage strategically' in a *contingent* fashion. These contributions emphasize the *variability* of strategic HRM policy choices under different business conditions. Three main types of contingent strategic theory have so far dominated – one links HR strategic choices to different 'stages' in the business life cycle; the second links HR strategic choices to different strategy/ structure configurations in the Chandlerian mould; (Chandler, 1962) the third links HR strategies to different business strategies of the type identified by Michael Porter (1980, 1985). We review each of these in turn.

## Business life-cycle stages

The first of these, the business life-cycle approach, essentially seeks to link appropriate HR policies to different 'stages' from business start up, through early growth and maturity and eventually to business decline. There are a number of examples of the 'stages' approach (Kochan and Barrocci, 1985; Baird and Meshoulam, 1988; Lengnick-Hall and Lengnick-Hall, 1988). Table 3.3 shows Kochan and Barrocci's link between four different business life-cycle stages (along the top horizontal axis of the figure) and the appropriate HR policies in the spheres of resourcing, compensation, employee training and development, and labour relations (shown vertically in the left column). The business life cycle can be posited as progressing through four stages from initiation to growth through maturity and then to decline. At each stage a business might be hypothesized to have different priorities. These different priorities, in turn, require their own appropriate human resource strategies.

At the start-up stage a business is deemed to require recruitment and selection strategies which quickly attract the best talent; a reward strategy which supports this by paying highly competitive rates; a training and development strategy which builds the foundations for the future; and an employee relations strategy which draws the basic architecture and puts in place the underlying philosophy for the new business.

If one contrasts this with the kind of human resource and industrial relations strategy suitable for a mature business, the differences easily become apparent. Under mature conditions the emphasis in HRM is upon control and maintenance of costs and resources. Hence, the recruitment and selection stance might be geared to trickle-feed new blood into vacant positions created by retirements. There might also be a policy of encouraging enough labour turnover so as to minimize the need for compulsory lay-offs. Meanwhile, the pay and benefits policy is likely to be

**Table 3.3** Critical human resource activities at different organizational or business unit stages

| Human resource functions | Life-cycle stages | | | |
|---|---|---|---|---|
| | *Start-up* | *Growth* | *Maturity* | *Decline* |
| Recruitment, selection and staffing | Attract best technical/professional talent | Recruit adequate numbers and mix of qualified workers. Management succession planning. Manage rapid internal labour market movements | Encourage sufficient turnover to minimize lay-offs and provide new openings. Encourage mobility as re-organizations shift jobs around | Plan and implement workforce reductions and reallocation |
| Compensation and benefits | Meet or exceed labour market rates to attract needed talent | Meet external market but consider internal equity effects. Establish formal compensation structures | Control compensation | Tighter cost control |
| Employee training and development | Define future skill requirements and begin establishing career ladders | Mould effective management team through management development and organizational development | Maintain flexibility and skills of an ageing workforce | Implement retraining and career consulting services |
| Labour/employee relations | Set basic employee relations philosophy and organization | Maintain labour peace and employee motivation and morale | Control labour costs and maintain labour peace. Improve productivity | Maintain peace |

*Source:* Kochan and Barocci (1985: 104).

geared to a keen control over costs. Training and development might be expected to have as their priority the maintenance of flexibility and the adequate provision of skill levels in an ageing workforce.

However, business life cycle is not the only critical variable which is likely to influence the choice of appropriate HRM strategies. Another major contingency is likely to be the configuration of business strategies and structures.

### Strategy/structure linkage

The most noted example of the second type of contingency theory – the strategy/structure linkage – is the work of Fombrun et al. (1984). Their model (see Table 3.4) is evidently of a contingent nature, that is, there is no *one* best way. Rather, the 'best' practice will vary depending upon the particular situation.

The table shows a range of 'appropriate' HR choices suited to five different strategy/structure types ranging from single product businesses with functional structures, through diversified product strategies allied to multi-divisional organizational forms and on to multi-product companies operating globally. For each of the five types of situation the key HR policy choices in the spheres of selection, appraisal, reward and development are delineated.

The links between business strategy and structure are very close, as Chandler (1962) and Channon (1973) have shown. So closely intertwined have they been found to be that much debate has in fact ensued as to whether 'strategy follows structure' or 'structure follows strategy'. Whichever way this may be, the two are evidently mutually related. What is interesting from our perspective, however, is the further linkage with human resource management strategy. The figure suggests for instance that in a company following a single-product strategy with an associated functional structure, the HRM strategy is likely to be traditional in appearance. Selection and appraisal may well be conducted in a subjective fashion and reward and development practices may veer to the unsystematic and the paternalistic.

By way of contrast, a company pursuing a diversification strategy with a multi-divisional structure is likely to be characterized by a human resource strategy which is driven by impersonal,

**Table 3.4** Human resources management links to strategy and structure

| Strategy | Structure | Human resource management | | | |
| --- | --- | --- | --- | --- | --- |
| | | Selection | Appraisal | Rewards | Development |
| 1 Single product | Functional | Functionally oriented: subjective criteria used | Subjective measure via personal contact | Unsystematic and allocated in a paternalistic manner | Unsystematic largely job experiences: single function focus |
| 2 Single product (vertically integrated) | Functional | Functionally oriented: standardized criteria used | Impersonal: based on cost and productivity data | Related to performance and productivity | Functional specialists with some generalists: largely rotation |
| 3 Growth by acquisition (holding company) of unrelated businesses | Separate self-contained businesses | Functionally oriented, but varies from business to business in terms of how systematic | Impersonal: based on return on investment and profitability | Formula-based includes return on investment and profitability | Cross-functional but not cross-business |
| 4 Related diversification of product lines through internal growth and acquisition | Multi-divisional | Functionally and generalist oriented: systematic criteria used | Impersonal: based on return on investment, productivity, and subjective assessment of contribution to company | Large bonuses: based on profitability and subjective assessment of contribution to overall company | Cross-functional, cross-divisional, and cross corporate/divisional formal |
| 5 Multiple products in multiple countries | Global organization (geographic centre and world-wide) | Functionally and generalists oriented: systematic criteria used | Impersonal: based on multiple goals such as return on investment, profit tailored to product and country | Bonuses: based on multiple planned goals with moderate top management discretion | Cross-divisional and cross-subsidiary to corporate: formal and systematic |

*Source:* Adapted from Fombrun et al. (1984).

systematic devices which are, however, adaptable to the different parts of the organization. Reward systems are likely to be formula-based with a tendency towards a built-in response to return on investment and profitability. Selection and even appraisal may be found to vary between the different constituent business divisions. Where the multi-divisional approach is, however, accompanied by a business strategy built around interrelated, interdependent businesses, it is postulated that it is more likely in these circumstances that the human resource management strategy will foster and take advantage of that interrelationship. Hence, training and management development practices will operate cross-functionally and cross-divisionally. Senior managers and a select group picked out as probable future senior managers may be handled separately as a company-wide resource rather than their development and other conditions being left to the (variable) chance occurrences of separate, divisional, policies (or lack of them).

## *Matching HR/IR with business strategy*

The third type of strategic HR/IR contingency theory links policy choices in HR/IR with different types of business strategy. Most of the theorists in this category draw on Michael Porter's work on corporate strategy (e.g. Schuler and Jackson, 1987) or on Miles and Snow (e.g. Williams et al., 1990). Porter suggested that there are three basic strategic options in order to gain 'competitive advantage'. These are: innovation, quality-enhancement or cost-reduction. Tracing through the logic of these for HR strategy, Schuler and Jackson (1987) suggest that each one has an associated set of 'needed role behaviours'. These are employee behaviour patterns which are at a premium under each given circumstance.

Schuler (1988) elaborates 31 dilemmas which constitute the key 'human resource management practice choices'. For example, in terms of staffing choices will the bias be towards mainly using internal or external sources of labour supply? On appraisal, will behavioural criteria or results criteria be used? Will the short-term or the long-term be the chosen time-frame? Will the focus be on individual or group performance? Regarding compensation arrangements, will there be a simple base salary with no extra incentive payments or will there be many? Awareness of this constellation of dilemmas among policy choices opens up the possibility of elaborating the connections between different business strategies, their associated 'needed role behaviours' and, in turn, the appropriate practice choices for these particular situations. This is illustrated in Figure 3.2.

Thus, Schuler and Jackson's (1987) model suggests that where a firm has opted, say, for innovation as a means to gain competitive advantage, this sets up certain predictable required patterns of behaviour, or as Schuler and Jackson term them, requisite 'role behaviours'. Prime among these are creativity, a capacity and willingness to focus on longer-term goals, a relatively high level of collaborative action, a high tolerance of ambiguity and a high degree of readiness to take risks. On the other hand, concern for quality and for achieving output need only be at moderate levels.

This theory of the link between business strategy and human resource strategy goes on to identify the HRM policy choices which will be needed in order to evoke and maintain these requisite behaviour patterns. Hence for each of the main behavioural dimensions as listed in the central column there is also an accompanying HRM policy-option as shown in the third column. For example, a longer-term focus might be encouraged through the use of different criteria in performance appraisal. The required levels of cooperative, interdependent behaviours might in turn be facilitated through HRM policy choices in the realm of job design and through the installation of group-based payment systems.

As a way of illustrating the contrasts with other strategic choices one might note that where a cost-reduction business strategy is chosen then the behaviour patterns at a premium will conversely hinge around a short-term focus and a willingness to perform and tolerate repetitive and predictable job cycles in a standardized undeviating way. The associated HRM policy choices to encourage this set of behaviours will include (Tayloristic) job design principles, close monitoring and control, and an appraisal system which rewards and punishes in accord with short-term results.

Arguably, the most out-and-out 'matching' approach is taken by Miller (1989). He seeks to tighten-up what he sees as the rather

| Strategy | Employee role behaviour | HRM policies |
|---|---|---|
| 1 *Innovation* | A high degree of creative behaviour | Jobs that require close interaction and coordination among groups of individuals |
| | Longer term focus | Performance appraisals that are more likely to reflect longer term and group-based achievements |
| | A relatively high level of cooperative, interdependent behaviour | Jobs that allow employees to develop skills that can be used in other positions in the firm |
| | | Compensation systems that emphasize internal equity rather than external or market-based equity |
| | A moderate degree of concern for quality | Pay rates that tend to be low, but that allow employees to be stockholders and have more freedom to choose the mix of components that make up their pay package |
| | A moderate concern for quantity | |
| | An equal degree of concern for process and results | Broad career paths to reinforce the development of a broad range of skills |
| | A greater degree of risk taking | |
| | A high tolerance of ambiguity and unpredictability | |
| 2 *Quality enhancement* | Relatively repetitive and predictable behaviours | Relatively fixed and explicit job descriptions |
| | A more long term or intermediate focus | High levels of employee participation in decisions relevant to immediate work conditions and the job itself |
| | A moderate amount of cooperative, interdependent behaviour | A mix of individual and group criteria for performance appraisal that is mostly short term and results orientated |
| | A high concern for quality | A relatively egalitarian treatment of employees and some guarantees of employment security |
| | A modest concern for quality of output | Extensive and continuous training and development of employees |
| | High concern for process | |
| | Low risk-taking activity | |
| | Commitment to the goals of the organization | |
| 3 *Cost reduction* | Relatively repetitive and predictable behaviour | Relatively fixed and explicit job descriptions that allow little room for ambiguity |
| | A rather short-term focus | Narrowly designed jobs and narrowly defined career paths that encourage specialization, expertise and efficiency |
| | Primarily autonomous or individual activity | Short-term results orientated performance appraisals |
| | Moderate concern for quality | Close monitoring of market pay levels for use in making compensation decisions |
| | High concern for quantity of output | Minimal levels of employee training and development |
| | Primary concern for results | |
| | Low risk-taking activity | |
| | Relatively high degree of comfort with stability | |

**Figure 3.2** Business strategy and HRM policy choices. Employee role behaviour and HRM policies associated with particular business strategies
*Source*: Schuler and Jackson (1987: 209–13)

loose usage of the term HR strategy by suggesting that a HR approach is only 'strategic' if it 'fits' with the organization's product-market strategy and if it is proactive in this regard. This leads him to argue, for example, that in the case of British Coal the experimentation with local payment by results was *not* a strategic response because it did not align with British Coal's dominant customer base in the Central Electricity Generating Board (CEGB) and its consequent centralized marketing and pricing behaviour. The pit-based payment by results (PBR) scheme, says Miller, 'differentiated one small element of the business when the rest was integrated. It was not, therefore, a strategic response to human resource management' (p. 51).

Miller's position is crystal clear if somewhat stark. He contends:

> We can say that if managements manage their employees in ways which recognise their role in strategy implementation, it is behaving strategically. If on the other hand, it makes decisions simply in order to avoid trade unions, or better to control employees, it is operating in a fashion which is separate from the business and [is] non-strategic. (Miller, 1989: 51)

Few commentators have taken such an economical view of the issue. As will be demonstrated below, the meaning(s) given to the concept of strategy in general and human resource strategy in particular tend to range rather wider than Miller would wish.

Dyer (1983, 1985) and Tichy (1984) argue that the human resource management function should be integrated into the strategy formulation process as well as attuning HR practices at the implementation stage. Hence, they stress the importance of having a HR director at board level; they look for proactivity from the HR function; and they look for coherence between all the practices and policies within the organization's strategic thrust. Dyer (1983) concentrates on the outcomes of human resource strategies. As he says, 'the acid test' is whether there are 'identifiable combinations' of environments (and settings) and particular types of HRS which 'consistently yield better results than their alternatives' (p.165). His framework can be summarized in diagrammatic (and simplified) form as in Figure 3.3.

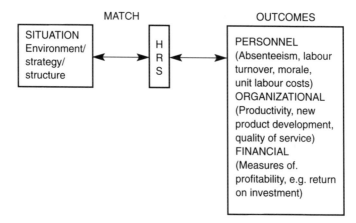

**Figure 3.3** Hypothesized linkages between the HR–business 'fit' and various outcomes
*Source*: Dyer (1983: 165)

## Issues and problems in the HR/IR strategy literature

As we observed at the outset of this chapter, if one judges by most accounts, managing strategically appears to be relatively straightforward. The 'best practice' scenarios seem clear enough and even the contingency approaches although seemingly more complex in some versions, amount in the end to 'matching' certain HR/IR policy options with particular corporate strategies. Yet, if it is all as straightforward as this, how does one account for (a) the empirical findings which reveal the wide-scale *lack* of strategy in British HR/IR (see for example the IRRU findings reported in Marginson et al., 1988); and (b) the record of comparative failure as recorded in 'The Story So Far' in Chapter 2?

The manager who seeks to act strategically in HR/IR will soon discover that the task is in fact far from being as straightforward as the theorists reviewed above appear to suggest. To begin with, both the best practice theorists and the contingency theorists, despite their other differences, seem to build their cases upon two assumptions which at first sight appear eminently reasonable. The first of these assumptions is that HR/IR managers will have easy recourse to a business strategy. The second assumption is that managers actually have a choice of strategy. We believe that both assumptions are in reality highly problematical.

Let us take the first one – that HR/IR managers can if they choose, have easy recourse to the 'corporate strategy' of their employing organization. This seemingly simple task is often an uphill struggle for a number of reasons. Where such strategies are available they are often extremely vague. There may well be financial targets and detailed budget plans but to translate these into operational terms can be very difficult. Even a specific statement from, say, a financial services institution to gain a 5 per cent market penetration in Europe for its range of products can carry numerous alternative implications from an HR/IR viewpoint.

But this is not all. Anyone interested in developing a strategic approach will face a further problem. Most of the strategic models typically lean towards rational planning assumptions in their conception of corporate strategy and HR strategy. The conventional, planned, rational model assumes that the formulation and implementation of business strategy occur in linear fashion. Chandler's (1962: 13) well-known discussion expresses this position clearly: 'Strategy is the determination of the basic long-term goals of an enterprise, and the adoption of courses of actions and the allocation of resources necessary for carrying out these goals.' As a number of recent analysts have shown, these sorts of assumptions present an unduly simplified and distorted view of strategic action. For example, Quinn (1980), Mintzberg (1978, 1987, 1988) and Pettigrew (1977) suggest that these 'rationalistic' models of strategy need to be replaced with 'processual' and 'incremental' models. For these analysts 'strategy' is seen to emerge through disjointed serial steps which are influenced by the social and political routines of organizational life. 'Strategy' is regarded as a far more complex affair than the simple idea of rational planning would suggest. As Mintzberg's (1978) classic formulation put it, strategy may best be seen as 'a pattern in a stream of decisions'. By implication, strategic choices are often being made on an everyday basis and by people at many levels in an organization. The interplay of influential complex factors both external to and internal to the firm is seen as requiring managers to make continual assessments, and continual adjustments. Managing strategy is thus an interactive process. Objectives themselves are likely to be unclear and post-rationalized. Under these conditions it is naturally going to be extremely difficult for an HR/IR manager simply to reach out for 'the' definitive corporate strategy and thence to construct a 'congruent' HR/IR version.

A position which is even more distanced from the formalistic rational-planning view of strategy is to be found in the 'interpretive' model (Johnson, 1987, 1990; Whittington, 1989). Here, strategy is seen very much as a social outcome. It is accordingly shaped by the prevailing ideologies, rituals, myths and symbols of the organizational culture. Changing the strategy therefore entails an exercise in the manipulation or management of meaning. Effecting such a shift is difficult because managers and other organizational members operate within deeply embedded 'causal maps', 'scripts' or 'ideologies' which may be hardly perceived at the conscious level.

In this perspective the emphasis is shifted to the highlighting of the intricacies in internal processes: how managers came to be sensitized to the need for a change in direction; what factors condition the formation of the range of options considered. These and other issues are seen as crucially influenced by social and political forces. Managerial motivations, their circumscribed sources of information and their frames of reference all came centrally into the picture as critical factors in the shaping of strategic choices (Johnson, 1987; Whittington, 1989, 1993).

Another and rather different type of challenge to the rationalistic model attacks the *assumption* that a grand integrated strategy must necessarily be more effective and efficient than the absence of such a strategy. It is certainly true that commentaries which note the lack of a strategic approach towards IR and personnel do tend to imply that this is a 'failing'. Even more explicit are those prescriptive models which purport to reveal how business strategy should be matched with HR policies. But some critics would challenge the bases for these claims. For instance, the strength of the linkage between competitive performance and sophisticated HRM has been questioned. Intuitively it seems logical that an 'integrated' approach should be 'better', but what evidence is there to support such a view? Ultimately, this is a question which has to be subjected to empirical investigation.

One of the difficulties in making bold claims about appropriate linkages between business strategy and HR strategy arises from the simple fact that few firms appear, in practice, to engage in strategic planning – particularly with regard to HR and IR (Rowland and Summers, 1981; Mills, 1985; Marginson et al., 1988). In industrial relations, the idea of managers exercising 'strategic choice' has been popularized as we saw above by influential figures from the MIT School (Kochan et al., 1986; Kochan et al., 1990). But, in the British context at least, empirical research (Marginson et al., 1988) has questioned the extent to which consistently applied policies lie behind recent initiatives. They suggest, alternatively, that pragmatic and opportunistic responses to changing economic and labour market conditions appear a more valid explanation. Indeed, they observe 'it is a moot point whether it is appropriate to dignify management's approach to industrial relations with the adjective "strategic"' (p. 10).

Work in the early 1980s (Purcell and Sisson, 1983; Deaton, 1985) suggested that in practice most British firms were essentially 'pragmatic' or 'opportunistic' when dealing with industrial relations. But in the light of the upsurge of interest in integrated and strategic approaches to the management of employees Sisson and colleagues took the opportunity in the Warwick company level survey to re-assess this judgement (Marginson et al., 1988: 116–20). Respondents at corporate and divisional levels were asked about the 'overall approach on philosophy' which they adopted in the management of employees and subsequently these managers were asked to describe the elements in their own words. On first consideration the results looked impressive: 84 per cent of head office managers claimed that their company did have an overall approach to employment management. Notably, companies which were financially centralized in terms of profit responsibility were significantly more likely to have an overall approach to IR; and service sector companies too were also more likely to have this characteristic.

However, when it came to the point where respondents were asked to describe this integrated approach many managers had great difficulty in detailing its features. Rather vague references were made to being 'forward looking' or 'caring'. Moreover, when categories of replies such as a stress on 'employee involvement' were compared with the detailed profile of practices drawn from other parts of the interview schedule there was found to be no correlation at all.

The authors observed: 'it is difficult to escape the conclusion that, although the great majority of our respondents claim that their organizations have an overall policy or approach to the management of employees, with the exception of a number of companies which are overseas owned, or financially centralized, or operating in the service sectors, it would be wrong to set very much store by this . . . the general weight of evidence would seem to confirm that most UK owned enterprises remain pragmatic or opportunistic in their approach' (p. 120).

This brings us to the second of the two big assumptions we identified above. This assumption is that managers have a genuine free choice of strategic stance. According to this, once a group of corporate managers is convinced that, say, the path marked out by Kochan et al. (1986) in the 'Transformation' book is the progressive position to hold, then all that remains following an act of 'will' to move in this direction, is to 'implement' the strategy effectively. This sort of assumption is again highly simplistic. Companies (and strategic business units or divisions) are not islands unto themselves. They find it very difficult to act independently of prevailing legal, social and political norms and structures. Even the harbingers of transformational change in American industrial relations (Kochan et al., 1986) have more recently noted that

> while important innovations in practice were accompanied by numerous calls for a paradigm shift toward a more 'strategic' focus for human resource management research, developments in both practice and research fell far short of expectations. (Kochan and Dyer, 1992: 1)

These authors have been forced into this reassessment of their earlier position by recent empirical studies in the USA which have revealed that there too the majority of firms do not achieve a high degree of integration between business strategy and human resource management (Golden and Ramanujam, 1985). The crunch point in explaining this shortfall goes to the very heart of the interplay between HR and IR which is the central thrust of this present book. Kochan and Dyer in their paper argue that the

> 'strategic' human resource management models of the 1980s were too limited . . . because they depended so heavily on the values, strategies and support of top executives . . . While we see [these] as necessary conditions, we do not see them as sufficient to support the transformational process. A model capable of achieving sustained and transformational change will, therefore, need to incorporate more active roles of other stakeholders in the employment relationship, including government, employees and union representatives as well as line managers'. (Kochan and Dyer, 1992: 1)

## Why is strategic human resource management so difficult to achieve in the UK?

Despite the apparent attraction of the HRM model and despite the enthusiasm with which the Tom Peter's roadshows are received, the plain fact is that everyday managerial practice fails to match the *beau idéal* by some considerable measure. The question to be answered at this point centres on why the ideal of strategic human resource management should be so difficult to achieve. In particular, what are the factors which limit its attainment in the British context?

Two main sets of factors can be identified. It is vitally important that both sets are taken into account by those managers who have determined to rise to the challenge of acting in a strategic manner. The first set comprises a host of what might be called 'situational' factors such as prevailing technology, the state of industrial relations and the like. The second set of factors is rather more generic to the British context as a whole.

Under the first heading, the situational factors, the implication is that some companies will, because of particularistic circumstances, find it relatively more difficult to practise in accordance with HRM tenets than will others. One of these factors is the extant production technology. If this is geared towards short-cycle repetitive activity then the whole managerial approach is more likely to be pulled towards the associated panoply of Tayloristic principles. There will seem little good reason to invest in extensive training. The need for the exercise of discretion and innovative behaviour will be reduced and 'commitment' other than that required to report for work will seem superfluous.

Technology is of course not entirely a 'given'. It is designed and shaped in accordance with social assumptions and expectations. It forms part of the wider set of choices associated with a production strategy. In those circumstances where the thrust is towards cost-reduction rather than quality enhancement or differentiation built on some other principle such as innovation, then minimum specifications may easily result. These can quickly extend across the span of methods, materials, employee selection, reward packages, training and the rest. In these conditions the prospects for HRM are clearly not propitious.

Large, multi-union 'brownfield' production sites might also be expected to be less conducive to HRM change than a small-scale, non-union or single union 'greenfield' site. The trend towards re-directing investment towards conditions of the latter variety can largely be explained by this extra malleability in such cases. The extent to which the accumulation of custom and practice and of outdated plant are the true sources of inertia rather than multi-unionism and 'traditional industrial relations' *per se*, is a very moot point. David Guest's (1989) analysis of this issue leads towards the conclusion that the latter is in itself a factor. So much so, it appears, that Guest seems to doubt whether the full-blown HRM approach is, or could ever be, compatible with traditional trade unionism (1989: 54–5). He writes: 'there is an incompatibility between the essentially unitarist HRM and pluralist tradition of industrial relations in the UK.' But he also notes that 'there have been initiatives in many companies to increase employee involvement and to take other steps on the path towards HRM'. Given the assumed incompatibility of these approaches, how can we explain this? One obvious answer is that the underlying assumption of incompatibility is wrong. This is essentially the view of Kochan et al. (1986). But, says Guest, their analysis applies largely to single-union plants in the USA and, in any case, their timescale is not sufficiently long to allow for the possibility that the incompatibility thesis is true in that the American unions may be 'colluding in their own gradual demise' (1989: 54).

There are also other possibilities. It may be that the two systems could coexist (providing that the full implications of HRM are not pushed to the limits). Alternatively, the tentative signs of coexistence may simply result from the fact that even where senior managers are thinking strategically about HRM the actualization of this thinking tends to be opportunistic because of problems of implementation. 'As a result', Guest says, 'HRM issues are rarely pursued to the point where the industrial relations' system is seriously challenged. At some point, any company pursuing HRM will confront the industrial relations institutions in areas like flexibility, job design and reward systems' (p. 55).

These two latter arguments are broadly the same. Guest is able to maintain his assumption of 'incompatibility' by, in the first instance postulating a conscious holding back by senior managers for strategic reasons, and in the second instance by a rather less well thought-through behaviour pattern where the two 'incompatibles' are able to rub-along together because of difficulties of implementing the full logic of corporate visions.

In addition to the above set of particular, situational, factors there are also the more generic impediments to HRM in the British context. The evidence from cross-national studies of productivity and managerial behaviour leads towards the conclusion that elements which may express themselves in sharp form in certain specific cases may also be endemic in a broader fashion in this country. For example, the National Institute of Education and Social Research (NIESR) has conducted a series of comparative productivity studies at the level of the firm (see for example, Prais and Wagner, 1988). These reveal how, in industry after industry, German companies tend to conduct themselves in a manner which plans for the longer term and allows competition at the higher value-added end of the market. British companies fared badly in comparison. These generic limiting factors can be summarized as resulting from a complex of interconnected characteristics of the British industrial scene. We will try to disentangle these as follows.

First, there is the problem of 'short-termism' in Britain. This means that managerial performance horizons are adjusted to meet annual, half-year, and even quarterly reporting schedules. The exigencies of this regime place a premium on behaviours and investments which have an immediate pay-back. This, up to a point, may act as a useful discipline. But, a consequential effect is to discourage, and even penalise, actions which are geared to a beneficial return over a longer time horizon. Many HRM initiatives would fall into this latter category – most notably those which relate to training and development and investments of time and resources in winning commitment.

Conversely, short-term reporting periods tend to put pressure on managers to have recourse to opportunistic quick-fix agreements, firefighting solutions; and Tayloristic job design methods which are built on command and control rather than the more time-consuming consensus-seeking methods. Little wonder then, that these are the managerial devices and methods which have come to be so characteristic of the British scene.

It is worth recognizing that the endemic character of short-termism is interconnected with other features associated with British management. They are, in their own right, inimical to strategic human resource management. The occupational structuring of senior British management is one such. The accountancy qualification has, for some years, been one of the few recognized routes into managerial positions. In recent years the dominance of accountants on company boards and executive management boards has, if anything, actually increased. Many a large British company such as British Telecom has sought to sharpen its commercial acumen by ejecting the home-grown engineers from the most senior policy-making echelons and replacing them with accountants recruited externally. For example, on the BT main board, of the 24 members, only three (as at November 1991) were BT engineers who were promoted through the traditional route. Just eight years previously the majority on the board had arrived through this route.

Nor is it just a question of numbers of accountants. Arguably, even more important is the dominance of accountancy logic and accountancy-driven managerial control systems which have come to be pervasive in British companies (Armstrong, 1989). It becomes very difficult for an alternative logic, such as that contained within HRM, to gain a foothold and to prevail over the incessant demands of the accountancy-driven tune. In the absence of well educated and trained managers, fully equipped with a wider vista, the managerial accountants' way of thinking will prevail. Longer term planning in HRM especially will be difficult to practise when, in the experience of most British managers 'planning' simply means 'budgeting'.

These features of the British scene are supported still further by the basic strategies and structures finding favour here. As the McKinsey (1988) consultants showed in their report on the electronics industry, there is a predilection for the M-form, multi-divisional structure. The headlong rush to this form across a whole range of British industries is not to be doubted. But the McKinsey consultants were scathing about an approach, the 'state of the art' in America in the 1960s and 1970s, which had come, belatedly, to dominate thinking in Britain in a way which serves to impede, they say, strategic planning. The British electronic companies which they investigated were, in consequence, failing to take advantages of the opportunities for synergy which large company status should confer. Fragmentation and devolution to constituent businesses had become so prevalent that, when wedded to the often associated financial control system (Goold and Campbell, 1987), the result was a set of small businesses having to respond to short-term financial goals. Under such a regime, HRM can be expected to find the climate inclement.

Moreover, much of this corporate-dictated behaviour is shaped exogenously by the expectations of the City. The structure of ownership of companies in Britain, unlike say Germany and Japan, relies heavily on large investments from trusts, pension funds and other institutional shareholders. The account managers employed by these bodies tend to be judged by their short-term returns and this therefore again serves to fuel the short-term bias.

In the light of the above analysis it might be assumed that organizations in the public sector are likely to be immune to these

HRM-limiting pressures. In fact, while public sector organizations escape many of these forces they are none the less subject
to yet others which can be equally limiting for the human
resource management approach. Public sector organizations are
more typically highly unionized, are often multi-union in character and they are expected to follow due process and procedure
and to be even-handed and fair in the treatment of all employees
as well as members of the public. These features tend to limit the
scope for the exercise of flexibility and discretion.

# Conclusions

We began this chapter by noting that it has now become
conventional wisdom to view HRM as a *strategic* endeavour. It
was further noted that most of the accounts of strategic HRM
seemed to present it as a relatively straightforward affair. This
point applies alike to both the 'best practice' models and the
contingency approaches. We suggested that managing strategically is not simple either at the conceptual or the practical
level. Some of the more important contributions to the debate
were reviewed, in particular the range of recent American models
which have sought to link strategic HR and IR with various
business conditions.

The argument of the chapter then moved on to challenge two
central assumptions which underpin most contributions to the
discussion: the first that HR managers normally have a business
strategy to which they can relate; and the second that managers
are free to select and to enact their chosen strategies. On each
count, the business of acting strategically in HR and IR was found
to be far more complex and difficult than the normal glib
commentaries would suggest.

The central messages arising from this chapter may be summarized as follows. Developing a strategic approach to managing
HR/IR is not nearly so easy as some pundits seem to assume. No
organization is an island unto itself. Because of the wider context
in which they have to work – and, in particular, because of the
pressures towards short-termism and ironically, because of the
'tradition of voluntarism' in UK labour law – those persons

running organizations in the UK who want to move up to a strategic plane in HR/IR face an uphill struggle. Moreover, the range of options open to them will usually turn out to be more severely constrained than they had imagined or had been led to expect.

We suggest, none the less, that they do have some 'choice', and that there is often a great deal that can be done by managers who are prepared to question conventional wisdom. Examination of the specific areas in which action can (and should) be taken is what the rest of the book is about. It remains to emphasize here, however, that before embarking on initiatives in any of these areas, it is important to ensure that close attention is paid to three critical points. The first of these is that the business strategy must be capable of being translated into operational action plans. Second, it must be made absolutely clear to whom the responsibility for developing the strategy actually belongs: does it rest, for example, at corporate headquarters, the divisional office, or at each individual business unit? Third, some decision has to be taken about the overall thrust of the approach – will it, for example, aspire to match up to one of the 'best practice' models or will it reflect in contingency fashion, the particular needs of the organization?

We commence the detailed analysis in the next chapter by tackling an issue which is rarely addressed in textbooks on industrial relations or human resource management – i.e. the strategic decisions to be made about organizational and work structuring.

# 4

# ORGANIZING FOR HIGH PERFORMANCE: RESTRUCTURING AND INVOLVEMENT

The pressure from increasingly competitive environments and the changing nature of that competition have led to a perceived need for extensive re-structuring. The search for adaptable, lean, and responsive organizational forms has been hotly pursued. Businesses and public service organizations alike have been changing the way they allocate and organize work in significant ways and these carry human resource and industrial relations' implications. High on the agenda of many managers have been the issues of 'de-layering', 'downsizing', 'flexibility', 'team-working', 'service level agreements', 'high performance work systems', 'strategic business units', 'core and periphery', 'tele-working', 'franchising' and other similar organizational devices and issues.

Already, the restructuring of big corporations such as ICI, BP and BT has occurred on a massive scale. In 1991, even the erstwhile monolith of IBM embarked upon a massive restructuring by dividing itself into 13 autonomous units each responsible for its own profitability. National Westminster and the other clearing banks have sought to decentralize and delayer. In the public sector too, the civil service, local government and the NHS have undergone extensive re-structuring. Agencies in the civil service, Service Delivery Units in local authorities and self-governing Trusts in the NHS all witness the drive towards devolution.

Beneath the variety of forms there are certain common themes and many of these are central to human resource management and industrial relations. The central drive appears to be towards devolved accountability. This is supposed to bring with it adaptability, energy and involvement. It is the purpose of this chapter to draw these out and to explore their implications.

The chapter is divided into three main sections. The first examines the nature and implications of wide-ranging corporate re-structuring such as divisionalization and strategic business units. The second section attends to task-level reorganization of work – focusing especially on the numerous experiments in 'teamworking'. The final section continues the theme of employee involvement which is central to the idea of teams by exploring forms of participation and organizing for quality which cut across the various corporate levels.

## Corporate re-structuring

The purpose of this section is to examine the main types of corporate re-structuring and to focus on their HR and IR implications. A central concern will be to highlight the choices facing managers today. Among the variation two key themes stand out: first, a drive towards *devolution* of accountability and second, a search for *flexibility*. Each of these can be interpreted as being in themselves impelled (at least in part) by human resource management assumptions. We now consider each in turn.

### Devolution

Despite the promotion of, and the attention given to small firms in the 1980s, the UK economy is still dominated by large enterprises. Given that decisions in a few corporate centres could shape human resource and industrial relations policies across wide swathes of the economy, the overall neglect of corporate structuring in HR/IR debate is little short of remarkable. This is particularly so when it is noted that corporate governance and structuring have been undergoing considerable change in recent years. The implications of structural forms for the way management of human resources are conducted have been largely left unexplored. One notable exception is Purcell (1989) and another is the Warwick company level study referred to earlier which examined the management of industrial relations in the multi-establishment enterprise (Marginson et al., 1988). This study sought to uncover which IR decisions were taken at the corporate centre, the divisional tier and the operating units. We want to point up the findings of that study and add to it a set of human resource management issues as well.

As organizations grew whether by acquisition, merger or organically, into large corporations the problem of their governance and their structuring became a pressing issue. As Channon (1982) observed, large corporations were increasingly diversified and divisionalized. Structures built around management functions such as finance, engineering, personnel and marketing were perceived as incapable of coping with the complexities of diverse markets, processes and products. In order to handle this complexity separate divisions were typically created and to these were devolved much of the responsibility for handling the strategy in their field of operations. Hence, for example, ICI would have its paints division and its pharmaceutical division; Lucas would have its aerospace and its motor-components divisions. This 'divisionalization' meant that intermediate levels of strategic decision were interposed between the corporate centre and the operating units. In consequence, the question of the appropriate roles for each tier came to be asked and the range of options concerning how to manage these multi-divisional forms became a crucial agenda item in the corporate strategy literature (Chandler, 1962; Hill and Pickering, 1986; Goold and Campbell, 1987). The implications of this re-structuring for HR and IR have, however, hardly been considered.

It is vital to recognize at this stage that there is no one correct answer to the problem of centralization and decentralization. The rationale for centralization stems from the need for coordination. Why then should any organization decentralize? Mintzberg (1979) offers three classical answers: because issues are too complex for the central brain to comprehend; because local managers may be able to respond more quickly to local conditions; and third: 'decentralization is a stimulus for motivation' (p. 183). Decentralization thus becomes a means to attract and retain creative people. (For managers a fourth reason is advanced – decentralization allows middle managers to practise decision-making skills which one day they will need for senior management roles.)

The problem of centralization or decentralization is in fact part of a bigger one which concerns the ways in which an organization manages the twin needs of differentiation and integration (Lawrence and Lorsch, 1967). The precise balance can be expected to shift as different pressures and different priorities arise. For example, at the time of writing, the chemicals giant ICI, which has 120,000 employees across 40 countries, is wrestling with the decision as to whether to split (in effect to de-merge) into two separate companies each with its own board of directors and each with its own set of shareholders. One company would focus on bulk products such as fertilizers and paints, the other on bio-science products such as pharmaceuticals. Championing the proposal is the Chairman, Sir Denys Henderson. The reasons he gives for supporting it include the following: it would give each company greater 'focus' and shorter lines of communication; each would be closer to its shareholders and customers; it would allow for the exercise of more entrepreneurial flair, would facilitate quicker action – and, by removing the security of cross-subsidy, would allow less 'comfort' and hence sharpen awareness of opportunities and threats. As Sir Denys is keen to point out, this is all business-driven and is not to be confused with the 'financial engineering' of a Hanson Trust. What is notable, however, is that a great deal of the rationale for the move hinges on certain calculations about how managers and employees will behave differently under the new structural order.

When the manager comes to focus on HR and IR in a very particular way, he or she will be faced with four main decisions (Ahlstrand and Purcell, 1988). These are:

1 What should be the structure for collective bargaining?
2 How should the personnel function itself be deployed across the various levels?

3 Whether, and how, a corporate culture should be promoted across the different units and levels.

4 Should managers and certain other employees be treated as a corporate resource or should the management of their careers and their terms and conditions be left to the separate businesses?

We examine collective bargaining problems in Chapter 9; the issue of corporate culture in Chapter 8; career planning and the corporate managerial resource problem are dealt with in Chapter 5. Here we want to discuss the overall issue of the link between structure and IR/HR. Two main stances are assessed: the first rests on the contention that the multi-divisional form is itself a major obstacle to strategic HRM, whereas the second suggests that even M-form structures contain the potential for a variety of HR and IR approaches – it all depends upon how they are used.

The clearest exposition of the 'pessimistic' scenario is made by Purcell (1989). The trend towards corporate restructuring and strategy based on diversification, divisionalization and portfolio management from the centre is inimical, he suggests, to strategic human resource management. Portfolio planning, he argues, 'tends to drive out, or at least drive down, questions of style and non-economic issues and positively encourages different approaches to employee relations in different segments of the business' (Purcell, 1989: 76). It not only becomes more likely that the corporate level will disavow a need to develop integrated HR strategies but, in addition, because of the forces generated towards short-run review of performance by the separate business units, it becomes 'harder at the unit level to develop and maintain long-run human resource policies'. Purcell admits this is a pessimistic conclusion but he maintains it is unavoidable. His summary judgement is uncompromising: 'current trends in corporate strategy in many large diversified companies render the ideals of human resource management unobtainable' (1989: 90).

There is arguably something about the British way of managing the multi-divisional corporation which lies at the centre of the problem. McKinsey & Co., the international management consultants, appear to have made such an analysis in their critical report on the UK electronics industry (NEDO, 1988). They suggest that too many companies continue to rely on structures and strategies which were 'state of the art' in the 1960s but inappropriate now. In theory, responsibility for strategic planning in many of these companies is delegated to individual business units. In practice, however, there is too often a crucial conflict between the general responsibility of the business units to devise medium- and long-term strategies and the immediate imperative resulting from performance controls imposed by the corporate centre. In consequence, there is, in effect, a more or less total reliance on short-run profit indicators and the neglect of measures such as market share which emphasize the longer term. McKinsey consultants suggest that the predominant approach, at least in the electronics industry, is 'numbers-driven' rather than 'issue-driven'. The mutually reinforcing structure and style characteristic of GEC, Plessey, Ferranti and Racal, lead to very limited real planning and the inability to capture 'the potential synergies and scale of a large company'. Among the consequential losses, they say, is the capacity to 'attract and develop highly talented management' (NEDO, 1988: 49). The message is clear: the way the British use the multi-divisional and SBU structures is inimical to strategic management – and this includes strategic action in the spheres of human resources and industrial relations.

The analyses by Purcell and McKinsey perhaps lead to a position which is too adamant and pessimistic. Not all multi-divisional companies manage their businesses in the same way. This point is well illustrated in the research conducted by Goold and Campbell (1987) who bring to the fore companies which use strategic planning as well as companies which rely on financial control. Likewise, Hendry (1990) takes issue with Purcell and also shows the variety of human resource practices in decentralized and divisionalized corporations. He notes how GKN and IMI which both used 'financial control' mechanisms to handle corporate – subsidiary relations, had adopted different internal labour market strategies to match their contrasting product markets. Of particular interest is that IMI, despite having a more diversified business than GKN, had developed a greater range of corporate level internal labour market policies and practices.

Hendry's explanation is that IMI's diversified businesses are built around a relatively common 'engineering base' and a belief that a general set of skills is appropriate for running these businesses.

One consequence was that IMI 'put a premium on the adaptability of its managers (in terms of skills and mobility across the Group)' and therefore it developed a set of corporate HR policies and practices designed to allow this interchangeability and to take advantage of it. GKN on the other hand saw itself as having a more recognizable 'core business' but one built on a set of differentiated clusters of expertise. To this extent it was more functionally structured and each function and business was responsible separately for its own human resource development; in consequence there was less of a perception that there was any need for a corporate-wide internal labour market (Hendry, 1990: 97).

It would appear that the sheer fact of being an M-form does not, in itself, preclude the development of human resource practices. None the less, other things being equal, it is probably true to say that it is relatively easier for a 'single-product' business such as a retailing chain (Sainsbury, Marks & Spencer) to formulate and implement a human resource strategy than is the case for a conglomerate or a multi-divisional corporation. This point was noted by Sisson and Scullion (1985).

But devolution and its related forms such as divisionalization and the strategic business unit have not been the only vital theme in recent moves towards corporate re-structuring. Another dominant theme is to be found in the idea of the 'flexible firm'.

*The flexible firm*

The 'flexible firm' model devised by the Institute for Manpower Studies has provoked extensive interest in managerial circles (Atkinson 1984, 1985; Atkinson and Meager 1986). The analysis suggests that in order to be adaptable to market changes and to hold labour costs down, different *types* of labour flexibility are being simultaneously pursued. The three main kinds identified by Atkinson (1984) were: functional, numerical and financial. Functional flexibility refers to the capability of employees to switch between different tasks. Thus it includes, for example, multi-skilled craftsmen moving across mechanical and electrical job boundaries; it denotes also workers switching between indirect and direct production jobs. In large measure this type of flexibility equates with the long-standing search for easing of job demarcations.

Numerical flexibility is the term used to denote the employer's scope to adjust easily labour supply to meet immediate needs. It includes freer use of hire and fire as well as various forms of loose 'contractual' arrangements such as sub-contracting in place of the normal employment contract so that labour is more readily on tap to be drawn upon or dispersed with more easily.

Financial flexibility is pursued so that pay costs for various groups of workers can more freely reflect current external labour market conditions. It implies a switch away from collective negotiations based on cost of living and indeed away from across-the-board rate for the job, towards new pay systems which take account of immediate local conditions.

Atkinson takes the analysis further by then advancing the notion that these different dimensions to flexibility can be brought together in the concept of the 'flexible firm'. This idea hinges on the distinction between separate strategies towards different segments of the labour force. Thus, it is suggested that 'many UK firms are trying to introduce' (p. 29) a new organizational structure which involves the break-up of the workforce into a series of 'peripheral', therefore numerically flexible, groups of workers clustered around a numerically stable 'core'. The 'core' group performs the organization's critical firm-specific activities in a functionally flexible manner. Figure 4.1 shows the lay-out of these groups.

Under conditions of market growth the periphery expands; under reverse conditions the periphery contracts. The core workforce by contrast is shielded from market fluctuations. They are full-time permanent career employees. An example would be the large construction companies such as John Laing which now actually employs very few manual building workers whether craft or labourers. The main permanent workforce comprises managers, technical staff, surveyors and similar other professional-technical employees. The people who actually build the

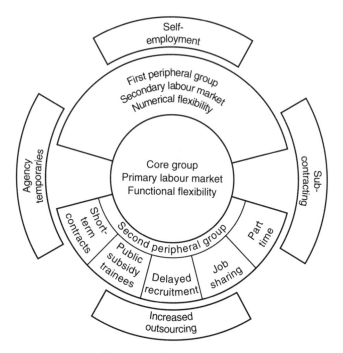

**Figure 4.1** The flexible firm
*Source*: Atkinson (1984: 29)

houses and construct the hospitals and bridges are predominantly short-term contract workers – mainly supplied by subcontractors. Core group specialists are less readily available on the external market; most of them, as in Laing's, are home-grown by the employing company and their commitment is sought through preferential treatment and enculturation programmes.

The 'first periphery group' shown in the figure consists also of full-time employees but they have less access to career opportunities. They are likely to include secretarial, clerical and assembly workers. A lower level of functional flexibility is sought from this group and, although not numerically flexible in the full sense, these jobs are likely to be filled on the open labour market and there may well be a relatively high degree of turnover. The 'second peripheral group' is a catch-all for the groups shown on the figure and includes part-time employees, short-term contract staff

|                            | Core group              | Externals                      |
| -------------------------- | ----------------------- | ------------------------------ |
| Focus for management       | Employee                | Job                            |
| Instrument of control      | Effecting deployment    | Delivery against specification |
| Management style           | Participative           | Directive                      |
| Remuneration system        | Wage for time worked    | Fee for work done              |
| Motivation/incentive system | Performance appraisal   | Delivery on schedule           |
| Supply                     | Recruitment and training | Competitive tender/ severance  |

**Figure 4.2** Managing the flexible firm
*Source*: Atkinson (1984: 31)

and similar categories. Job security and career development for these sub-groups will be slight – if not indeed entirely absent.

Beyond this is a third set of workers who are outliers to the firm. This labour source includes agency temporaries, self-employed workers, and sub-contractors. The reference to in-creased 'outsourcing' in the model is strictly speaking a rather different arrangement which lies beyond the normal concept of the labour market because outsourcing of components and services takes one into the arena of commercial supplier con-tracts.

As Atkinson observes, there are significant managerial impli-cations arising from the adoption of such a strategy. Figure 4.2 gives a brief summary. The nature of the human resource and industrial relations problems associated with the diverse groups means there will be quite different policies for them (for sim-plicity the various 'peripherals' are combined here under the label 'externals').

For the core, the focus of personnel attention is arguably the person rather than the job – hence, for example, management trainees recruited into a large company are not employed with just one specific job in mind. For the externals, however, the situation is reversed. The means of control vary also: the core group are measured against cooperation and progress; the externals are evaluated against timely delivery to specification. A participative management style for the core is contrasted with a 'directive' one for externals though in the case of sub-contractors this may be an oversimplification of the true situation because labour control is arguably removed from the main employer under these arrangements.

Payment systems may also differ with the core employed on an incremental salary basis whereas the peripherals are likely to be paid for units of work completed to standard. For example, penalty deductions for late completion are standard practice in the construction industry. Calculation and negotiation of these adjustments is indeed a function of the core group! Labour supply for the core is taken care of through the recruitment of graduates and school leavers; for the externals it may result from job-by-job competitive tendering.

The 'flexible firm' model is clearly intuitively appealing. It has, however, been extremely controversial. Doubts have been expressed as to whether the Institute of Manpower studies is describing a trend or prescribing (i.e. recommending) a line of action (Pollert, 1988). Evidence of actual adoption is very patchy. The incidences of flexible employment practices such as sub-contracting which are uncovered are often of long-standing and hardly sufficient evidence of a new departure. Even where a new trend does seem to have been detected – as with the growth of part-time work in the 1980s – it is questioned whether this is evidence of a new employer-led 'strategy' or rather simply a response to supply-side problems. For example, many retailers appeared to have been forced into offering part-time work in areas of relatively full employment simply because of the difficulties of attracting and retaining full-time staff. The reality appears to be an admix of pressures – part-time working seems to have been partly employee-led but also partly employer-led – the latter having their own set of reasons for its introduction, and these not necessarily being part of a wide 'strategy' towards a 'flexible firm'.

The attempt by banks, building societies and retail outlets to find pay and conditions formulae which will enable them to offer extended opening hours is an example of the practical personnel and IR aspects of core and periphery flexibility. Core flexibility in particular may be restricted by union agreements.

Peripheral workforces may offer a different kind of flexibility – but at a cost. Such employees may have a lesser reason to show commitment to the organization. They may, in consequence, require greater degrees of supervision and control than other staff. This could be expected to present particular problems to those organizations aspiring to shift their culture away from traditional control mechanisms. 'Casual' staff may also be less skilled. And there is likely to be a disinclination to avoid investing in them by offering training. The outcome may well be an overall level of poorer performance which could eventually threaten the firm's competitive position in the market place. One way to test out this assumption is to consider how 'peripherals' would fit within that other major employer-led initiative of recent years – the 'team'.

## Teams and cells: task level organization and involvement

Teamwork has been one of the key ingredients of the new industrial relations and human resource management movements. *Fortune* business magazine in the United States heralded it as 'possibly *the* productivity breakthrough of the 1990s'. It is difficult if not impossible to disentangle the employee involvement (EI) aspects from the re-organization of work aspects and some of the elements appear to have been around for quite some time. But *Business Week* has sought to counter such scepticism with the bold claim that while EI has in some form been around for years it was, they say, 'merely sloshed in thin coating across an ageing industrial base by timid US companies'. But now there are signs that real employee involvement is pervading the core of corporate America (*Business Week*, 1989: 36). Beneath the journalese there is an important issue. Arguably, one of the most radical questions facing managers is the need to bring about a shift away from Tayloristic work organization principles because of the extent to which they are incompatible with current market needs.

Despite some resistance from supervisors and middle managers the team concept is reported as taking significant hold in many US companies including, for example, GM, Ford and Chrysler. General Electric is said to have 20% of its 120,000 employees working in teams. And in the UK, Buchanan and McCalman (1989) give a favourable review of the team-based 'high performance work systems' at Digital in Ayr and the re-organization into teamworking by Birds Eye Walls has been described by Storey (1992).

What are the main features and dimensions of teamworking? There are variations but essentially they typically comprise between 5–14 multi-capable workers who can and do switch between tasks, organize and allocate their work, take responsibility for performance levels and quality, may even select new members to their unit – and all without (or with very little) formal supervision.

New technological capabilities and associated new wave manufacturing strategies such as just in time (JIT), manufacturing resources planning (MRPII) and total quality management (TQM) carry profound implications for human resource and industrial relations' management. This point has even been recognized by those analysts working at the hard systems end of the new management. Thus, one of the most influential of such commentators R. J. Schonberger, has shown that 'world-class manufacturing' standards and status require far more than investment in the latest equipment. Schonberger (1986) suggests a socio-technical model which entails the recombining of the shopfloor tasks of set-up, operation, maintenance and quality control.

Job or task level re-structuring has appeared over the years in a number of guises. One of the most important of these has been the concept of 'socio-technical systems' as advanced by the Tavistock Institute. This idea suggests the importance of finding an appropriate alignment between the technical and the social organization of work. The advantages offered by autonomous work groups tend to be highlighted by this approach.

There are strong continuity links with later work on job enrichment and the job characteristics model of Hackman et al. (1975). The latter theory suggested that the 'outcomes' of high work effectiveness and job satisfaction were products of critical 'psychological states' such as the experienced 'meaningfulness of work', the responsibility allocated and the 'knowledge of results' of work activities. These in turn are positioned as products arising from a set of job characteristics which include skill variety, task identity and significance, autonomy and feedback. The model implicitly suggests certain prescriptions for restructuring. These relate to the combining of tasks to allow variety of experience; the formation of natural work units to facilitate identity with task; establishing client relationships by encouraging as many employees as possible to be in contact with the customer; and improved vertical integration of jobs by allowing employees to get involved in work scheduling, execution, quality checks, training other employees and problem-solving.

One of the fullest accounts of teamworking in Britain is given by Buchanan (1993) and Buchanan and McCalman (1989). Buchanan sees the new forms devised in the mid to late 1980s as distinct from, and more significant than, the earlier Quality of Working Life (QWL) movement which *appeared* to flourish in the 1960s and 1970s. The new re-organizing is driven by different forces, is more comprehensive in approach and more impactful in practice. His account of the Digital experience with high performance work systems in Ayr calls attention to the following key features. There was a package of changes to support the increase in worker responsibility and control. Management had a clear vision of the kind of products, market-strategy, organizational design and work systems that were necessary in order for this site to compete and survive under the new conditions. This clarity of view was shared fully with all employees and this sharing was part of the management of change process.

At the core of the new system were the 'high performance teams'. These were autonomous groups each with about 12 members who operated without supervisors. The teams had responsibility ranging from production, fault tracing and problem solving to certain equipment maintenance functions. The teams were 'multi-skilled' insofar as there were no separate job titles and all members were helped and encouraged to develop a range of capabilities and to practise them. They shared experience and problems. The payment system was geared to skills' acquisition and use. The teams were self-disciplining. They engaged in new member selection and peer evaluation.

The supporting climate included an open lay-out, flexi-time, an absence of clocking, and an open managerial style. This all added up to a new role for managers. Managers had to learn to stand back and relinquish their traditional directive functions. In place of these redundant roles managers were expected to shift their priorities towards market issues (such as identifying new business opportunities, improving sales forecasts, liaising with customers) and to improving operational logistics (including materials management inventory and supply). The shift from conventional manufacturing to the new system was successful along a number of dimensions at Digital. There was improved productivity, speedier product launch, and acceptance of responsibility.

Buchanan (1992: 153) argues that the high performance approach marks a new departure from the job enrichment techniques of the 1960s and 1970s. The aim under job enrichment was to reduce labour turnover and absenteeism; under the high performance work system it was to gain competitive edge through flexibility and quality. The change period also took longer under the latter system and the change was more far-reaching in nature.

How does this account stand up against other research? The first thing to note is that the Digital case study was conducted in a non-union plant. Moreover, given disruption in the market conditions for its previous products, the site looked over the brink to see a real and imminent threat to its very existence. And it must also be noted that the study of the degree of change occurred within a couple of years of the change programme – indeed, given the long-term nature of the changes described it might even be argued that the positive results pick up some of the optimism and momentum which are part of the initial enthusiasm of planned change. Sustainability of the positive attitudes and behaviours is likely to be another issue.

Relatively under-explored have been the reactions of cell members themselves to this form of organizational arrangement. One exception is the report made by Buchanan and Preston (1992) concerning the results of a study into cell operations in a

British aero-engine components manufacturer. The company had introduced cells as part of its drive towards manufacturing systems engineering. This involved changes to production control, to organization and to materials flow. The operation of the cells was found to be deficient in a number of respects. Morale was low – it seemed that expectations had been raised which had not been met. Flexible working was inhibited, in part because the company's centralized payment system did not allow for cross-skills working and additionally because cell members were not permitted to make adjustments to CNC programmes to resolve minor equipment problems. Although the researchers found some positive consequences arising from the move to 'autonomous' cells the most crucial finding was the extent to which unrevised human resource policies and practices served to undermine the initiative.

Quality circles can be viewed as one type of team. Indeed, many companies which now use them have preferred to re-label them 'problem-solving-teams'. But, whatever the title, these devices depart in the critical respect from the job re-design team experiments discussed so far: they typically operate in parallel with the normal work arrangements rather than replacing them. None the less, the quality circle concept has enjoyed considerable influence in recent years. There have been a number of attempts to chart their 'evolution'. New configurations are projected for the future. The American magazine *Business Week* (July 10, 1989) tried to map a trajectory from 'problem-solving teams' which mushroomed in the 1970s to 'special purpose teams' (early to mid 1980s), to 'self-managing teams' which 'appear to be the way of the future' (p. 37).

The unresolved HR and IR aspects of re-structuring into 'teams' have been partly explored by Charles Leadbeater (1989) in the *Financial Times*. He cites the case of GTE telecommunications in the USA which introduced a new payments system to overcome the tension between collaborative teamworking and performance-related pay. The company has introduced project teams, problem-solving teams and cross-functional teams extensively. The collaboration involved in teamworking is reported to induce loyalty and commitment which bring efficiency gains in their own right (in addition to those gains accruing from flexibility).

The difficulty that was encountered stemmed from the individualized nature of traditional performance-related pay schemes. These tend to fragment rather than bring together the workforce. To surmount this the company piloted a team-based payment system which is linked to performance. Teams are paid according to a 'competitiveness index'. This means that a team's pay is linked to how well it does in relation to benchmarks drawn from the company's main competitors such as General Electric. The benchmark criteria include cost and quality targets. Such unit-based pay systems could eventually replace agreements arrived at for entire plants. Leadbeater comments (1989: 4): 'A modernising union movement could easily put itself on the side of efficiency by supporting the new collectivism of teamworking and insisting that individual performance should play only a limited role.'

The implication is that the future of payment systems under these teamwork conditions moves the debate on from the traditional union collective approach versus the new individualistic approach. The 'most important tension will be within new approaches to human resource management – between the new collectivism of teamworking and the new individualism of performance-related pay' (Leadbeater, 1989).

Leadbeater's analysis, although thought-provoking, does not go far enough. There are fundamental issues at stake here. If the 'competitiveness index' was to be more widely proposed it would raise the question of feasible measurement. Which 'unit' of production would be deemed suitable? How would interdependencies be taken account of? Would sufficient relevant data about team and unit performance be released by competing companies? Moreover, reliance on the 'competitiveness index' would be likely to provoke disputes about the relative levels of capital investment in the affected plants.

For trade unions and managers the attention paid by this mechanism to (selected) external relativities are likely also to raise questions about their impact on internal relativities. The initiative is a further step in the introduction of the market into organizations. While market 'realities' and market 'discipline' may be brought into the firm the move could be said to undermine the logic of social organization by the modern corporation and the general logic of bureaucratic control. What relative weight should be given to positive and negative sanctions and internal rules governing how work should be done in comparison with the information deriving from market comparisons? If personal power has been replaced by the exercise of organizational power what then are the implications of seeking to install market logic?

A similar set of concerns is raised by O'Dell (1989) who argues the need to align the reward system with team organization. He seeks to illustrate how American companies such as Honeywell, Eastman Kodak and GE have introduced incentive payments fitted to the team situation. Notably, however, he reports unresolved problems at managerial levels where unreconstituted appraisal and merit pay schemes have come into conflict with the drive for managerial teamworking.

## Employee participation and organizing for quality

Employee involvement has been one of the hallmarks of the new management. The idea, and indeed various manifest forms, of 'participation' have of course been around for a long time: the issue is seemingly an ever-recurring one on the management agenda. But the 1970s'-style workers-on-the-board industrial democracy proposals were pushed aside in the 1980s and management led the way in devising new forms of employee involvement on its own terms. EI in its modern sense is characterized by its focus on the individual employee; by the fact that the impetus for its introduction comes from management and not from union or legislative pressure; and by the underlying intent to use it as a way to increase commitment and ultimately to seek competitive advantage through its use. EI in this form is often closely linked with the idea of 'open management' and with customer care programmes and other 'quality' initiatives.

Employee involvement comes in a variety of forms. These include team briefings, quality circle and problem-solving teams of various kinds, and employee communication devices such as newsletters and special reports. Whatever the precise form, the notable point is that there appears to have been a considerable increase in initiatives of an EI kind during the 1980s. This gathering pace is confirmed in a recent report to the Department of Employment, *New Developments in Employee Involvement* (Marchington et al., 1991). This report makes the point that 80 per cent of the EI schemes studied during the research had been introduced in the 1980s. Likewise, the third workplace industrial relation survey (Millward et al., 1992) reveals that in the late 1980s whereas there was a fall in the proportion of workplaces with joint consultative committees, there was conversely a 'substantial' growth since the mid-1980s in a wide range of new initiatives for employee involvement. Newly introduced arrangements for EI were reported in 45 per cent of all establishments in 1990 compared with 35 per cent in 1984. The increase was largely accounted for by new initiatives which had been launched in the service sector.

There is also further evidence of an increasing use of various techniques in employee communication and participation. For example, Carrington (1991) reports that the use of employee attitude surveys in Britain has been growing despite the ever-rising cost of conducting them. Even more optimistically, Müller (1991) describes how a range of initiatives including teamwork and other forms of EI has recently been 'integrated' at Rover into a total system approach.

One argument is that participative methods are increasingly becoming not an optional 'nice to have' but a functional necessity given the rise of the new 'knowledge' workers (Harris and Harris, 1989) and the technological and organizational restructuring which puts a premium on adaptability, spontaneity and commitment. Whether there is in fact a simple equation between the launch of EI programmes and these particular outcomes is a question we address later in the chapter.

In the main, most practitioners use the terms 'employee involvement' and 'employee participation' interchangeably. It is possible to make a conceptual distinction by reserving 'participation' for instances where employees share some decision-making with managers but the utility of forcing such a distinction seems limited. Rather more useful is the succinct way in which Lammers (1967) captures an often sought-after set of distinctions between the *level* of *involvement* and the *scope* of involvement.

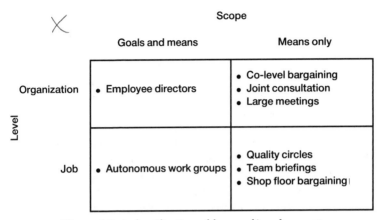

**Figure 4.3** A classification of forms of involvement
*Source*: Adapted from Lammers (1967)

'Level' is classified primarily into job level versus organizational level, and 'scope' is divided into decisions about goals and means versus decisions about means only. The model is shown in Figure 4.3.

Forms of participation at the organizational level normally entail indirect participation through elected representatives whereas job level forms can directly engage every employee. Illustrative types of involvement are shown in each cell.

## *Reasons for EI*

The main *reasons* for this revitalization of interest are easy enough to identify. If all workers are to be pulling in the same direction they need to be aware of key organizational objectives and of the threats and opportunities facing the enterprise. To some extent then there is a simple communication issue underlying the 'involvement' theme. Clear communication could, however, also of course be pursued even under highly directive managerial styles. In circumstances where there are attempts to install devolved forms of organization of the types discussed earlier in this chapter, the need to 'involve' employees rather more fully in the problematics of the task become more sharply apparent. In fact it could be said that employee involvement is a necessary corollary of team forms of work organization – in marked contrast to Tayloristic forms where strict conformance to assigned standardized task was the prime requirement.

The rise of EI on the managerial agenda could therefore be ascribed to the wider move to reorganize working arrangements. One suspects, however, a further reason. On the back of popularization of ideas of 'ownership' and involvement by Tom Peters, many managers have been tempted to pick up this part of the message without being persuaded to depart from traditional ways of organizing work. In consequence, the techniques and appurtenances of involvement are frequently simply larded on to unreformed structural forms and cultures. It is hardly surprising that in these circumstances involvement and participation are rightly seen as cosmetic and that the initiatives have a high mortality rate.

Apart from the aim to communicate information about targets, options, priorities and dilemmas, involvement perhaps may also carry the objectives of tapping into the knowledge and inventiveness of each person and group; and to engender and harness their enthusiasm and commitment. At a more cynical level some schemes might be seen as rather tokenistic attempts to ward off potential demands for more far-reaching arrangements whether proposed from Brussels or elsewhere.

The European Commission is pressing for employee participation through a number of channels – most notably the Social Charter, the Fifth Directive, and the European Company Statute. Essentially, these approaches would install obligations on employing organizations to provide mandatory consultative and participatory institutional arrangements. The British government and the Confederation of British Industry have vigorously opposed what they regard as the 'rigid requirements' emanating from the European Commission. As a countermove the government has published its own report (*People and Companies: Employee Involvement in Britain*), which extols the merits of voluntary arrangements. Companies such as Marks & Spencer and the John Lewis Partnership are portrayed as role models (Department of Employment, 1989). This stance is also adopted by the CBI. This can be seen from various of its reports such as *A Europe of*

*Opportunities for All* (CBI, 1989) and *Involvement: Shaping the Future for Business* (CBI, 1990). The European trade union confederation (ETUC) on the other hand contends that mandatory measures are required in order to cajole the less progressive companies.

Members of the British Institute of Management appear rather more open to the idea of EC legislation on employee participation. A BIM survey, reported in the discussion paper 'Involved in Europe', found that 76 per cent of BIM members seemed to accept some EC measures in this area. The Institute of Personnel Management also still stands by its code issued in 1983 which recommends that companies should establish consultation procedures. In fact the IPM would now like to see statutory backing for this code.

## *Evidence of EI practice*

In the light of the 'voluntaristic' British approach to employee involvement it is really hardly surprising that actual practice is extremely variable. Reliable hard evidence about take-up and impact is sparse. There are, however, some pointers to current practice. The Marchington et al. report (1992) cited above was based on a case work in 20 organizations. The pattern of employee involvement methods being deployed in these cases was found to be as shown in Table 4.1.

The types of practices counted by these researchers as part of EI can be seen to be very wide-ranging. They include three types of downward communication methods (in-house newspapers, employee reports, team briefings); four types of upward problem-solving (suggestion schemes, attitude surveys, quality circles and TQM-type schemes); two types of financial participation (joint consultation, collective bargaining and 'change programmes'). In the body of the report they actually exclude collective bargaining as being part of EI proper and the way they conceive of EI leads them to concentrate almost entirely on the downward communication and upward problem-solving types. One of the main findings was that most of the companies utilized a mix of these techniques – a feature illustrated in the figure. Twenty-four of the 25 organizations operated at least two of the devices.

**Table 4.1**  EI in practice: forms of employee involvement and participation

| Organization | Downward communication | | | | Upward problem solving | | | Financial EI | | Representative participation | | Change programme |
| | Newspaper | Employee reports | Briefing | Suggestion schemes | Attitude surveys | Quality circles | Customer care/TQM | Profit sharing/share scheme | Unit-wide bonus | JCC/Works council | Collective bargaining | |
| --- | --- | --- | --- | --- | --- | --- | --- | --- | --- | --- | --- | --- |
| Chemco | × | | | × | × | | × | × | | × | × | × |
| Multichem | × | × | × | × | | | × | | × | × | × | × |
| Photochem | × | | × | × | × | | × | | × | × | × | × |
| JapanCo | × | | × | | | | × | | | × | × | |
| Mactool | | | × | × | | × | × | | × | × | × | × |
| Precision Metal | × | × | × | × | | × | × | × | | × | × | × |
| Northern Shoe | | | × | × | × | × | × | × | | | × | × |
| Southern Shoe | × | × | × | × | | × | × | × | | | × | × |
| Weaveco | × | × | × | × | | × | | × | | × | × | × |
| Trustport | × | × | × | × | | | × | | × | × | × | × |
| NTC | × | | × | × | × | | × | | | × | × | × |
| South East Health | × | | × | | × | | × | | | × | × | |
| Midbank | × | | × | × | | × | | | × | × | × | |
| Finance House | × | × | × | | × | | | × | | | × | × |
| Retfinco | × | | × | | | | × | × | | × | × | |
| BuSoc | × | × | | × | | | × | × | | × | × | × |
| Hiclas | × | × | | | × | | × | × | | × | × | × |
| Storeco | × | × | × | | | | × | × | | × | | × |
| 4-star | × | | | | | | | | | × | × | |
| LeisureCo | × | | | × | | | × | | | | | × |
| Computer plc | | | × | | | | | | | | | × |
| Housing Association | | | | | | | | | | | | |
| Waterco | × | | × | × | | | × | × | | × | | × |
| MNT | | | × | × | | | × | | × | × | | |
| MarkAd | | | × | | | | | | × | | | |

*Source:* Marchington et al., (1992).

The individualistic/collectivistic theme finds some reflection in this work for the research revealed that where union membership was high there tended to be a wider range of EI techniques deployed (in addition to the collective bargaining machinery). This was particularly the case in manufacturing companies where, over time, different initiatives had been introduced. Hence, Joint Consultative Committees, quality circles, profit sharing, suggestion schemes, videos and so on had come to operate alongside each other. In contrast, the non-union companies tended to have a narrower range of EI techniques. This should not be inferred to mean that EI was, however, less important in these cases; rather it simply seemed to mean that they were focusing their energies around one or two devices. In part, however, the correlation may not be as strong as is implied because the unionized organizations also tended to be the larger ones and so the wider range of EI techniques deployed might be a function of size.

In his research on developments in human resource management Storey (1992) also found that organizations were generally pursuing multiple forms of involvement. However, this research pointed up the considerable difficulties which the case companies had experienced in launching and sustaining certain key EI techniques. In particular, quality circles had faced difficulties stemming from suspicion from union representatives and many employees. The motor companies were found to have been especially keen to establish quality circles. Rover had made a very determined effort. It had used external consultants, appointed a QC coordinator and a separate full-time facilitator, and it had also trained dozens of potential circle leaders. But despite these efforts, nearly five years after the launch date only 20 circles had been successfully started. This represented in total approximately 120 people. The Longbridge workforce at the time was 11,000. Moreover, none of these circles had been established in the two main assembly buildings and it was in these problem areas that senior managers most desired to see them.

Peugeot-Talbot at Ryton had also tried to launch circles but the scheme was aborted. Later in the 1980s, however, 'problem-solving groups' which in some instances amounted much to the same thing, were installed with some considerable success.

At Ford, EI was the officially adopted term for a distinctive initiative. This had been designed by the American parent company and was being 'rolled-out' throughout the world. At the heart of EI, for Ford, was the establishment of problem-solving groups. These groups were, however, to be supported by an elaborate infrastructure which, included training, local steering committees and management-trade union agreement. Significantly, EI at Ford was conceived of not simply as a quality circle 'add-on' which would not disturb existing work organization arrangements. On the contrary the company defined EI as meaning 'working in a different way than we have in the past. It is about including employees in the decision-making processes which affect their everyday life. It is not a panacea or a management tool but rather a joint process to create teamwork.'

Ford's EI scheme involves national and local management-trade union agreement. In Britain, while the staff unions agreed to the scheme at a national level, the blue collar unions such as the TGWU would not do so. A further feature is the establishment of local joint (i.e. management and union) EI steering committees. Local joint groups are supposed to form and meet regularly. A third element is the briefing of employees on EI. This is to be done, notably, by the steering committee members in labour-management pairs meeting with small groups of employees. A fourth feature is the appointment of an EI coordinator at each site. This person, to be selected by the joint steering committee, is supposed to be drawn from interested applicants from the site. The coordinator's role is to train and support problem-solving groups and provide a link between them and the rest of the organization. The next element is the training of mixed groups of middle managers and union representatives at each site exploring EI in depth. Following this phase there is skill-training workshops for nascent problem-solving groups at all levels in the organization. And finally, the scheme requires monitoring and support of these groups by the coordinators and the spreading of the process across all parts of the company.

What is especially noticeable about this Ford Motor Company example is the extent to which joint management-union ownership and sponsorship of EI are emphasized. Take-up of the scheme in Britain, however, has been patchy. The reluctance of the manual unions to endorse it has, to date, seriously undermined its impact.

## EI: key issues of managerial concern

One of the central debates about quality circles concerns their instability or alternatively their potential for maturation. The pessimistic side of this points to the tendencies of QCs to decline and cease to function. Liverpool (1990) notes this tendency in three American factories which he studied. Dale (1986) reports a high mortality rate of QCs in Britain. Lawler and Mohrman (1985) also note from their experience in the USA that, most commonly, decline sets in. However despite their tendency to 'self-destruct', Lawler and Mohrman argue that this does not mean that management should avoid them. On the contrary, these researchers see potential for further use of quality circles even at the mature stage of their life cycle. Essentially, they see an opportunity to progress quality circles into wider forms of problem-solving bodies. They envisage the 'transition' of quality circles into self-managing teams as a possibility. Such transformation though, the authors stress, does not occur naturally; rather it has to be planned and consciously managed. None the less, they warn that the transition is a difficult series of steps and that managers committed to participative approach might be better advised to begin with work teams in the first place rather than taking the quality circle route. Where, however, an organization already has embarked on a quality circle programme managing the transition to a new form of participation might be considered a better option than letting them die.

A further issue in relation to EI which attracts managerial concern is the implication for payment systems. This in large measure reflects the discussion earlier about the problems of designing appropriate reward packages for teams.

All this emphasis upon employer-led attempts to engage employee involvement might suggest that managers were on the whole in favour of the idea and workers on the whole reluctant partners. This may, however, be misleading. One leading

American authority on industrial relations, Jack Barbash (1979: 456), made the following observation:

> Management prefers the adversary relationship because it fears that union collaboration will dilute management authority and thereby impair efficiency. The union prefers it that way, because the adversary relationship is most consistent with the maintenance of the union as a bargaining organization, and bargaining is what the union is all about. (cited in Bate, 1992: 228)

Bate observes that while these pluralistic outlooks have largely been developed and maintained in order to serve the 'survival interests' of the parties, they may well work against the 'need to develop effective problem-solving processes' (p. 228).

## The impact of EI

Michael Cross (1990) sought to quantify the impact of team-working by drawing on studies in a range of organizations. He claims that, overall, there was a productivity gain of some 20 per cent. This resulted from reduced overtime working (from an average of 11 to 5 per cent), reduced absenteeism (from 7 to 4 per cent), improved customer service and competitiveness through reduced factory lead-times (an overall mean average improvement of 10.9 per cent), increased machine outputs (mean average of 18.5 per cent), and a reduced supervisory/management structure estimated at between 2 to 5 per cent reduction.

The Marchington et al. (1992) survey for the Department of Employment found it difficult to produce these sorts of quantitative findings. But they did offer other evidence in support of employee involvement. For example, they note that employees themselves, in the main, wished to see particular forms of EI in their organizations continue. The majority also thought that communication and involvement had improved in the previous five years. Interestingly, while the majority perceived that EI overall had made a positive contribution to their organizations, when quizzed about each separate EI technique only a minority said that their own commitment had increased as a result. For example, only a fifth of the sample reported that there had been an increase in commitment as a result of the introduction of team briefing.

In the context of our analysis of individualism and collectivism it is significant also that the study found that the majority of 'ordinary' employees identified managers and supervisors as the prime source of information about 'what is going on here'. Trade union representatives hardly figured at all. If these findings are representative of organizations in the country at large then this suggests an important shift in employee relations since the 1970s.

The various difficulties in operating EI should not, however, be underplayed. There are many warnings in the studies about the problems which can be expected and our own experience tends to reinforce these messages. Adverse reactions from middle managers is one of the more common experiences (e.g. Carrington, 1991b). But wider disillusionment and cynicism is also a not uncommon finding in situations where 'team' programmes are not fully followed through and supported by the wider personnel systems (Buchanan and Preston, 1992; O'Connor, 1990). Raising expectations but failing to meet them can thus be dangerous.

## Conclusions

We began this chapter by noting that organizational restructuring has recently taken many forms and has occurred on an extensive basis. Underlying the variety of measures are certain common themes – the most central of which is the desire to devolve accountability to small, definable and self-managed units. The thinking behind this is that the managerial tasks of controlling, winning commitment, allocating responsibility, empowering, and energizing can all somehow be made more attainable by focusing activities in this way.

The analysis in the chapter was organized in three main sections. In the first, we reviewed corporate restructuring – focusing in particular upon the human resource and industrial relations issues arising out of the multi-divisional form and out of the creation of strategic business units. The main concern highlighted here was the difficulty in devising and delivering a strategic approach to human resource and industrial relations management under circumstances where business units were monitored and controlled by reference to short-term performance measures. A related point was made in connection with that other fashionable device, namely the flexible firm. Here too it was pointed out that while the division of the workforce into 'core' and 'periphery' had proved to be a very attractive idea for many employers it should not be expected that human resource and industrial relations problems can easily be surmounted through such a move. Determination of what is 'core' to an organization can be difficult and shifting. Withdrawal of investment in the designated 'peripherals' can also exacerbate what is often the real problem, that is, a comparatively unskilled and uncommitted workforce.

The second part of the chapter concentrated on organizational strategies at the task level – and most especially on the idea of teamworking. Teamworking was seen to be pivotal to the new 'high performance' work systems of a number of businesses in the United States and Britain. Their place in the scheme of things stemmed from the rationale that competitive advantage could be gained through the premiums which flow from flexible working and quality. 'Self-managing' teams are at once therefore a strategic device and a way of managing human resources and industrial relations – but, as was pointed out in the chapter, a pre-requisite for the successful installation of teams is the need to get human resource and industrial relations management onto a sound footing.

Central to the teamworking idea is the importance of employee involvement and participation. This topic was the focus of the third and final section of the chapter. In line with the previous discussion, it was noted that task-level involvement initiatives had grown significantly in the past few years. This is encouraging. But these employer-led initiatives were accompanied by a more general neglect of higher-level forms of consultation. Unless the balance can be found between micro-level participation and involvement and macro-level (in many respects mirroring the balance between the individualism and collectivism of HR and IR) then it seems unlikely that the initiatives will be sustainable or will have much real impact. Fortunately, there are some recent signs that a number of organizations have begun to take steps of this kind and the prospects for a more balanced approach seem rather brighter than was the case even a few months ago. This is a theme to which we return in Chapters 9 and 10 in particular.

# 5

# PLANNING AND RESOURCING

---

The subject matter of this chapter embraces two of the activities which have traditionally been seen as the stock-in-trade of personnel managers. The first, 'manpower planning' comprises the activities of forecasting the future demand for labour and the supply of labour, comparing the two profiles, and making action plans to 'reconcile' them. The other process covers the recruitment and selection of new employees.

Why do these processes deserve examination in a book which is primarily concerned with raising and examining issues which are likely to be high on the agenda of managers concerned with the *strategic* direction of their organizations? The clue to this can be found in the classic human resource management declaration: 'People are our most important asset.' This suggests that ensuring the right people are in the right place at the right time is a critical factor in gaining and maintaining competitive advantage. It further suggests that definite steps must be taken in order to ensure an adequate supply of the 'right people'. This in turn means that attention will have to be paid to job and people 'profiling' and the provision of a suitable mechanism to match the two. When couched in these terms, the processes of planning, resourcing, recruitment and selection are evidently central to the concept of human resource strategy and to business strategy alike.

One particular reason why these processes have taken on a new prominence is the example of the Japanese companies which have set up operations in Britain. The seriousness with which these new-comers have been seen to treat these issues (and the amount of resources they have devoted to them) has proved to be especially influential. The most publicized of these cases have been Nissan and Toyota. Both have been seen to operate highly systematic and carefully structured recruitment processes for all levels of employee. In its first round of recruitment for supervisors, Nissan invited no fewer than 200 applicants to be interviewed for just 22 jobs. The initial 'shortlisting' to reach the 200 figure was itself undertaken by senior managers. A week-long period of selection exercises followed and 75 were invited back for a further battery of tests. This second phase of selection included attitudinal and personality profiling as well as competence testing. Reports and assessments were fed to senior managers who themselves conducted the final interview. The process of resourcing the production staff was similarly meticulous and also involved multiple tests and interviews.

Similarly, Toyota used what have been described as 'decidedly un-British recruitment practices' (*The Guardian*, 17 December 1992) to staff-up its new plant at Burnaston near Derby. Employees spent six months in the extensive recruitment and selection process, undergoing assessment for a total of 16 hours. Toyota used a five-page application form followed by a series of mental and physical tests, an interactive video test to judge how candidates would respond to different types of situation, a 75-minute targeted interview and then six hours on a simulated production line. The Toyota Director of Human Resources at Burnaston said, 'We didn't want the traditional 20-minute interview and the you-go-to-the-same-football-match-as-me-so-you-must-be-OK line. We want people who can work as a team and who have ideas for improvements and can demonstrate an ability to learn' (ibid.).

The publicity given to demographic changes has also made an impact. Most large employers such as the banks, the civil service, and telecommunications have traditionally relied upon recruitment from school leavers. But this source of supply is forecast to diminish very rapidly. The total number of under 25 year olds in the labour force will decline by 1 million between 1990 and the year 2000. In the EC as a whole the working population will actually fall by 20 per cent between now and 2040 (Johnson, 1992: 27). This means 45 million fewer labour market participants. The forecasted reduction in supply is particularly notable in Germany. The 1990 workforce total of 53.5 million for the combined former West and East parts of that country is projected to fall massively to just 36.9 million by 2050 – that is a workforce reduction greater than the total population of the former East Germany. These figures on the shrinking size of the age group actually understate the degree of change. Because of the higher numbers of young people going into higher and further education the proportion available for employment will be even smaller.

This chapter is structured in two main sections. The first brings together in a novel way current developments in the techniques involved in HR planning and resourcing. The second analyses critically the key issues and problems which have to be faced in planning and resourcing and which rarely, if ever, receive the attention they deserve in traditional textbooks.

## Emerging techniques in human resource planning and resourcing

### *Planning*

The textbooks present human resource planning (HRP) as if it were a rational-linear mathematical exercise undertaken by a central singular planner. Typically, the idealized account shows it as a sequence of activities as illustrated in Figure 5.1.

The elements in this idealized sequence can be discussed in three phases:

1  the calculation of the demand for labour (demand side techniques)
2  the calculation of labour supply (planning for labour supply)
3  the matching process leading to action plans (reconciliation of supply and demand).

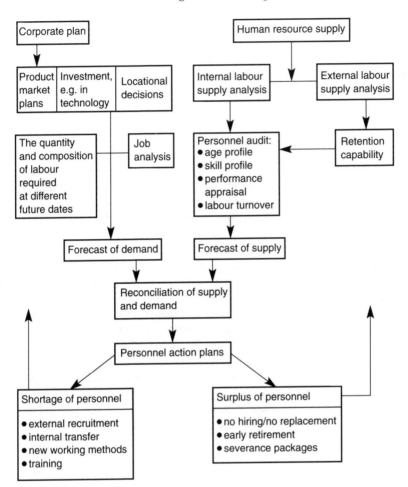

**Figure 5.1** An idealized HRP model

*Demand side techniques*
The first phase of activity for the planner is supposed to be the evaluation of the factors shown in the top left of the figure. This requires initially an understanding of the organization's corporate plan. This in an idealized case would have a long-range character perhaps comprising a five-year rolling programme. Armed with such details, the HR planner should be able to derive

information about the projected nature and scale of operations over a stipulated time period.

A range of methods is nominally available for forecasting future demands for staff. These include current-base-plus forecasts, ratio-trend analysis and regression analysis. The first of these, 'current base plus', is perhaps the most common. It means beginning with the present organization and using scrutiny procedures to review proposed changes. The realities of organizational politics are soon realized under this approach. A formal staffing committee which reviews proposals for staff replacement or staff additions is a common device. Unit line managers have to 'make a case' for incremental change.

A more formalized approach is the use of budgets to control staffing. Authorization for change requires application under a specified budgetary code associated with each and every position. This procedure makes it difficult for departmental managers to manoeuvre by using extra temporary staff or by having a 'transition' period with two people doing very much the same job. Staffing may additionally be controlled by formal rules such as specified ratios of types of staff such as secretarial to managers or maintenance engineers to production workers.

On the assumption that past ratios between production levels and labour demand will remain broadly valid then a simple calculation could potentially translate a business plan into a labour demand forecast. A ratio-trend analysis can be refined by adding extra information derived from work study techniques. The demand for people can be assessed in a range of ways including, for example, a ratio of output, sales, clients, patients, or crimes. In a service organization such as health care, a ratio analysis based on bed occupancy and its relationship with staffing might, at least initially, be expected to apply. Sometimes regression analysis can be used to measure the degree of relationship (correlation) between variables. Multiple regression can identify patterns among numerous variables simultaneously.

*Planning for labour supply*
Managerial activity under this heading relates to what is known as 'stocks' and 'flows' analysis. That is, managers can benefit from an audit of the current composition of the labour force and

from a tracking of various movements such as people leaving the organization, being promoted or simply undergoing internal transfer. An analysis of the 'stock' will usually be done along the dimensions of: numbers in various grades, skills, age profiles, work loads and productivity. An understanding of the distribution of employees across departments and functions will also usually be included. To ensure compliance with equal opportunity policies an analysis of the ethnic and gender composition of the stock may also be appropriate.

The case of Abbey National PLC offers an example. They have a computerized human resource planning system which contains details of the 'competency' profiles of its staff and competency requirements of the various jobs to be done in the organization. When vacancies arise the twin databases can be searched and prospective 'matches' made. The catalogue of names which is constructed is only used for short-listing purposes and not for arriving at a final decision. After over twelve months of operation the most notable feature is the considerable confidence which most managers in the organization seem to have in the system.

Increasingly, there is a trend towards the use of staffing ratios as a tool to help in HRP. The main ones include revenue/per employee; net income/per employee; direct labour/indirect labour; management/employees; and personnel specialists/payroll costs. These ratios along with other key indicators, such as average remuneration, can be used to make comparisons with other similar organizations. Variances may then be the stimulus for scrutiny of a particular area and for subsequent action to pull that part of the organization's staffing into line with the norm.

Modelling may be used to forecast future labour supply and to simulate the drawing of different scenarios. A supply-push model is based around a matrix where rows indicate grade levels and columns define functions, projects or other organizational units. All current employees can be assigned to the cell of the model. If, based on past mobility, employees are assumed to be 'pushed' out of their current positions through promotions, and transfers at a certain rate, forecasts over different time periods can be generated from the model. The forecast for all cells can then be compared with projected future demand and shortfalls or surpluses identified (Walker, 1992: 170–6).

### 'Reconciliation' of supply and demand

Having collected data and analysed it and then having made forecasts, the next stage is to take action and to seek to exercise some control over events. Assuming a less than perfect fit in the various forecasts of supply and demand, a 'gap' analysis can be made and policy options reviewed. Possible influencing steps include organizational restructuring, alteration of working methods, re-focusing activity onto selected areas of the business and withdrawing from, or scaling-down, others.

If a labour shortage in some or all categories of labour is forecast, then managerial strategic responses can take a range of different forms. Atkinson (1989) of the Institute of Manpower Studies classifies four main types of response. These are illustrated in Figure 5.2.

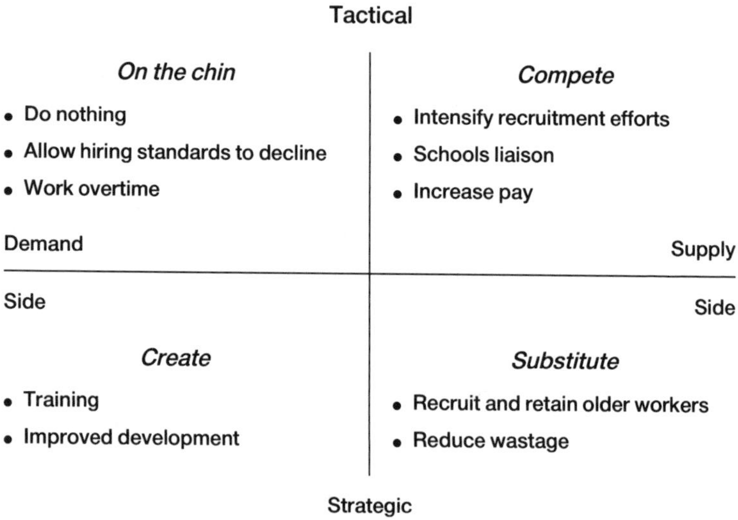

Tactical

|  |  |
|---|---|
| *On the chin* | *Compete* |
| • Do nothing | • Intensify recruitment efforts |
| • Allow hiring standards to decline | • Schools liaison |
| • Work overtime | • Increase pay |
| Demand | Supply |
| Side | Side |
| *Create* | *Substitute* |
| • Training | • Recruit and retain older workers |
| • Improved development | • Reduce wastage |

Strategic

**Figure 5.2** Four types of response to labour shortages
*Source*: Atkinson (1989: 23)

| Name | Job title | Age | Grade | Performance rating | Personal qualities (Key: 1 = High 5 = Low) | Assessment of potential |
|------|-----------|-----|-------|--------------------|--------------------------------------------|-------------------------|
| A. Smith | Production Manager | 50 | M2 | Adequate to above av. | Job knowledge 2, Planning/organization 4, Creativity/initiative 4, Ability to get results 3, Acceptability to others 3, Financial awareness 4, Development of subordinates 4 | Potential list 'D' |
| G. Dawson | Manager Site Services | 58 | M3 | Adequate to above av. | Job knowledge 3, Planning/organization 3, Creativity/initiative 4, Ability to get results 3, Acceptability to others 3, Financial awareness 3, Development of subordinates 3 | Potential list 'C' |
| B. Lee | Engineering Manager | 38 | M2 | Exceptional | Job knowledge 1, Planning/organization 2, Creativity/initiative 1, Ability to get results 1, Acceptability to others 3, Financial awareness 3, Development of subordinates 1 | Potential list 'A' |
| J. Brown | P & MC Manager | 40 | M3 | Adequate to above av. | Job knowledge 3, Planning/organization 3, Creativity/initiative 5, Ability to get results 5, Acceptability to others 3, Financial awareness 5, Development of subordinates 5 | Potential list 'C' |
| B. Jones | Process Engineer | 41 | M2 | Adequate to above av. | Job knowledge 2, Planning/organization 2, Creativity/initiative 3, Ability to get results 3, Acceptability to others 3, Financial awareness 4, Development of subordinates 3 | Potential list 'D' |

Key: 1 = High 5 = Low

**Figure 5.3** Manpower audit sheet

He suggests that firms' responses to shortages tend to be sequential – with the more difficult and far-reaching ones only being taken after the easier and less expensive ones have been tried. The hypothesized progression is from tactical responses to strategic ones. The first quadrant of the figure depicts a collection of responses which are minimalistic. Notably, however, Atkinson suggested that 'most businesses in the UK today are still in this quadrant' (1989: 22). The second type of response sees firms more actively competing with each for scarce types of labour. The third involves rather more imaginative steps while the fourth involves a return to making the best use of their own available resources. Central here is the role of training and development so that talents can be used to the full.

*Career planning*
An array of specialists, professional, and technical employees as well as managers per se are usually given special attention in organizations. A key part of this special treatment is the management of their deployment, retention, utilization and career planning. Professional engineers, for example, will often have their own distinct career ladders. Managerial tools and techniques to handle these matters are much sought-after.

In one electronics firm known to the authors, the General Manager of one of the constituent businesses had himself drawn up a handbook containing the basic instruments to help him undertake succession planning. At the heart of his system were two figures. The first was a manpower audit sheet and the second was a managerial succession plan. These are reproduced as Figures 5.3 and 5.4 respectively.

Figure 5.3 succinctly captures the basic data on key individuals and scores them in terms of current performance, personal qualities and assessment of potential. In the illustration it may be seen that Lee had an excellent performance rating and a good scoring also across all dimensions of perceived personal qualities. This person was also given the highest ranking on assessed future potential. On the basis of each departmental categorization the managerial succession plan was constructed. This is shown in Figure 5.4.

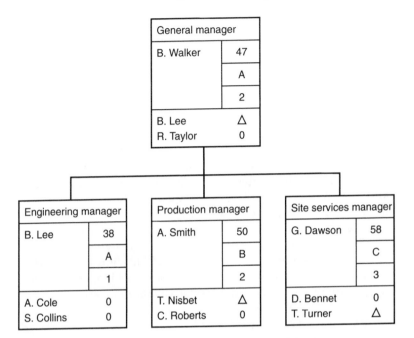

Key

38 Age

Present performance
A. Outstanding
B. Satisfactory
C. Needs improvement
D. Unsatisfactory, replace when possible

Promotion status
△ Ready now
0 Almost ready

Potential
1. Excellent
2. Promising
3. Doubtful
4. Not to be promoted

**Figure 5.4** Management succession chart

*Resourcing*

Resourcing is defined here as the recruitment, selection, deployment, redeployment and redundancy activities which are designed to maintain balanced inflow, throughflow and outflow of labour. The central thrust is to determine and then to profile requisite behaviours. The upsurge in interest in codifying 'competencies' can be seen as expressive of this concern.

## Methods of recruitment

An organization has just two sources of labour supply – the internal and the external labour market. Recruitment internally has typically involved word-of-mouth recommendation or the copying of some of the methods used in recruiting externally, for example, noticeboard advertisements. More recently, appraisals and career development reviews are providing much of the information on which decisions are made. Recruitment in the external labour market involves a variety of methods. Courtis (1985: 15) lists the main ones: advertising; employment agencies and job centres; registers; selection consultants; introductions by existing staff; people who have left the organization; people who applied on previous occasions; casual callers and respondents.

## Methods of selection

Organizations are increasingly encouraged to adopt a multi-method approach involving application forms, biodata, interviews, psychometric and aptitude tests, interviews and assessment centres.

In terms of new developments, the accent has been on the take-up and utilization of techniques which are rather more systematic than the traditional interview. Accordingly, managers have been keen to know a great deal more about psychometric testing, biodata techniques, assessment centres and criteria-based (or targeted) interviewing.

A second key feature has been a concern with behavioural and attitudinal characteristics of employees. The coming-into prominence of the particular techniques mentioned above also fits with this trend. For example, the biodata method, with which organizations such as National Westminster Bank have experimented, involves a highly structured series of multiple questions much like an elaborated application form. These questions, which appear in innocuous form such as how many brothers and sisters the candidate has, whether the candidate was the first or last born, how mobile the family has been, and so on, are derived by 'profiling' the current successful incumbent population. In broad terms, the idea is to replicate those characteristics correlated with success and to exclude those profiles associated with lack of success. For example, senior corporate lending managers in international banking might be found to share a profile which includes the following features: moderate but not outstanding academic success, parents who were geographically mobile, study patterns which were/are methodical rather than inspirational or haphazard. Supermarket chains have been experimenting with a similar approach for the selection of their store managers.

Likewise, psychometric tests are used not only to select on the basis of ability but also to construct 'profiles' which show interests, and behavioural tendencies such as a preference for working alone or with others, the need for achievement, sensitivity to criticism and so on. While there are no absolute pass/fail, right/wrong 'answers' when scoring these tests there will be cut-off points and preferred scoring ranges for different jobs. Ultimately they rest on the claim that certain 'types' of people make better bank managers, sales staff or executives than others. The 'appropriate' or 'guideline' profiles will be provided by the test providers (usually private consultants who devise, trial, and market their test products). These guidelines will be based on population 'norms' – i.e. typical score patterns for the 'relevant' occupational group. Precisely how relevant the normal group actually is to the particular situation in hand can be a critical question: jobs that superficially sound the same such as 'technical trainer' can be very different in practice.

Tests can be expensive to purchase and administer, although test providers invariably respond to this 'sales objection' by pointing out the costs of using poor selection methods! Test administration may be in part rationalized by using computer-based testing. Here, candidates respond to questions (in a booklet or on a computer screen) usually using simple yes/no buttons on a keyboard. The programmes, supplied by test providers, can be capable of furnishing an almost immediate scoring and can even print 'individualized' profiles using complete essay style reports with names of the individual candidates automatically inserted at appropriate points.

## Issues and problems

So much for the technical account of how planning and resourcing might 'ideally' be. Reality is not quite so straightforward. Even in the standard literature certain difficulties do get raised. A key one is that of reconciling supply and demand in rapidly changing business environments. Another is the question of reliability and validity in selection methods: i.e. do the chosen methods give consistent results and do they adequately measure the characteristic that they are supposed to? A third, is the question of bias and discrimination in the selection process more generally.

Important though these problems are, they are not the main focus here. Rather, our intent is to discuss some of the more basic issues and problems the would-be HR planner faces and to show how these are shaped by organizational contexts. In particular, in tune with the main theme of this book, we want to highlight the interplay between HR practices and industrial relations' considerations.

For, despite the rhetoric of 'people are our most important asset', the not untypical practice in Britain has been to treat planning and resourcing in a very *ad hoc* and peremptory fashion. In a highly unregulated legal environment 'hire and fire' has been common practice. Until very recently line workers in car plants, for example, were often 'requisitioned' by production managers merely a matter of days before they were deemed to be required. Thus, the request to the personnel department might be to 'find' 20 workers by 'next Monday'. Erstwhile painters and decorators registered at the labour exchange could thus find themselves on the production line within a very short timescale. In the event of a cut-back in production these people would just as speedily find themselves laid-off.

### From business plans to human resource plans

The most basic problem of all facing HR planners may be, as Chapter 3 has indicated, in securing access to a coherent business plan. This may simply be because a formal usable document does not exist. In practice we find that in many organizations there may be a set of 'motherhood' statements or, much more likely, financial ratios, but very rarely are these translated into operational plans covering the immediate future, let alone the next five or ten years. Or, if they are, they might take the form of a single-minded policy to drive down headcounts as a paramount, measurable, objective. Even if a plan is made available it can be a complex task to translate the investment and marketing strategies into operational plans for people.

For example, the executive board of a building society or insurance company may plan to extend operations in continental Europe. The HR implications are typically given little consideration. Does a corporate intention to grow in Europe mean local recruitment, preparation for managing expatriates or simple acquisition? Even when some forward HR planning is conducted this is very often limited to certain specific groups – for example, key technical experts. Moreover, planning appears to be often spasmodic. It may be triggered by a crisis or championed by an influential individual, but the evidence suggests that HRP in Britain is extraordinarily difficult to sustain.

The message is simple. The business plan has to be translated into operational plans if there is to be any meaningful HR planning. Those who are doing the HR planning must also have the necessary organizational power to make these fundamental decisions. Ideally, this means that those who draw up the business plan should simultaneously draw up the HR plan.

### An adequate personnel base

As the Department of Employment (1968: 11) recognized a quarter of a century ago, the quality of planning depends on the 'adequacy of . . . personnel records and statistics'. The assumption implicit in many of the prescriptive texts is that not only will the quantitative data that the planner needs be readily available, but the qualitative information will be to hand as well. That is to say, the planner will have information about the competences of existing employees, their career preferences and aspirations, and so on. More than that, there is an increasing assumption that much of this information will be computerized and so readily available at the press of a key.

Not only is this usually not the case, but worse still, the would-be planner in the typical UK organization is faced with a classic 'catch 22' situation. He or she desperately needs this kind of data but the problem is that in the absence of practices such as appraisal and testing, the data is unavailable. The only answer is to start with those practices such as appraisal, that will begin to generate the required data sets.

## Breaking with tradition

As the introduction to this chapter pointed out, the trends in the availability of younger workers – the traditional recruiting ground for most British employers – received a great deal of emphasis in the late 1980s. By contrast, relatively little attention was paid to what, potentially, were the off-setting developments: the increase in the 25 to 54 year old age group and, the potential of older workers who could be economically active. By 1995 there will be 1.2 million more people in the 25–54 year old group than there were in 1990. Moreover, the figure will continue to grow until the year 2000. Similarly ignored was a further shift in the employment profile – over 90 per cent of the extra workers who are recruited during the decade will be female.

Faced with labour shortfalls, a number of British employers began to adopt innovative and novel recruitment and retention policies before the recession took a hold. The building societies and banks, for example, launched more generous maternity leave and child-care schemes in order to attract and hold onto female employees. These and other organizations introduced flexi-time working and leave arrangements to recruit and retain more female employees. Stores, such as B&Q and Tesco began to 'rediscover' the 50-plus age group. They found that the performance of retirees was far superior to what they expected. Moreover, they also found that many of these returning retirees were willing and able to use new technologies – and that their training in this respect takes no longer than for younger workers. The favourable experience with the policy of actively recruiting older people has led to its continuance despite the newly available supply of unemployed young people due to the recession.

Unfortunately, these examples are the exceptions rather than the rule. In the main, there was little questioning of traditional resourcing practices. Corporate attitudes towards women and older people, let alone ethnic minorities or the unemployed, remain rather negative. Thus, trends indicate an acceleration in the long-standing decline of older workers' participation rates in the economy. Moreover, the entrenched HR systems conspire to ensure this. Earnings gradients related to age make the over-50 age group expensive – especially when the productivity of most employees over this age does not normally increase. Current policies and practices are pitched towards early retirement offers; flexible re-deployment is in contrast almost unknown in the UK (Johnson, 1992: 33).

## Market or hierarchy?

For many, the key issue in breaking with tradition is likely to revolve around whether to manage the activity internally through hierarchy or whether to put the emphasis on the market in the form of a commercial relationship. This dilemma picks up the issue of 'core and periphery' as discussed in the previous chapter. The hiving-off or subcontracting of so-called peripheral activities offers considerable attractions. At the very least, the tendering process offers the advantage of getting a realistic 'market' price; but other motives include the opportunity to cut costs and to concentrate resources on core groups.

There are also significant changes occurring at other levels which seem to point in the same direction. Recent advances in technology are expected to lead not only to an increase in the current half million Britons engaged in 'teleworking' from home but also the 'export' of data-processing jobs overseas. Communications with company head offices can be instantaneous using satellite or fibre optic links. The Philippines has already built up a formidable expertise in this area of work. And, in Belfast, the staff of a company called Dataprep Services do the typing for the Prudential's executives who are based in London.

It is not as simple as it is made out, however. It is often forgotten why employers shifted from a predominantly casual to a permanent labour force over the last 100 years. The main reason was to achieve greater control over the work process. Managing a market relationship is also very different from managing an employment relationship. First, there is the problem of negotiating the contract: the subcontractor may act opportunistically in tendering at a price to get the contract, but which he or she knows is unrealistic. The second problem is in managing the contract on an on-going basis. Experience in the NHS, for example, suggests that this can be something of a nightmare for the uninitiated. The net gain in terms of costs and value for money may not necessarily materialize from this. Alternatively, cost-cutting can all too easily result in lower levels of customer service and product quality – with a consequent reduction in demand. This, in turn, may trigger a further downward spiral of cost-saving measures.

There are other considerations as well. When an economic upturn comes the combination of demographic pressures and technological change may force employers 'to reverse the move towards flexible employment contracts which has been so pronounced over the last decade' (Johnson, 1992: 35). British employers have been much attracted by casualization of labour in the past few years but the demographic and technological logic might point in the opposite direction – that is, towards long-term employment contracts with a commitment to long-term continual retraining. This logic will be heightened if the Single European Market leads to greater labour mobility across the continent. Poaching by German firms where the declining workforce will be especially felt could lead either to continued downward pressure in Britain on skills training or, a more fundamental HR policy reaction involving a switch from the short-term, least-cost options, to longer-term contracts built around the enhancement of human capital.

### Whose responsibility?

As Chapter 4 has detailed, one of the notable changes in the structure of organizations has been a marked shift away from large corporate bureaucracies to multi-divisional structures in which there is a considerable devolution to individual units. In this context it is now increasingly argued that it is vital to take at least some HRP away from the preserve of the remote head office.

Planning and resourcing are now also more likely to be viewed as essential activities for local managers. Unit level managers can, for example, usefully maintain up-to-date information on varying work loads, the utilization of labour, labour turnover and other similar patterns in labour supply and demand. Such databases and records can be expected to be of assistance in the scheduling of future work and in the gauging of the implications of varying levels of peaks and troughs. The result could be an enhanced ability to match supply and demand for labour of all types. It could be said that every manager should therefore be engaged in some aspect of HRP.

For illustration, it is useful to return to the Abbey National example. This company's 'Self-Help Guide to Manpower Planning' for its line managers is part of its wider strategy of devolving HR responsibility. Bottom-up manpower planning is seen as consonant with this. The self-help guide urges all managers to 'give at least as much time to planning of human resources as we would give to the planning of other resources. In this way we will be better prepared to recruit, retain, motivate and deploy the staff that are most appropriate for the achievement of corporate goals. If one organization plans, and subsequently utilizes its human resources more effectively than another the resultant strategy will give that organization a competitive advantage.' The guide provides a set of forms to help collect appropriate data and formulate a coherent plan. The whole point about the decentralized approach to HRP is that it seeks to meet broad corporate objectives with the specialist knowledge about staff activities which only departmental managers process.

Such examples remain relatively rare, however. It is not so much that companies retain the HR planning at headquarters – although there is some evidence of this. Rather there is simply a vacuum. Managers at headquarters, when asked by interviewers like us what is happening in planning and resourcing, typically say that responsibility for such matters has been devolved to individual units. In practice this is rarely made explicit, however. Nor are unit managers given much assistance in getting to grips with what is involved. Even when they are, the emphasis on short-term financial results very often crowds out attention from medium- and long-term planning. Such attitudes can be infectious too.

### Trade union involvement?

Historically, British trade unions have played a significant role in the supply of labour. In some industries, notably, the docks, printing and parts of the engineering industry, the trade unions have been the effective labour exchange. In many others, they have *de facto* been the main source of recruitment under the informal system of word-of-mouth recommendation. In some cases such practices have been open to abuse. It must not be forgotten, however, that they have mostly operated with management's tacit if not open support. They have, after all, saved management the time and resources which are involved in the process.

The role of trade unions in planning and resourcing is, however, rarely, if ever, mentioned in the prescriptive texts. In Mayo's (1991) book, for example, which is regarded as one of the most authoritative in the field, there is not a single reference to trade unions. The reason, one suspects, is very simple. Planning and resourcing is largely seen as a question of managerial responsibility. Involving trade unions is likely to raise fundamental issues which, as we have seen throughout this book, most current employers have preferred to evade. Most notably, the question of employment security would be placed much higher on the agenda. Similarly, the underlying issues relating to flexibility would need to be addressed more fully. In the current climate most British employers have preferred to avoid a consideration of such far-reaching questions. They are the kinds of issues which, however, will need to be addressed if a secure basis for sustained recovery is to be constructed. They are issues to which we return in subsequent chapters.

Proactive human resource planning means attending to opportunities for improved labour utilization. This therefore involves an examination of work design and the allocation of levels of skills (and therefore tiered labour costs). It also involves a review of how available skills might be better utilized, and how other skills might be added to enhance job performance. To engage in these issues inevitably takes HR planners into the realms of labour relations. Typified depictions of HR planning are of a 'data gathering' activity. In this way the process is invariably seen as de-politicized. But in fact of course the choice of which areas of work to target for study is itself a 'political' issue in organizational terms. Certain jobs or units might be selected for special attention because these are seen as wielding too much power. These 'bottlenecks' might be circumvented or broken up by out-sourcing these services, by dispersing the members, by de-skilling the jobs, by automating the process or by duplicating the function at other sites and thus reducing dependency on the group in question. Each of these options produces winners and losers and thus takes the staffing process out of the purely technical realm.

In one NHS Trust hospital we studied, the Human Resource Director instanced as one of his major successes the elimination of agency staff costs which formerly had accounted for 20 per cent of the staffing budget. This had been achieved through a new collective agreement which involved the hospital's full-time employees in working more flexible hours and relinquishing many of their premium rates for overtime.

A key issue in this and other cases is employment security. Most British managements, faced with the kind of pressures to deliver short-term financial results identified in earlier chapters have been extremely reluctant to enter into agreements guaran-teeing security of employment. Many even refuse to compromise on their right to make compulsory redundancies. Yet there is a strong case, which will be developed in more detail in Chapter 10, for arguing that agreements on employment security and ways of ensuring it, far from being the barrier to change can actually facilitate it. Experience in Germany, for example, where the issue is the subject of works council involvement (see, for example, the discussion in Streeck, 1985) or in the large companies in Japan, where there has been *de facto* 'life-long' employment, suggests that it is a key to the virtuous cycle. Employees are more likely to go along with proposals for change if they genuinely feel that everything is being done to maintain employment. It is when they feel they are a commodity to be 'hired and fired' at management's whim, as in the UK, that most resistance to change seems to have built up. If management does not have a clear policy relating to trade unions, they are unlikely to take this on board. This is a point to which Chapter 9 returns.

## Conclusions

The British tradition in the spheres of planning and resourcing has been to operate in an essentially piecemeal, *ad hoc* manner. In the 1980s, the concurrence of publicity about the demographic dip and the influence of Japanese implants, led to the placing of HR and resourcing much higher on the agenda than had normally been the case. While the recession which followed undid much of this work, the basic lessons are still broadly in evidence and can be fairly easily identified. HRP and resourcing means treating staffing issues far more seriously than heretofore. This also means giving them adequate resources of managerial time and money. It means rather less informality and not trying to do the job 'on the cheap'. It means being increasingly alert to changes in labour supply and demand. As we have seen in this chapter this is not solely a question of demographics: changes in technology and in organizational form can also drastically recast the demand and supply of labour. It means, finally, being prepared to adapt policies to fit ever-changing situations – be this 'new' sources of labour (such as the over 50 year olds) or the flexible utilization of labour. But with increasing acceleration in the rate of change and with the move to more flexible organizations there is an extra temptation among managers to avoid human resourcing planning altogether and to act pragmatically. The prospect of strategic HRM thus recedes even further.

# 6

# PERFORMANCE MANAGEMENT AND PERFORMANCE RELATED PAY

---

The idea of 'performance management' has accelerated up the managerial agenda in the past few years. It is a phenomenon which we will show is intimately linked with the growth of HRM in general and with the individualization of the employment relationship in particular. The meaning of the term is open, however, to a number of different interpretations. On a continuum, two extreme divergent meanings can be identified – one being very wide and all-encompassing, the other very narrow and constricted. Under the first it is sometimes used more or less to refer to the totality of HR practices ranging from planning, training, coaching, customer care, total quality and reward – i.e. almost anything which could influence performance. Under the second, at its narrowest, the term is used virtually synonymously with individual performance related pay (PRP).

In this chapter, our treatment of the term will be more circumscribed than the catch-all conceptualization but not quite so narrowly drawn as the second. The chapter is structured into three main sections. In the first, the meaning of performance management is examined and the reasons for its popularity are traced. In the second, evidence about its practice is presented and certain key issues are examined. The final section focuses on what some would see as the central feature of performance management – the operation of performance-related pay.

## The meaning of performance management

Performance management in its current sense connotes an interlocking set of policies and practices which have as their focus the enhanced achievement of organizational objectives through a concentration on individual performance. The key elements may be identified as:

1 The setting of clear objectives for individual employees (these objectives are derived from the organization's strategy and a series of departmental purpose analyses (DPAs).
2 Formal monitoring and review of progress towards meeting objectives.
3 Utilization of the outcomes of the review process to reinforce desired behaviour through differential rewards and/or to identify training and development needs.

These three critical elements may be underpinned with further initiatives such as enhanced communication practices and the building of a 'shared vision'. But it is the three elements of objective setting, review and follow-through which appear, in one form or another, in most accounts to constitute the heart of the concept of 'performance management'. Two features are especially noteworthy. First, attention to the management of individual performance is elevated to a higher plane: it comes to be regarded as an issue of strategic importance. Indeed, arguably the whole point about the concept of performance is that it promises or offers a way to link the micro activities of managing individuals and groups to the macro issue of corporate objectives.

Second, while few if any of its constituent elements are new, it is the way in which they are placed together into an interlocking whole which is claimed to make the difference. In effect therefore, most commentators when talking of 'performance manage-ment' are by implication referring to a performance management

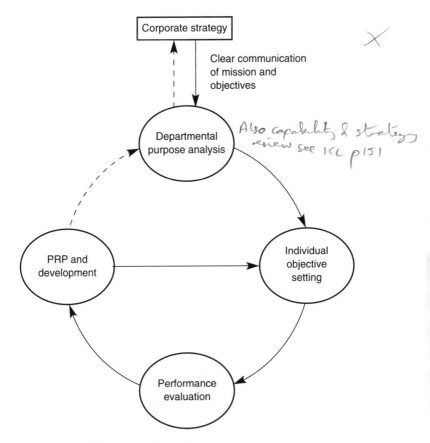

**Figure 6.1** Elements of a performance management system

system (PMS). Figure 6.1 shows how the main elements of such a system might interlink.

This reveals the significance of the clear communication of mission and objective from the corporate strategy level. Each department reviews its purposes and activities in relation to this overall business strategy. A feedback loop is allowed for at this point – the corporate strategy may be amended in the light of considerable strengths or weaknesses in particular key departments. Individuals have their objectives set in accord with the DPA and following evaluation of their performance either differential performance related payments are triggered and/or coaching and other development steps are taken. Renewed individual objectives are established at this stage in the cycle and a feedback loop is allowed for so that the department as a whole may adjust its mission in the light of enhanced performance levels achieved. The reasons why performance management has come to attract so much attention in recent years (Addams and Embley, 1988; Fowler, 1990; Bevan and Thompson, 1991; Neale 1991; IPM, 1992; Sheard, 1992; Fletcher and Williams, 1992a,b) can be traced to a number of factors. Chief among them are increased competition; in the public sector, governmental pressure; organizational restructuring with an emphasis upon decentralization of accountability; and an intent to reshape industrial relations so that individualization displaces collective arrangements.

The first of these, increasing competition, has prompted companies to examine how their operations in every detail contribute to effectiveness or detract from it. To this extent, performance management can be seen as part of a move to pay more attention to detail. It can also be regarded as part of the wider idea of 'value-added' and the associated scrutiny of what contribution is being made by every part of the organization.

The second, governmental pressure on public sector organizations, is absolutely critical. It is no accident or coincidence that performance management philosophy and practice are particularly marked in public sector organizations such as hospitals, schools and local government. Here, accountability and measurement form a clear part of the political agenda.

Third, organizational restructuring which involves an emphasis upon the decentralization of accountability to strategic business units, profit centres and cost centres as discussed in Chapter 4, can be seen as part and parcel of the rise to prominence of performance management. Indeed, performance management might even be seen as the key to making these devolved structures work. The IPM (1992) survey, for example, found that 31 per cent of divisionalized companies were claiming to operate a full formal PMS whereas none of the single site companies did so.

The intent to redraw and redefine the boundaries of employee relations which we list as the fourth reason is of course a continuing theme throughout this book. It is worth stating at this point, however, that performance management offers one of the clearest examples of the attempt to individualize the employment relationship. Just about every element within it – from individual goal setting, through to individual performance appraisal and on to individual performance-related pay – serves to render erstwhile collective rules, terms and conditions, increasingly irrelevant.

## The practice of performance management

The variations in meaning of the term 'performance management' makes the measurement of its actual take-up and practice a fraught affair. Attempts to research it raise many methodological problems. Its elusiveness makes large-scale surveying especially problematical. One of the most representative sample surveys, in Britain at least, was that conducted by the Institute of Personnel Management (Bevan and Thompson, 1992). Their survey had usable returns from 794 employers covering 4.3 million workers – that is, nearly 20 per cent of the UK workforce. The survey found that 20 per cent of employing organizations reported that they did have a 'formal performance management programme'. Nearly three-quarters said they used performance-related pay, over a third reported having a Total Quality Programme and nearly 60 per cent said they had 'policies and practices aimed at managing employee performance' (Bevan and Thompson, 1992: 15).

The organizations claiming to have a fully-developed formal performance management programme were found to be larger in terms of employment size and they were more likely to be foreign-owned. The data also showed a tendency for those employers with PMS to have considered and changed the levels at which pay and personnel policies are determined. Interestingly, there was no association found between the adoption of formal PMS and overall organizational performance. 'Such programmes are as likely to be introduced by poor performers (in relative terms) as high performers' (Bevan and Thompson, 1992: 17).

Employers with formal performance management systems were also more likely than the rest to be introducing other initiatives such as total quality management and performance-related pay. They also tended to be the organizations most likely to have mission statements which are communicated to all employees. Their level of employee communications also appeared to be above average. It should be noted, however, that the application of formal PMS was often directed mainly at managerial – especially senior managerial – employees rather than necessarily being across the board. There was an association also with the use of formally documented appraisal systems. Nearly three quarters of all organizations in the survey had some type of performance-related pay. The utilization of this type of payment system was especially notable in those organizations claiming to have a formal PMS.

In addition to the large-scale postal survey, the IPM also sponsored a qualitative case-study research programme. This work (Fletcher and Williams, 1992b) involved visits to 26 organizations. What was most notable about this 'follow-up' to the postal questionnaire study was that many of the organizations identified by the first study as practising formal PMS turned out to have very little justification for making such a claim. As Fletcher and Williams (1992b: 77) observed: 'Many of those claiming to operate performance management do not have in place procedures which meet the wide-ranging definition offered in the IMS report' (i.e. the Bevan and Thompson 1992 report described above). Fletcher and Williams found it necessary to seek out additional new cases which were reputed to be operating a PMS. Nevertheless, as they admit, even their case-study work revealed that 'the nature of performance management remains elusive' (1992b: 77). For Fletcher and Williams, appraisal and PRP are 'at the heart of what most organizations do'. On the positive side their work, which included a number of employee surveys, suggested that a comprehensive, and well-integrated approach to performance management which is directed and linked to clear strategic goals 'can have its benefits in terms of positive affective responses on the part of staff, e.g. greater organizational commitment, clarity of work goals, job satisfaction, etc.' (Fletcher and Williams, 1992b: 78).

In a case study of performance management in ICI Pharmaceuticals, Sheard (1992) argues that the system was introduced as part of a wide-reaching culture change. Previous ways of managing were, she claims, ill-suited to the increasingly competitive environment facing ICI at the end of the 1980s and early 1990s. An internal review revealed an organization where four problems were endemic: decisions were being taken at too high a level and were thus out of touch with the market place and customer needs; the culture was task-orientated in the sense that people concentrated on task inputs and methods rather than being output-orientated; people-management skills were undervalued and therefore undeveloped; and employees were disconnected from the business.

Sheard, who is a training and development consultant at ICI Pharmaceuticals, describes how performance management was used to tackle these four problems. She reports how the chief executive led the way to a new performance improvement strategy in 1989. This entailed, for example, the communication of strategic objectives throughout the business. Explicit mention was made of the importance of people in attaining those objectives. People at every level became familiar with the objectives. There was a cascade process so that managers at every level were asked to review their own and their unit's objectives and to place these within the frame of the corporate objectives. Departmental purpose analyses were conducted, and objectives were explicitly stated for units and departments for the next 12 to 24 months. Employees were then fed business results and these were discussed with employees 'in a way which encouraged interaction and debate by relating them to their own areas, supplemented with a review of departmental activities' (Sheard, 1992: 40).

Integral also was the introduction of a new 'development of people, work and reward' system. Crucially, for ICI, the performance management system focused on *developing* people rather than assessment. As part of this, line managers were involved in coaching, encouragement and motivation. Thus, Sheard claims, ICI has focused on a development-driven model but a more performance-related rewards system has also been introduced.

137

The focus, however, in ICI's performance management system is upon: clear objectives, an emphasis upon contribution not task, agreed individual targets, development plans based on these targets, and the involvement of individuals in setting objectives. These features in many ways summarise the essence of an 'ideal' PMS with a particular emphasis in this case upon the developmental aspect. One final feature of this leading-edge case in PMS is worth noting – the performance-related pay element is itself decentralised. Each department devises its own reward plan which reflects its priorities and business goals. Implementation is also managed locally within agreed budget constraints. Local managers therefore are encouraged to use this discretion to determine the type, scale and timing of the rewards.

Certain key issues emerge from this review of the evidence on the use of performance management. First, the meaning of the term continues to be relatively open rather than precise. None the less, there would appear to be the kernel of an idea worth preserving – that is, there is seemingly a set of policies and practices which when entwined can refocus attention on issues of goals, achievement, evaluation and action. Second, appraisal and/or other performance review methods are pivotal to the concept. Third, the actions which ensue from such evaluation can tend towards either differential payment or towards further training and development. We attend to the payment issue in the remainder of this chapter before addressing the training and development theme in the next.

## Performance-related pay

Two main types of individual PRP scheme are to be found: one involves the linking of pay to performance as measured by the achievement of specific individual objectives and the other – sometimes known as merit rating – assesses performance in terms of certain behavioural traits such as problem-solving, reliability, initiative, cooperation, and so on (see Figure 6.2 for examples). A number of recent surveys, which are reviewed in Kessler (1993), confirm substantial growth in both types especially among non-manual employees, many of whom have

1 Fixed incremental scales with limited flexibility, i.e. there is a standard increase for the majority of staff, but the manager can increase payments for exceptionally effective staff or reduce the increase for poor performers.
2 Performance pay linked to an incremental scale, i.e. attainment of the next point on the scale is dependent on the employee reaching a satisfactory performance rating.
3 Pay increase based on performance rating and awarded by a series of fixed percentage points, e.g.:

|  | % increase |
| --- | --- |
| Unsatisfactory | 0 |
| Satisfactory | 2.0 |
| Above average | 3.5 |
| Excellent | 5.0 |

**Figure 6.2** Examples of individual performance related pay
*Source*: Based on ACAS (1988a: 31)

traditionally been paid salaries with automatic annual increments related to length of service. Unlike some previous trends in pay systems, the public sector as well as the private sector is affected; for example, among the 500,000 non-industrial civil servants, assessed performance is now integral to salary progression for most grades.

However, despite the outpouring of advice and consultancy that is available, the signs are that in many organizations individual PRP is leading to major problems. Not only is the introduction of PRP being badly handled. The near-obsession with individual PRP means that other features essential to performance management are being ignored or not being given the attention they deserve. We suggest that the single-minded determination to install individual PRP (despite the lack of firm evidence concerning its efficacy) is reflective of the wider move towards individualism and away from collectivism which has been highlighted elsewhere in this book. As the argument in this chapter unfolds it will be possible to witness some of the limits to the individualization strategy.

1  It focuses effort where the organization wants it (specified in performance plans, objectives or targets).
2  It supports a performance-orientated culture (pay for results not effort).
3  It emphasizes individual performance or teamwork as appropriate (group-based schemes foster cooperation, personal schemes focus on individual contribution).
4  It strengthens the performance planning process (the setting of objectives and performance standards will carry more weight).
5  It rewards the right people (high rewards to those whose performance is commensurately high).
6  It can motivate all the people (a well-designed scheme will be motivating to all participants).

**Figure 6.3**  The logic of performance pay
*Source*: Brading and Wright (1990: 1)

If one ignores for the moment the substantial body of evidence which casts doubt on the links between pay and performance, the case for individual PRP sounds very plausible. It is difficult to quarrel with the overall objective of performance pay which has been described as 'to improve performance by converting the paybill from an indiscriminate machine to a more finely tuned mechanism, sensitive and responsive to a company's and employees' needs' (Brading and Wright, 1990: 1). Equally, there appears to be nothing exceptional about the kinds of specific objectives which organizations are said to be looking for in introducing PRP (see Figure 6.3), especially if the possibility of group as opposed to individual PRP is taken into account.

However, as Kessler's (1993) review of the research evidence suggests, there is a significant gap between assumptions and reality in those many organizations which have introduced individual PRP. A common feature is a failure to think through the introduction of performance-related pay in a coherent manner. Thus, in many cases the establishment of formal performance criteria leaves a great deal to be desired – 'objectives' and 'behaviours' which bear little relationship to work practice are being engineered purely for the purposes of having an individual PRP scheme. In the performance assessment process, which lies at the heart of individual PRP, there are complaints about subjectivity and inconsistency which are often compounded by lack of attention to the training of managers in carrying out appraisal and to the administrative procedures for monitoring arrangements. The links between performance and the level of pay are not always clear and effective – in many cases, it is argued, the amount of the incentive element is far too small to make any material difference. Few organizations, it seems, have built in arrangements to monitor the impact of individual PRP on productivity; or, indeed, to estimate how much such schemes cost to run (see also Thompson, 1992, for further evidence on many of these points). It has also been noted that excessive emphasis on extrinsic motivation in the form of pay can result in damage to intrinsic motivation (Deci, 1975). Motivation which comes from pride in work may be undermined. A recent ACAS report makes the same point: individual performance-related pay schemes are actually demotivating. The system tends to be disliked by those carrying out the appraisals and those who are appraised. Ted Riley, a principal adviser in the ACAS Work Research Unit says that in some specific instances performance-related pay can be successful, for example, 'In a small organization with highly dynamic whizz-kids it might work', he says, 'But most organizations are not like that' (Riley, 1992).

Perhaps the most worrying aspect, however, is that individual PRP would seem to contradict or sit uneasily with a number of other policies and objectives which managers profess to be pursuing. One of these is the emphasis which many organizations are putting on teamwork. In many cases, notably where operations are inter-linked, individual PRP would appear to be totally inappropriate. Focusing on individual performance goals in such situations can undermine team spirit and cooperation. At the very least, employees may focus their attention on individual targets (especially if they are artificially contrived for the pay system) at the expense of the performance of the unit. Even so, there currently appears to be a widespread insistence on having individual PRP – come what may. Arguably, this clamour for the latest flavour of the month is as good an example as any of the kind of *lack* of strategic thinking in HR and IR which we have commented upon elsewhere in this book.

In the circumstances, one is reminded of the experience of individual and small-group individual payment by results systems in the car industry in the post-Second World War period. Given the nature of car assembly work, in which the pace of work of individual employees is largely determined by the pace of the track, a car assembly line would hardly seem to be the place in which to have individual and gang systems of payment by results. Despite this, and despite the commitment of US manufacturers to alternative systems, such as measured daywork, the UK manufacturers persisted with individual PBR throughout the post-Second World War period. The result was that by the late 1960s, the payment system was out of control. There was little or no relationship between effort and reward, there was considerable earnings drift and a much-publicized pattern of strikes which was seen as being highly damaging to the ability to meet delivery dates. It was to take another decade, during which measured daywork was introduced followed by plant-wide incentives systems, to get things into some semblance of normality. By this time the UK car manufacturers had suffered a considerable loss of market share (for further details about the experience with individual payment by results schemes, see NBPI, 1968a).

It may be going too far to suggest that similar mistakes are being made with individual PRP. Yet there are signs that this may be happening in some cases. Why? The discussion in Kessler (1993) is extremely helpful here. He identifies two analytical approaches to understanding managers' choices of pay systems which draw attention to the confusion of motives that appear to be present in many organizations. The first approach sees the choice of pay system as part of a relatively ordered and rational process in which managers pick the scheme which is appropriate to its needs. This, the contingency approach, has a long tradition in the writing about pay systems in the UK (Lupton and Gowler's, *Selecting a Wage Payment System*, which was published as long ago as 1969, is a well-known example and is still probably the best guide there is). The second approach sees the choice of the payment system as a far less ordered or rational management process. Rather, it is a largely political or ideological process acquiring symbolic value to support particular interests or values. In this case the details of the scheme, and how it is introduced and monitored, are likely to be seen as largely irrelevant by decision makers. It is the message sent by the introduction of the scheme that matters most.

It is difficult to escape the conclusion that it is the second view that it is most appropriate to adopt, namely that individual PRP is being introduced for largely ideological reasons. The messages which senior managers would appear to be wishing to give are also fairly clear. First, there is to be a change in the culture of the organization. It is no accident, for example, that some of the most publicized individual PRP schemes have been in the newly privatized public utilities – senior managers have been as anxious to impress the stockmarket analysts with their commitment to the 'commercialism' of the private sector as they have their own employees. Second, managers must manage. A key implication of individual PRP is that managers have to take responsibility for performance management: <u>requiring them to take tough decisions</u> about the payments that are going to be made to individual employees is seen as a critical element in the process. Third, and perhaps most important, there is the focus on the individual; the implication, at the very least, is that trade unions and collective bargaining will play a lesser role in pay determination. Indeed, in some well-publicized cases, for example, management grades in British Rail and British Telecom, the introduction of individual PRP has been directly associated with the withdrawal of collective bargaining rights over pay.

It is also possible to suggest two further and related considerations. One is the inherent belief of top managers – it seems to be almost an article of faith – that pay is the prime motivator in performance. The second is their conviction that not only is managing through the payment system the most effective means of managing HR and IR, but it is also sufficient for doing so. This last point is worth stressing because it has much wider implications. Much is made in the personnel management literature of different types of 'contract'. UK management, it seems, feels much more comfortable – largely because of historical reasons – with the cash nexus or subcontracting relationship than it does with the other forms of contract which carry mutual obligations.

## Key issues in reward management

There is no dispute about the overall significance of the reward system in performance management. In the words of Collins (1991: 78), the reward system is important in attracting and retaining employees of the required quality, underpinning the drive to improve performance, and supporting the ability to change.

However, as will be clear from reading any standard textbook (see, for example, Torrington and Hall (1991)), one of the great debates in personnel management is whether the system of rewards, in Herzberg's (1966) terms, is to be seen as a 'motivator' or 'hygiene' factor. Is the system of rewards, in other words, to be seen primarily as a positive incentive to greater performance or, if employees feel that it is unfair, as a source of disincentive? Our view is that it is sensible to start from the second position. This is because, in the head-long rush to individual PRP, there has been a tendency in many UK organizations to neglect other key components of reward systems. Certainly the research evidence suggests that there is considerable scope for improvement in a number of the areas involved; these will therefore be considered before returning to the issue of individual performance in the final section.

### An appropriate pay structure

Two main aspects are involved. One relates to internal pay relationships or differentials; the other to external pay relationships or relativities. Both these are fundamentally important because they are inextricably tied up with notions of fairness. The problem is that fairness is not an absolute but a relative concept. Pay relationships provide the critical measure of the worth or status which the individual is accorded in the organization and in society more generally; their fairness is judged in comparison to others. If they are felt to be unfair, they can be a major disincentive. In Brown's words:

> The most ingenious of bonus systems and the best of supervision are of little use if the underlying pay structure is felt to be unfair. Consequently, the prudent personnel manager devotes far less time to devising new pay incentives than to tending old notions of fairness. (Brown, 1989: 252–3)

The recommended method of setting the basis for pay differentials which are felt to be fair is job evaluation. This is simply a procedure for allowing comparisons between jobs in a systematic way. A variety of methods is available, but four main types can be found: ranking; paired comparisons; grading or job classification; and points rating (ACAS 1988a: 7–8; and NBPI, 1968b).

The starting point in each case is the preparation of a description of the jobs being compared using common headings or factors. The first three methods are often referred to as 'non-analytical'. The simplest, ranking, is fairly rudimentary and involves a number of judgements: should job A be paid more than job B, C, or D? Paired comparison is very similar – the difference is that each job is compared with every other job in turn. Grading reverses the process: a decision is taken to have so many grades and then the jobs are allocated to the different grades. Points rating is referred to as an analytical method. This method involves deriving a number of factors and the relative weighting to be attached to them. Each job is then considered factor by factor to give a points total which can be used to determine the position in the job hierarchy.

Typically, UK companies have operated with a minimum of five or six grades. A number of the Japanese companies who have invested in the UK, notably Nissan, have chosen to work with only two major grades. If a major objective is to improve flexibility, it is argued, too many grades can present major obstacles – job evaluation, by definition, involves the preparation of job descriptions. The tighter these are drawn for the purposes of distinguishing one job from another, the greater the inflexibility.

External pay relationships or relativities, the second aspect of pay structure, have in the past been an issue of considerable controversy especially during the periods of incomes policy in the 1960s and 1970s. Currently, to return to the point made earlier about the ideological explanation of management behaviour, they are supposed to be a non-issue. The main considerations in pay determination, it is argued, ought to be the specific circumstances of the individual organization – the ability to pay, in other words, is of paramount importance. The problem is that the issue will not go away. Organizations have to have regard to what potential competitors for their employees are paying. Otherwise, they risk losing their best people. In the main they do this through market surveys. In the case of managers, for example, considerable use is made of the Hay system to judge the appropriateness of pay levels. In the case of manual workers the local employers' organization is very often the source of the data. In the public services, groups like the armed forces, senior civil servants, doctors, nurses, and teachers have formal review bodies responsible for making recommendations on the basis of comparisons.

### Single status

Most commentators accept that the division between manual and non-manual workers, which is grounded in history, cannot be justified and makes little sense. A key reason is that the very existence of these status differences makes it extremely difficult to win the kind of cooperation and commitment that organizations claim to be seeking. There is no defensible reason, for example, why a 50 year old skilled craftsman, who has worked 30 years with an organization should have inferior sick pay or pension arrangements to his 18 year old offspring who only recently joined as a junior. A second reason is that in many organizations it is increasingly difficult to distinguish on any objective basis between manual and non-manual jobs. A third reason is that, as the non-pay items increase in their cost, management want greater return from them. Indeed, in the USA the so-called 'cafeteria principle' is becoming increasingly important: in the attempt to draw attention to the costs and benefits of these elements, employees are encouraged to choose between different combinations of non-pay benefits instead of taking them for granted.

Such concerns have not been translated into practice, however, despite predictions about the decline of the status gap (Price and Price, 1993). Certainly throughout the 1980s there have been moves to harmonize some of the terms and conditions of manual and non-manual workers. Sick pay is a case in point. Examples of single status arrangements, however, remain the exception rather than the rule. In the ACAS survey of 667 workplaces in manufacturing and services in 1988, for example, of the respondents who used some form of job evaluation in determining payment, only one in eight reported that they had an integrated scheme covering manual and non-manual workers (ACAS, 1988a: 7).

Admittedly, there are some major problems in moving towards single status arrangements. One is cost. Sizeable increases may be involved and many organizations are in no position to pay the bill. Especially important is the cost of security that would be involved in many organizations as a result of different notice provisions which would arise. Another is trade union opposition. Much of this has come in particular from non-manual unions who are afraid of losing their particular advantages or who fear that they will be 'held back' while others catch up. In many cases, there is a suspicion that managers simply do not perceive the status divide to be a major cause for real concern. On the contrary, the divide could be seen as bringing positive advantages to management. Rightly or wrongly, managements in some organizations feel that it enables them to enjoy the tactical advantage of playing one group off against another.

### Group performance pay

Kessler's (1993) review of the recent surveys notes that the incidence of collective performance schemes, especially those which cover the unit or the company, is relatively low. Indeed, the ACAS (1988a: 18) survey referred to earlier suggested that just over half of the establishments in the sample had some form of group or collective bonus system. The majority of these affected the immediate work group only, however. A mere 13 per cent of workplaces had schemes which covered the workplace or the enterprise as a whole.

There is a widespread view that the direct incentive in group schemes is low because the performance–reward link is too remote. Even so, the relatively low incidence of such schemes is surprising for several reasons. First, there are a number of important variables which can be the basis of performance schemes such as output, cost reduction, sales and quality (for further details, see ACAS, 1985: 14–7; 34–7). Second, much work is team work and many of the problems associated with individual PRP schemes are overcome with appropriately designed group schemes – especially if the low level of the payment in many individual PRP schemes is taken into account. Third, group bonus schemes are one of the most effective forms of communication to employees about such key issues as productivity, costs and quality.

### Profit sharing

A further possibility in the private sector is profit sharing. Profit sharing, which has received considerable support from the government in the form of tax incentives through the Financial Acts involves linking pay or some element of pay to profits either in the form of direct cash payments or shares.

The empirical evidence also provides a useful starting point here. There has, it is true, been a significant increase in the coverage of profit sharing since the early 1980s. It is by no means extensive, however. Only 36 per cent of the workplaces in the ACAS (1988a: 20) survey which has already been quoted, reported some form of profit sharing and share ownership. Significantly too, in the light of the discussion above about the status divide, the majority of these schemes affected non-manual workers only, however. Only about one-third of the workplaces with profit-sharing schemes or between 12 per cent and 13 per cent of the total applied them to both manual and non-manual workers.

The nature of the Inland Revenue arrangements may have been a deterrent here. But this applies only to government schemes. Here too then there would appear to be considerable scope for improvement in the performance management stakes.

*Managing individual performance*

In this final section we examine some of the essential mechanics which are involved in the attempt to manage individual perform-ance. Most commentators are agreed that an effective appraisal system is essential to any serious attempt to manage individual performance. Appraisal serves two main purposes: performance review (which allows managers and employees to identify possibilities for improvement in the current job) and potential review (to predict the level and type of work which an employee is capable of doing and to consider how the person might best be prepared for this). The problem is that the two have become inextricably tied up with a third, and what many people see as the most important, purpose of appraisal, namely a reward review to determine the basis of individual PRP. Indeed, such has been the pressure of this view that many texts are equivocal about having separate processes or a single process – it is often presented as a matter of preference or convenience. In our view, an organization which is serious about performance management will keep the reviews of performance and potential separate from any reward review. If the three processes are mixed up, there is an inevitable danger that none will be done properly.

There are a number of types of appraisal system. Under the 'rating' approach a range of factors, such as quality and output of work, are graded on a numerical scale according to the level of performance, e.g. outstanding, exceeds requirements of the job, meets the requirements of the job, shows minor weaknesses, shows some significant weaknesses, or unacceptable.

A second method is to compare achievements with objectives: the manager and the employee agree objectives at the beginning of the appraisal period and the subsequent appraisal is based on how far these objectives have been met. A third method uses 'critical incidents'. With this the appraiser records incidents of the employee's positive and negative behaviour during the appraisal period and the record forms the basis of the appraisal report. A fourth method is the narrative report – the appraiser describes the employee's work performance in his or her own words either in the form of an open 'essay' or of answers to certain questions or guidelines. And a fifth method is the 'behaviourally anchored rating scale'. With this the appraiser uses a 'custom-built' set of characteristics or 'anchors' derived from analysis of the particular job to rate the performance of the employee (ACAS, 1988b: 12–8).

In terms of styles of appraisal, there has reputedly been a move from 'tell and sell', though 'tell and listen' to more open 'problem solving' approaches (see, for example, Holdsworth, 1992: 69–70). If the manager is serious about performance management this last style would seem to be imperative. It needs to be noted, however, that the process is time-consuming if applied to all employees and it presents many managers with considerable difficulties. Not least among these is how this type of individual-based planning will be integrated with any collective processes which are in train and with the plans emanating from the business unit and the department. Clearly, operating in this way places a high premium on managerial competence.

To assess the potential of employees, some large organizations use assessment centres. These may involve the organization's own staff or those of an external agency. Here assessors are likely to use a combination of appraisal methods, together with the kind of individual and group psychological and psychometric tests as discussed in Chapter 5, to gauge potential.

In the case of managers' performance, a recent development in some organizations, for example, British Airways, BP and W.H. Smith, is 'peer' and 'subordinate' assessment. The individual manager is not simply appraised by his or her superior, but also by colleagues and the employees in his or her department. Attitude surveys can also be used for this purpose; IBM, for example, uses a section of its regular survey of employee attitudes to get feedback on managers' performance.

All the signs are that individual performance related pay is going to grow in its coverage for some time to come. It is important therefore that the mechanics introduced to facilitate it are as effective as possible. For those managers determined to press ahead with individual PRP despite the difficulties, one model to bear in mind might suitably be that used in ICL (see Figure 6.4).

This shows how the different purposes of appraisal might be linked together. The model is based on a four-step cycle. The first involves the setting of individual objectives – each of which is

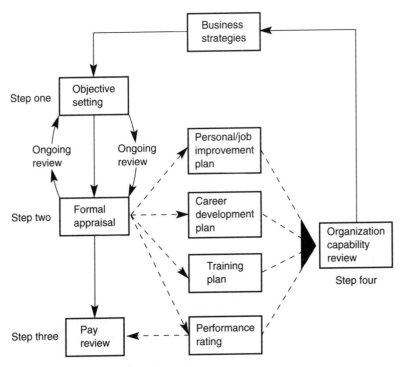

**Figure 6.4** The ICL performance management system
*Source*: Neale (1991: 27)

supposed to support the attainment of the overall business strategy. The second step is the formal appraisal which centres on what was achieved in relation to the objectives set. The outcome of this meeting should be as shown in the middle column of the figure, i.e. a personal improvement plan, a career development plan, a training plan and a performance rating. Step three is a pay review in which the level of pay is based mainly on actual achievement as measured against pre-agreed objectives. Step four, the 'organization capability review', focuses attention on the capability of each part of the organization to achieve the business strategy. A feedback loop allows for emendation of that strategy.

A second source of advice to which managers might turn could be the ACAS guide for organizations thinking of introducing individual PRP (ACAS, 1988b and 1988c). The ACAS recommendations are important not only because they touch on one of the central themes of this book – the need to manage 'individualism' and 'collectivism' both – but also because all too often they have been forgotten in much recent writing on 'performance management'. Essentially, what ACAS advises is that full consultation should take place with managers, employees and trade unions – and agreement reached – before the scheme is introduced; that systems should be relatively simple to understand, operate and monitor; that managers are properly trained and have sufficient time available to carry out the reviews; the appraisal system should be kept separate from the reward review procedure; that the system should be closely monitored by senior managers; that employees should have an opportunity to see and to make comments on their assessment markings; and finally, that an appeals procedure should be made available.

Clearly, many of these recommendations will not be palatable especially to those managers who seek, most centrally, to use the introduction of a PRP scheme as a means to individualize the employment relationship. The reference to agreement with the trade unions is therefore likely to be most unwelcome. But, where performance management is in fact the *real* objective rather than de-collectivization, then trade unions might usefully be involved in a number of the key stages of a PRP scheme. They can be involved in negotiating the principles, in helping to determine the global amount of the pay increase, and in helping to decide the distribution between general and individual increases. They also have a critical role to play in the appeals procedure.

Where this type of guidance is followed, one might expect that the kind of balance between individualism and collectivism which we have been talking about throughout this book, could be attained. It is, as we observed earlier, guidance which is undeniably some distance from the 'high-tech' end of HRM, but it is none the less valid for that. Indeed, as we have also been at some pains to stress, despite claims by many popular pundits to the contrary, no one set of prescriptions can be expected to have applicability for all types of situation. We are addressing ourselves here primarily to those mainstream, unionised and proceduralized British organizations, whether in the public or private sectors, where the fundamental issues turn on questions of survival in a hostile climate and where the most immediately pressing needs are in fact rather basic.

## Conclusions

In this chapter we have reviewed the rise of performance management and the resurgence of interest in performance-related pay. Both trends, we argued, reflect the current interest in individualizing the employment relationship. There is a dearth of sound empirical evidence to show that either system produces the kind of results which managers want from them. Nevertheless, enthusiasm for them remains very evident. Both systems are seen to be congruent with the other kinds of change in HR and IR which are explored in this book.

For those involved in the design of performance management systems, there are three main points to be borne in mind. First, the payment system, important though it is, constitutes only one element in performance management. All too often, it can be argued, British management has relied exclusively on the payment system – be it payment by results in the 1950s and 1960s, or individual PRP in the 1980s and the early 1990s.

Second, there is no such thing as a 'perfect' system. Certainly there are general considerations to be taken into account and many of them have been considered here. But there is really no alternative to deciding what is appropriate in particular circumstances. In the language of social sciences, there is a need to adopt a contingency approach.

The third point is no less basic than the others. As circumstances change, so do the pressures on the performance management system. A pay system or pay structure, in other words, is not for ever. Systems and structures which may seem highly appropriate in one period can be highly inappropriate in the next when products and services have changed or when new operating systems and technologies have been introduced. These and other elements in the performance management system, then, need constant review and the expectation must be that they will require substantial changes at frequent intervals. The Appendix to this book demonstrates how such reviews might be undertaken.

# 7

# TRAINING AND DEVELOPMENT

———

In this chapter we will examine the spectrum of activities aimed at improving the human capital within an organization. For many people, this translates into the skills and knowledge to do present and future jobs. Increasingly, however, training and development, or human resource development (HRD) to use the umbrella title, are being seen as important also in improving attitudes and approaches to tasks. Customer care and total quality management, which will be considered in more detail in Chapter 8, are good examples.

There are grounds for contending that HRD deserves to be viewed as 'the vital component' in human resource management (Keep, 1989). If HRM is largely based on the treatment of labour as a strategic and valued resource rather than merely a cost, then it would seem to follow that training and development would offer the surest expression of the investment in, and nurturing of, that resource.

The crucial importance of training and development in a HR/IR strategy can be also argued in other ways. Managerial commitment to training is significant, for example, in its symbolic value. Where managers fail to train they send a message which suggests that labour is easily dispensed with and of little value. Where significant training is undertaken it indicates a commitment to people and the recipients are more likely to feel valued. Depending on its nature and extent, training may also signal the choice of a value-added business strategy in place of a lowest-cost strategy. The research by the National Institute of Economic and Social Research has demonstrated very clearly the contrasting conditions, possibilities and consequences in Germany and Britain where companies have respectively followed these paths (Steedman and Wagner, 1987).

There is also a demonstrable link between training and the wider issues of industrial relations. The nature of this connection has been effectively explored by Lane (1990). She reveals how the vocational and educational training (VET) system in Germany forms a pivotal role in the virtuous circle of high investment in training, effective utilization of advanced technology, high levels of skill, high wages but low unit costs, and high levels of competitiveness – especially at the premium end of the market. These in turn are all linked with functional flexibility and low levels of labour conflict.

Sadly, while it is increasingly accepted that training and development are critical in any high value-added competitive strategy, as Chapter 2 has demonstrated, the UK does not possess the infrastructure at national level which other countries have in order to deliver the needed levels of competence. Certain new initiatives have recently been launched, such as the Training and Enterprise Councils, in an attempt to correct for this state of affairs. Already, however, it is clear that these initiatives do not go anywhere far enough to deal with the long-standing failings of the UK's traditional market-based system. Like it or not, this means that managers who recognize the vital importance of training and development to the strategic direction of their organization are going to have to take the necessary steps themselves.

In the light of these preliminary observations, the first section of this chapter describes the steps that are involved in identifying and satisfying training and development needs. The second section gives details of a clutch of initiatives and innovations in training and development at organizational level which offer pointers to what might further be done by managers in their own organizations. The third and final section considers some of the issues and problems that may be faced, however, by managers who try to follow suit.

## The training and development 'cycle'

As in the case of planning and resourcing discussed in Chapter 5, the steps involved in 'doing' training and development are relatively straightforward and have been exhaustively reviewed in the traditional textbooks. Typically, these textbooks depict the management of training and development as a 'cycle' or series of logical steps. Figure 7.1 gives a brief outline of what is involved.

The cycle ideally commences at the top with the identification of training needs. This process known usually as 'training needs analysis' involves an assessment of the gap between desired levels of knowledge, skills and competencies and the actual pattern of current levels. The usual recommended approach is to focus, in turn, on the company, the department or unit, and then the individual. In this cascade fashion one is led from an assessment of the overall company trajectory and its future plans, down through the implications of these plans for sectional skill needs, and then on to the disaggregated individual training needs.

The emphasis in the prescriptions on training needs analysis is always to follow a logical sequence. This means, for example, at the individual job level beginning with the current job description, reviewing its contemporary relevance and adequacy and then, identifying key task areas and their associated needed competencies. In turn, this leads on to an assessment of the job holder's current level of competence in each of the identified key task areas. This information may be collected in various ways including, for example, direct observation, performance appraisal documentation and actual performance records. Discussion with the job holder is invariably also recommended as the vital information about impediments to effective performance and about training needs is often best gleaned directly from the person doing the job.

Increasingly in the case of management jobs, for example, development needs are being revealed by the use of self-analysis

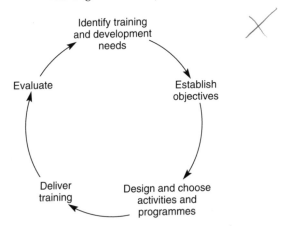

**Figure 7.1** The training and development cycle

techniques, testing, and personality and behavioural profiling. Many training courses for managers are built on an initial review of each individual's personal traits and orientations. Multiple-choice instruments designed for self-completion are frequently used and from these, individual managers are presented with a summary depiction of their 'style' or tendencies. Similar profiles are arrived at through the use of peer and subordinate assessments.

The second step in the cycle is to identify learning objectives. In effect this means being able to state what capabilities a trainee will be able to demonstrate following completion of the training. The desired objectives are obviously supposed to stem from the key tasks as identified under stage one. The successful listing of learning objectives is critical because, in effect, the resulting agenda forms the outline guide to the training content of the programme to follow.

The third step, the design and choice of activities, relates to the selection of learning methods deemed most appropriate to meet the list of learning objectives. The actual choice of method will be shaped by the kind of learning which is supposed to occur. A classic distinction is often drawn, for example, between practical how-to-do capabilities versus knowledge based on an understanding of underlying principles. Neither is inherently superior to the other; each has its place depending upon the trainer's ultimate objectives. Other important choices which have to be made include decisions about on or off-the-job training and the detailed mix of activities to be undertaken by the trainee.

The fourth step is the delivery of the training. At this implementation stage all of the issues concerning teaching and learning styles come into play. Again, the watchword from all the prescriptive texts is to match these with the previously assessed objectives.

Here it is important to note that technological advances have facilitated the growth of distance-learning techniques such as interactive video. Such devices have so far found most use in technical training. None the less, the momentum should not be underestimated. The open learning provisions at Jaguar and at Midland Bank, to take two examples, have met with a response from across these companies. Midland Bank's so-called 'Leap' programme is, in effect, a mail-order system which allows staff to have direct access to a wide array of learning materials from a central library. The take-up has been extraordinarily high and the well-ordered provision and its promotion have helped to generate a culture which is conducive to staff and management development.

Evaluation, the fifth stage in the training and development 'cycle', is increasingly being viewed in the training literature as an integral part of the training cycle. In other words it should not be regarded as an optional add-on, something which comes outside of, and after training proper has been completed. If handled carefully, evaluation can be built into the programme and can help shape the progression of learning.

Finally, it is worth mentioning that, for some, this training and development 'cycle' is but the preliminary to creating the 'learning organization'. This has been defined as 'an organization that facilitates the learning of all its members and continuously transforms itself' (Pedler et al., 1991: 1). Training and development, in other words, are not to be seen simply as a set of processes, but part of the very essence of the organization. Viewed from this perspective, each and every experience is something from which people learn and draw the appropriate conclusions for their future behaviour. It ought, however, to be made clearer than its proponents seem willing to do, that in truth the learning organization represents an idealized end state rather than a working model.

## Innovations in training and development

As we argued at the beginning of this chapter, although the national scene is not particularly propitious for training and development in Britain, there are certain hopeful indicators of initiatives being pursued at company level. Managers searching for a competitive edge built on HRD, can look to these examples as sources of inspiration. Paradoxically, recession and resultant rationalization have in some circumstances acted as catalysts for change which have had repercussions on training and development. Reductions in manpower have prompted the re-combining of jobs in various ways. Craft differences have been reduced; balanced labour force initiatives have sought to compensate for shortages in one craft area with surpluses in another; team-working has led to a certain amount of interchangeability and flexibility; there has even been a diminished distinction between blue and white collar jobs especially at technician level.

Recession apart, increased international competition has also impelled certain changes which carry implications for staff development. New technology has often been introduced to keep pace with foreign competition and this may mean that there is little option other than to embark on the training of existing employees. In addition, the shifting of the basis of competition to areas of quality in product and service delivery has meant an increased need to train staff in customer care and total quality.

The discussion that follows considers innovations taking place in a number of key areas: youth training, adult training, customer care, 'open' learning and management development. In view of the audience for this book and its vital importance, particular attention is paid to management development.

### Youth training

As Chapter 2 observed, the training of young workers in the UK has traditionally been associated with the craft apprenticeship system. Typically, this was exclusive and time-served. This meant that in the industries in which it predominated, notably construction, engineering, and printing, if young workers did not gain access in their teens they were more or less condemned to semi-skilled or unskilled status for the rest of their lives. There was also no guarantee that even the privileged few had achieved any objective level of skill – it was enough to have served one's 'time'. In the industries without such arrangements, i.e. the great majority, this meant that there was little or no training available at all. Young workers simply picked things up by 'sitting next to Nellie'. This was above all true of the private service sector where, outside the banks and one or two of the large retailers, the vast majority of young people entering employment were offered little by way of structured job training.

Two things have happened in recent years. First, although there has been a dramatic drop in the number of apprenticeships, there have been radical changes in the arrangements. As Keep (1989: 196) points out, these include the revision of existing modules to allow for greater flexibility and transferability of skills, greater emphasis on practical experience, the incorporation of general elements through the Youth Training Scheme (YTS), and training based on the achievement of standards rather than on age or length of service criteria. Key examples are to be found in the chemicals and engineering industries.

The second significant development is that the training net has spread much wider. Here, the various government initiatives such as the YTS following the New Training Initiative of 1981, leading to Youth Training of 1989 have been catalysts. Criticism of these initiatives abound (see Keep, 1993). Even so, the numbers on such schemes have been impressive. By 1988/9, for example, there were, on average, some 389,000 trainees on the scheme during the year. Crucially, sectors such as health care, retail and catering have been encouraged to lay on induction and training programmes. In the better schemes there has also been a shift towards a 'competence' based rather than a process or time-served approach, thus emphasizing the outcomes of learning. Rainbird (1993) quotes a number of examples including the supermarket chain which has introduced a new national foundation scheme aimed at young recruits involving registration for the retail certificate. Woolworth, the stores chain, has recently embarked on a tiered educational and training provision in collaboration with Brunel University which can, in theory, take an unqualified junior from Certificate level, through Diploma level and on to degree level by means of a distance learning programme.

## Adult training

Rainbird (1993) is also a very good source for information about developments in continuous adult training, which had been a much neglected area. These initiatives are especially significant because most organizations already have in place 7 of the 10 employees they will have in the year 2000. She quotes cases from Incomes Data Services (1989) of progression from semi-skilled to skilled status (as at Sony) and of retraining leading to job enlargement and of manual to professional work (as at the *Financial Times*). She also discusses related developments in skills based pay, i.e. the progression to new grades being dependent on obtaining additional qualifications for dual or multi-skilling (see also IRRR, 1989d; IDS, 1989).

In her own case studies, Rainbird found a number of specific examples which suggest that some managements, at least, are taking adult training more seriously. Thus, she found a motor components manufacturer which had received support from the European Social Fund for the retraining of adults in new technology skills – a minimum of 100 hours for operators and 200 hours for young people on courses developed jointly with equipment manufacturers. In a contract caterers, she came across a Trainer Development Scheme to equip local managers to carry out their training responsibilities more fully. Alongside these skills, provision had been made for the production of a series of modular training packages with closely targeted content, related for example to health, safety, and hygiene.

### 'Customer care'

So far the focus has primarily been on skills training. A major development has been the use of continuous training to bring about shifts in attitudes. As Chapter 8 describes in more detail, in the early 1980s, organizations like British Airways and British Rail pioneered 'customer care' and 'customer first' campaigns. In the case of British Airways, for example, it is claimed that every member of its staff attended a two-day workshop devoted to raising awareness of the importance of the customer and what could be done to improve performance in this area.

In recent years a number of organizations have sought to bring about more wide-ranging shifts in culture through 'total quality management' programmes of the kinds that will be discussed in more detail in Chapter 8. These include British Airways, British Telecom, BP, ICI, National Westminster Bank, Philips Electronics and Shell (see also IFF, 1991).

It is not only the private sector and the public enterprises which have been involved. Similar developments have taken place in the National Health Service and local authorities. Here government pressure, notably in the form of the 'Patient's Charter' and the 'Citizen's Charter' has been important. In one local authority, for example, Rainbird (1993) found major changes brought about by the 'Citizen's Charter'. First, there had been a devolution of the responsibility for training and development to departmental level which embraced both operational responsibilities and budgets. Second, a customer care orientation was being developed which required the establishment of linkages between client and service departments as discussed in Chapter 4. In this process a key role was played by training officers who were as much facilitators as trainers. Significantly, too, she found that these arrangements were backed up by the introduction of performance management systems targeting the actual delivery of service.

### 'Open' learning

A fourth area in which there have been significant innovations is in the provision of wider opportunities through 'open' and 'distance' learning activities which are not immediately job-related. In the car industry, for example, Jaguar and Rover launched major initiatives in 'open' or 'distance' learning in the 1980s (Müller, 1991; Williams et al., 1990). Other companies at the forefront of developments in 'distance' learning include British Telecom and Lucas (Keep, 1989). Midland Bank's 'Leap Programme' quoted earlier is another example. Kodak Ltd is yet a further significant case.

One of the most interesting innovations in this area is Ford's 'Employee Development and Assistance Programme' (EDAP) launched in 1989. This allows employees to qualify for grants of up to £200 per annum for personal development activities (Hougham et al., 1991). In the words of the brochure introducing the scheme to Ford employees, 'EDAP is a joint union-management initiative aimed at developing Ford's most precious asset – people. Not just to improve their career prospects – though it can certainly help – but to make the most of them as individuals.' EDAP offers every Ford employee a wide range of course and other opportunities for personal and career enhancement, ranging from Open University degree funding to assistance with health-related programmes. Grants are decided, notably, by a joint union-management committee at each Ford location. EDAP-backed courses are voluntary and take place outside working hours. The scheme, it must be emphasized, is separate from the company's traditional job-related training provision which is on-going. It was anticipated that relatively few individuals would take up the opportunity. In the event, the numbers exploded and more than half of the approximately 40,000 employees have taken part (for further details see Hougham et al., 1991).

### Management development

For managers there has been, arguably, rather more evidence of increased activity than is the case for the majority of employees. In part this has occurred because management development has been seen as a vital device in the attempt to engineer organizational culture change. Examples include the attempt by building societies to promote innovative behaviour and greater willingness to take risks (Smith, 1987) and similar endeavours are reported in insurance (Stemp, 1987), railways (Thackway, 1984) and telecommunications (Smith et al., 1986). A further example is the use of management development as a tool in the pursuit of quality and customer service (Alexander, 1987). Management development is thus used not only to upgrade skills but to structure attitudes. In other words it becomes a collective personnel device.

We may consider recent developments at the organizational level by looking at progress across five main fronts:

1  company-specific work on management competencies
2  target setting
3  evaluation of performance and analysis of development needs
4  education, formal training and development interventions
5  support for self-development.

We can consider each of these in turn.

*Management competencies*
Even those companies with the gravest reservations about the feasibility of constructing a universal list of competencies for all managers are often found, none the less, working with, or working towards, a company-specific listing (such companies include Abbey National, Midland Bank, National Westminster Bank, British Telecom and Whitbread). The steps taken by National Westminster have been described in some detail in Cockerill (1989).

*Target-setting*
A different approach to tackling a similar issue (i.e. what is it that is expected of our manager?) is represented by the upsurge of interest in target-setting for managers. The serious endeavours to clarify and to make explicit, rather than leave implicit, 'objectives'; 'goals' or 'targets' is in itself a significant development. To some extent, companies have been here before with 'management by objectives' but this time around things are somewhat different. First, the participative aspect which used to figure fairly prominently in 'management by objectives' is now considerably de-emphasized. It has by no means disappeared but the thrust has shifted in that targets are now more likely to be derived in 'cascade' fashion out of a 'departmental purpose analysis' for example. The DPA in turn, is intended to stem from the corporate strategy. The second difference relates to the intimate connection

between target setting and the increasing significance of perform-ance-related pay for managers. Increasing numbers of managers are being 'invited' to move from collective-negotiated to personal contracts. This results not only in greater variation in levels of payment but also, in places, to moves towards fixed-term contracts. The third feature is that the targets are now more likely to be expressed in terms which are measurable and that the measured out-turns are seen to have real consequences.

A feature of target setting which links it to the 'developmental' theme is the 'stretching' element: the goals or target list are far more likely now to comprise items which represent achievements which go beyond the normal routine expectations of the job. In other words, it is not intended that the targets should simply itemize aspects of the job description – performance on these elements is supposedly monitored using the on-going appraisal system. The 'stretching' character of the target-based system focuses attention on entrepreneurial and innovative behaviour.

*Development needs*
With some form of competencies' list or target-setting system in place, any gap between high-level performance and actual performance should reveal itself fairly quickly. It is not as simple as this, however: the diagnosis of the underlying reasons for any such gap is often seen to require an appropriate array of instruments. In recent years there has been an increased use of a range of tools designed to meet this need. Thus, our case research tends to give substance to the survey results (Long, 1986; Storey, 1993) which suggest a marked increase in performance appraisal. Ordinary line managers are now more likely to take their responsibility for conducting systematic appraisals more seri-ously: as one manager explained, 'the worst thing you can do to a person in this organization is fail to conduct their appraisal properly'.

A number of the larger organizations are also now more likely to make use of assessment and development centres incorpor-ating many of the self-analysis techniques discussed in the previous section. Survey evidence in the US puts the growth in their usage from 100 companies in the early 1970s to over 2000 companies a decade later (Feldman, 1988). Our own work in

Britain would give qualified support to this kind of observation though it needs to be emphasized that, even for the more sophisticated of companies, the actual exposure of managers to these centres tends to be highly selective. They are often reserved for new graduate recruits or they may be found to be used heavily by certain specialized departments whilst being virtually ignored by most others.

*Education and training*
Although it is difficult to be precise about the level of management training being provided at any one time, our research would seem to indicate that recently there has been a marked increase in both the extent and quality of training. One development has been the growth in the number of company-sponsored master of business administration programmes. The MBA qualification weathered a period of critical comment in the early 1980s (see, for example, Sadler, 1989). While the debate continues within companies about the merits and pitfalls of hiring full-time MBA graduates, there has been a spate of company-led sponsorship of part-time, consortium, and single-company programmes. Many of the companies involved in these activities have sought to integrate this kind of course provision into their own internal management development portfolio. The organizations involved in the Warwick Consortium MBA for example, have insisted on calling it the 'Integrated MBA'. Typically, these types of MBA are used as a device to propel a limited number of high-potential candidates through the organization and to help produce more 'rounded' managers out of the functional specialists at the organization's disposal.

There have been parallel developments in the take-up of short-course programmes of, one, two or six-week duration at the management colleges such as Ashridge, Henley and Cranfield. These 'executive' programmes are supposedly tailored to the needs of particular companies and there is often a strong emphasis on team building. There has also been an increase in in-company one or two-day single-skill courses in areas such as time-management, communications, negotiation, presentation skills, interviewing and the like. Perhaps not surprisingly, one of the critical issues is the extent to which individual managers are sent on the right course at the right time. All too frequently it would appear that neither criterion is met; operating such a system tests the diagnostic and organizational skills of the managers of managers. It is not unknown for even the more expensive executive programmes to be used, in practice, as a preparation for the 'outplacement' of soon-to-be-made redundant managers. The crucial point is that the ambiguity with which many British managers view training and development persists even with regard to their own situation.

*Self-development*
Some commentators would suggest that it is in the realm of self-development that the most significant progress has been made. There has certainly been a welter of publications which offer guidelines to would-be followers of this approach (see, for example, Pedler et al., 1986). Moreover, it is true that most managers interviewed in the course of our research tended not to accord formal training a high ranking in the list of contributory factors in their own development. And yet, our work would also suggest that very few managers actually practise anything which could qualify for the title of 'self-development' either – unless, that is, one wanted to count the rather hit and miss 'reflection-on-what-has-happened' which Mumford et al. (1989) locate at the 'intuitive' end of their continuum of self-learning practices.

## Problems and issues

Two caveats have to be introduced at the outset of this section. First, as in the case of Chapter 5, our concern here is not with debates taking place about the techniques or processes involved in training and development – the reader who wants further details of these will find them in abundance in the prescriptive texts. Second, our assumption is that those running or going to run organizations at least recognize that training and development has a role to play. If they are irredeemably wedded to the 'low skills equilibrium' discussed in Chapter 2 – i.e. their business strategies are essentially founded on low quality and low cost – little of what follows will be relevant.

## The poaching problem

One does not have to talk to senior decision-makers for very long before the more basic issues (as opposed to the details of different training techniques) begin to emerge. The most common observation is that many of their colleagues argue that it is not worth putting serious resources into training and development because competitors will poach the upgraded staff. It is a variant of the 'prisoner's dilemma' – 'I will train but only if you do' – and reflects the lack of an adequate national training system which ensures a level playing field between companies.

There are only two things that can be said about this. First, it reflects a marked lack of confidence in the total employment package and experience that the organization has on offer; in which case many of the issues covered in this book – and not simply training and development – would seem to be in need of urgent attention. Second, the logical consequence of this pervasive viewpoint is that training will only occur in a highly constrained and pared-down fashion; the ultimate logical absurdity is to under-train so that no competitor will want to try to poach. If the organization is not already stuck in the 'low skills equilibrium', it will certainly very soon be so.

## Resources

A further fundamental impediment often also articulated by managers is that they cannot afford to commit significant resources to training because of the constant pressure from corporate and/or divisional level to show healthy financial results. Pay-back periods on training under these circumstances where performance is measured half-yearly and even quarterly are simply inimical to significant expenditures on headings which do not show an early return. This problem of short-termism as dictated by management accounting logic creeps into other attitudes too as will be seen below.

The interesting point is that it is not so obvious that British companies are as out of line with their international competitors in terms of training expenditure as once was thought. Companies in Germany, France and USA, it is said, spend a much higher proportion of their total employment costs on training than the British. Less than 2 per cent is a fairly typical finding in Britain (Hyman, 1992: 115); 3 to 5 per cent is not uncommon in Europe. But these sorts of estimates are challenged by the Cranfield/Price Waterhouse survey (Holden and Livian, 1992). This suggests that only in Sweden and France do more than one quarter of organizations spend above 4 per cent of the wages and salaries bill on training. The UK was shown to be broadly in line with the other 7 European countries surveyed. It is also relevant to note that in France legislation requires organizations to spend at least 1.2 per cent of the annual salaries and wages bill on training. Failure to do so results in a special tax.

The other traditional measure is to compare the average number of training days. Here again the same survey reveals that UK managers and other employees are broadly exposed to a similar degree of training as their counterparts in other European countries. But the UK did score rather worse in terms of the proportion of organizations providing their managers with fewer than 5 days training per year. Sixty-nine per cent of UK companies fell into this category – a higher proportion than any of the other countries (Germany reported 59 per cent as did France, Spain 32 per cent and Norway 46 per cent). It has to be remembered, however, that in Germany a great deal of training occurs outside the firm through state provision. In contrast, British training can be seen as fragmented.

In terms of actual amounts spent, the figures are revealed as very modest. The Training Agency (1989: 21) estimated a figure of £809 per employee but Hyman (1992: 116) found that companies' own figures on actual expenditures were much lower. Mean expenditure for small, medium and large companies were only £73, £87 and £111 per annum per employee respectively. These averages, however, masked considerable variation. For example, among the medium-sized companies the lowest spender only allocated £10 per employee per year to training whereas the highest spender had allocated £1,800. These variations were often related to sector differences – the catering hotel sector often spending low amounts and the high-tech consultancy companies spending the higher sums.

Two general considerations can be drawn from these sorts of figures. First, in whatever way the variation in the figures between the Training Agency and Hyman might be explained, the important fact appears to be that, overall, British companies are working from a fairly low training base. Hence, optimistic surveys which report managers as saying training is getting 'more' attention need to be put into this sort of perspective. The second consideration concerns the degree of significance which we ought to give to such data. It might be argued that training expenditure is not in fact a good indicator of training activity. Japanese companies which are known to provide exemplary training to their employees often record very low levels of overt expenditure on the training function. The reason for this is that so much of their training is fully integrated into everyday practice. Learning occurs on the job. In consequence, only relatively small sums appear under the heading of formal training budgets.

A final thought under this heading. If resources are a problem, there appears to be only one way of tackling it in the UK context. Where a particular range of training and development activities has been deemed to be essential to the strategy of the business, there must be a board-level decision to 'red-circle' the training budget to protect it from cuts – whatever the circumstances. If the board is not prepared to do this, or, our would-be change agent does not feel that the climate is right even to put this forward as a suggestion, then he or she may have to conclude that they are working for the wrong kind of company.

## A manager's priority?

Important though the question of resources is, it is not, in our view, the most important problem that has to be faced. All the indicators we have, tend to suggest that training in Britain is normally treated in the firm as a peripheral and low-level nonstrategic activity. It is in these respects that the 'short-termism' discussed in Chapters 2 and 3 wreaks its real damage. Managers and supervisors have not as yet as a matter of routine been inculcated with the Japanese practice of regarding staff development as one of their priority agenda items.

It is found, for example, in the hierarchy of measures (and consequently of objectives) which are deemed to be important. Rarely is it the case in British companies that the extent to which a manager develops his or her own immediate staff is regarded as the critical measure of how well that manager is doing the job. Yet in our research comparing British and Japanese managers (Storey et al., 1991) we found that the Japanese tended to place subordinate development as one of the highest priorities when defining the nature of the managerial role. In contrast, British managers would much more readily point to the need to be seen as shouldering 'responsibility' and to be meeting financial and production targets as the essence of their job.

An outcome of this basic difference in the understanding of what it means to be a manager is to be found also in performance appraisal criteria and evaluation systems in Britain. At best there is token and subsidiary reference to staff development in the evaluative systems used; often this facet of managerial work is simply omitted altogether. Under such circumstances it is of little wonder that training and development are in practice given low priority and regarded as peripheral.

From time to time a new training initiative may be launched and staff development becomes a relatively high profile activity. But, given the next downturn in the business cycle the traditional priorities reassert themselves and training once again becomes a mere nice-to-have but 'cannot be afforded, luxury'. Supervisors and staff themselves rarely act as a constituency to complain about this. On the contrary, they are far more likely to be complicit in the process. Reading the signs about 'what counts', ordinary members of staff routinely declare themselves 'too busy' to be trained. Their supervisors and departmental line managers resist attempts to take any of their staff away from normal duties. Here one witnesses the real, measured, priorities asserting themselves at all levels throughout the organization.

Ironically, when begrudgingly, training does take place, because it has been pared and timed to cause minimal disruption the resulting experience is often unsatisfactory. Trainees at first line management level, for example, will rightly observe that the training has come too late, or that it is insufficiently targeted at their specific needs. These problems are not purely technical failings of the kind the prescriptive texts warn about. On the contrary, they are logical outcomes of the endemic training problems in Britain of the kind outlined in this section. The poor training record (Coopers and Lybrand, 1985) is an integral feature of the actual human resource and industrial relations management context described in this book. Most of the voluminous prescriptive training literature is abjectly neglectful of this reality. It is little wonder therefore that its impact has been so marginal.

Fortunately most clouds seem to have some silver lining. One factor is the delayering of management levels discussed in Chapter 4. The 'action' manager who has been the dominant role model in British management is beginning to disappear – organizations simply cannot afford to employ managers to do or to control what other people are supposed to be doing. A second is the training and development which managers are receiving themselves. This increasingly emphasizes the limitations of the traditional role and the need for managers to become 'enablers', 'facilitators' and 'developers' rather than 'doers'. The missing link in many organizations is the structure of rewards to make this kind of thinking stick.

The importance of the coherent inter-locking of this range of techniques can perhaps best be illustrated by drawing upon the comparative Britain–Japan study referred to above (Storey et al., 1991). This revealed the significance of bringing into alignment the systems for monitoring and evaluating managers, the setting of goals and targets for managers, the way they are developed and the way they are rewarded. The study was conducted in four British companies in Britain matched with four Japanese companies operating in Japan. The objective of the study was to uncover how managers were 'made' in practice and in particular to trace the relative influence of national cultural differences and sectoral differences. The results of the study are relevant on a number of levels: they allow comparisons between Japanese and British management practices and they permit comparisons between and within particular companies. The major differences between British and Japanese managers are educational attainment, frequency of job change and the age at which they become managers. Not one of the Japanese managers had entered the workforce before age 18, whereas 45 per cent of the British sample had. Almost all of the Japanese managers (94 per cent) had undergraduate or postgraduate qualifications compared with 42 per cent of their British counterparts.

But the main message, apart from this higher level of education at start-up, was the consistent, careful and systematic way in which the Japanese went about making their managers. Many British managers may have experienced a greater volume of job change but it was relatively more random than was occurring in Japan. The British were more likely to encounter a deep-seated preconception that people either 'have what it takes' or they do not. In consequence, a certain sink-or-swim philosophy was allowed to prevail. A corollary was the emphasis placed on being exposed to responsible positions at an early age for a select few. The assumed power of this practice finds support in current conventional wisdom in Western management development literature (for example, Margerison and Kakabadse, 1985). What it neglects, however, is the often happenchance nature of the process. Those given such early challenges often just happened, as our respondents admitted, to be 'in the right place at the right time'. The corollary of this lack of planning is that large numbers of an equally talented cohort became disillusioned and key talents are lost to the company as those left out leave to look for opportunities elsewhere.

In contrast, the Japanese were far more likely to give weight to the importance of continuous development for the whole cohort of entrants over a prolonged period of years. Continuous adjustments might be made but the system remained essentially intact and known to all. The notable feature in Britain, by contrast, was the propensity to vacillate. New programmes and initiatives were launched and old ones swept away almost in their entirety. There were two damaging consequences: managers at all levels saw little point in committing themselves too heavily to a prevailing system because it was thought likely to be temporary; second, there was little inclination to invest time in learning about the current pattern of provision and so British managers (especially those out in the divisions away from corporate headquarters) were often remarkably unclear about what training packages and related development devices were available. Sometimes the centrally provided core courses were of the highest world standards but their promulgation often left a lot to be desired.

### Trade union involvement?

Like planning and resourcing discussed in Chapter 5, the question of trade union involvement in training is rarely discussed these days and for similar reasons. In this case the example set by the government has not exactly helped. With the abolition of the Manpower Services Commission, on which they had equal representation with employers, trade unions have effectively been excluded from representation on the new Training and Enterprise Councils. These, decidedly, are employer-led bodies.

Clearly trade unions (and their professional association equivalents) do have a significant interest in training and development. While it is true that unions have not always had a positive image in the area (training has rarely been a serious issue among trade union concerns when the real bargaining begins and, in the case of the 'professions' their main aim has often appeared to be to maintain exclusivity) there are currently some signs that stances may be changing. An increasing number of trade union leaders are beginning to locate training and development high up on their 'new agenda' (see for instance GMB/UCW, 1991 and TGWU/GMB, 1992).

In the circumstances, it is interesting to note that a key feature of Ford's EDAP scheme discussed above is its 'jointism'. Most recent initiatives, including 'open learning' have been largely management-inspired or, if not management-inspired, under management control. One of the significant features of EDAP is that it is a joint programme. The national committee is a joint body with co-management and trade union chairmen, as are the local committees.

It is important to appreciate the motives of the Ford management. As the Manager of Education and Training at Ford and one of the original EDAP coordinators has pointed out, underlying the desire to improve education and personal development, there was an implicit agreement between unions and management to the following programme goals: to make 'improvements in the industrial relations climate' by arranging for management and unions to work together on a range of 'non-adversarial' issues, and to change the 'climate' of the company at national and local level by delegating significant budget decisions to joint groups of representatives (Mortimer, 1990: 309).

Initiatives like this are rare in the UK, although more common in the USA (see, for example, Kochan et al., 1986). The great majority of British managers would no doubt prefer to wait and see if EDAP delivers on these objectives before taking any action themselves. This is a great pity and in large measure misses the point. It is the willingness to experiment in areas such as this which is important and which is so sadly lacking.

## Conclusion

In the light of the discussion in this chapter, it is apparent that there is now rather less cause for outright pessimism in relation to training and development than might have been the case just a few years ago. There are a number of significant initiatives being attempted. These, in turn, suggest that progress is possible even in the absence of the kind of infrastucture at national level which a number of competitor countries have put in place. Crucially, they suggest that it is possible for individual organizations to take initiatives. They do, in other words, have some measure of 'strategic choice'.

Although our sense is that more and more organizations are having to follow suit as rapid changes in technology and organization structures bite ever deeper, it remains the case that these are the exceptions to test the rule. Training and development are all too often given very low priority or lip-service only is paid to them. In relation to the point we made earlier, that the average organization already has seven out of the ten employees that it will have in the year 2000, this tendency is, quite frankly, alarming. How such organizations are going to rise to the challenges and changes that they repeatedly tell us face them is a mystery.

The key issue, we have argued, is not so much resources. These are obviously important, but there is some evidence to suggest that the gap in expenditure on formal training between British companies and their competitors is not so great as was thought. Formal training, however, is not really the issue. How people learn at work generally should be the issue of paramount concern. It is here that the role of individual managers is especially important. Typically, British managers do not see their role as being crucial in the training and development of the employees with whom they work. Nor is this simply a question of the inadequacies of their own training and development. The prime signal managers receive from the top (for example, in the form of appraisal criteria, reward systems and promotion patterns) is that what really counts is delivering short-term results in physical and (especially) financial terms. The message is implicit in the analysis: if senior managers seriously believe that training and development are necessary to delivering on the organization's strategic goals, they have to change the signals they are sending to their colleagues. Pious statements about the importance of the 'learning organization', are not going to be nearly enough; they have to bring their appraisal and reward systems into line with what they say they want to achieve. This constitutes yet another argument for having an integrated approach to managing HR/IR.

# 8

# VISION, MISSION AND CULTURE MANAGEMENT: CUSTOMER ORIENTATION AND QUALITY IN THE NEW MANAGEMENT OF LABOUR

The broad shift which we have described, from a reliance on proceduralism and collectivism to a preference for individualism and 'commitment', is itself indicative of a major culture change. This has not entirely been brought about in a planned way by organizational managers. Many of the conditioning features which allowed this to happen and to an extent impelled it to occur, resulted from major changes in the political, legal and economic environment. For example, fundamental re-structuring of industrial sectors with a dramatic decline in the heavy industries which were highly unionized (such as coal-mining, engineering, railways and docks) and a growth in lighter service industries which were not (such as hotels, retailing, and personal services) has entailed an overall de-collectivization of employee relations. But running in parallel with such changes has been an unusual, not to say extraordinary, upsurge in the number of managers seeking, quite consciously and deliberately, to shape, control and manage their organizations' culture, values and norms.

Throughout most of this century (i.e. in effect during most of the period of 'management') the idea of 'managing culture' was relatively unheard of. Managing was perceived to be about the administrative functions of planning, organizing and controlling. Following the accommodation with collective labour post Second World War, it was accepted that it was also about negotiation and compromise. In the 1980s all this was to undergo considerable change.

The previously peripheral OD-style notions of 'visioning' and 'culture change' came decidedly centre-stage. It has now become commonplace for senior managers in just about all sectors to talk routinely about their role in driving or desiring culture change and likewise to be engaged in constructing organizational 'mission statements'. The attempted reconstruction of 'mental sets' and the associated reshaping of behavioural patterns are built around the interlocking concepts of 'vision', 'mission', 'values', 'customer-orientation' and 'quality'. The management of these has become an issue high on many an executive's agenda. Expectations about what they can deliver often run extremely high. Reactions in other parts of the organization (at managerial as well as non-managerial levels) are increasingly likely to be deeply cynical.

Against this backcloth, the purpose of this chapter is to examine initiatives in the realm of culture change management and to evaluate their implications for HR and IR. The first section of the chapter discusses the meanings of the main terms and reviews the available evidence concerning their usage; the second section explores the practical ways in which organizations are attempting to 'manage culture'; the third section focuses on total quality management (TQM) as an example of a culture change initiative which deserves special attention because of its sheer pervasity. Finally, the HR and IR implications of all of these types of intervention are discussed.

## Vision and mission

Many of the terms highlighted so far in this chapter are often used, in practice, in overlapping ways. It will serve little purpose here for us to trace back the original sources and meanings or to seek to draw precise distinctions. Such exercises can so easily miss the point. Suffice it to say that certain broad differences are worth bearing in mind. The concept of 'vision' can be understood as the overarching view of where the organization could, and perhaps should, be heading towards. 'Mission' can be thought of as a rather more firmly agreed set of ideas (possibly in the form of a formal statement) concerning what the organization is trying to do in a relatively enduring way. This may be expected to cover the scope of the organization's operations and its distinctive focus.

In his book on *HR Vision*, Stephen Connock (1991) the then General Manager (Human Resources) for Pearl Assurance, isolated Human Resource vision as the vital precursor to the design of appropriate human resource strategies. Vision, for Cannock, provides a cohesive philosophy, a common thread running from business mission to HR activities. It provides a sense of direction and a source of inspiration; it expresses the organization's core values; and it provides a yardstick against which to measure behaviour and performance. HR vision, suggests Connock, can be developed 'from a thorough understanding of both the planning process and the way a business is evolving to achieve its objectives' (1991: 3). At the same time, the concept of HR vision is wrapped-up, in his analysis, with the related ideas of 'excellence' and 'quality'. Hence while there is an acknowledgement of the contingency of diverse business settings, there is also a hint of a new orthodoxy or paradigm of the kind extolled by Tom Peters.

As we noted earlier, there is, however, considerable scepticism and indeed cynicism about such ideas. Managerial employees who have once submitted to such notions and then found themselves redundant are particularly prone to take a cynical stance on these sorts of claims. But despite this there is some evidence of a growing recognition and acceptance of the importance of 'vision' to business survival and development – especially so in America (Collins and Porras, 1991). The idea has spread beyond the traditional territory occupied by IBM and Boeing. It may spread still further as it is recognized that the vital factor is not necessarily charismatic leadership but a catalytic leadership which encourages creative, forward-looking behaviours and thought patterns. The key to it all would appear to be a clear sense of the fundamental, overarching, objectives. Or, as Reyes and Kleiner (1990) put it, the baseline is the idea of 'organizational purpose'. This they see as a *force* which propels and guides the disparate organizational efforts towards a defined goal (see also *The Economist*, 9 November 1991).

The process of deriving or developing a 'vision' arises from continual questioning of, and active listening to, all the major stakeholders – customers, employees, suppliers, and so on. Indeed, the vision can only be kept vital and alive by continual questioning of this kind.

If vision is associated with 'purpose' or 'goals', mission is associated with a way of behaving (cf. Campbell and Yeung, 1991a). Accordingly, mission planning involves an analysis of employee behaviour. It focuses on identifying behaviour standards that are central to achieving implementation of strategy, and it encourages discussion among managers and other employees of the 'organization's commitment' to its stakeholders and higher level purposes. All this of course massively begs crucial questions about *whose* commitment and how this is to be achieved.

Campbell and Yeung (1991b) argue that there are two main approaches to company mission statements – one focuses on business strategy while the other attends to aspects of ethics and philosophy. These two aspects can, however, be reconciled they suggest. This is achieved when the 'four elements' of mission (purpose, strategy, behaviour standards and values) reinforce each other. Crucially, however, this depends upon matching the values of the organization with those of individuals. Management's initial steps are to clarify the need for a mission and to encourage the thinking in order to achieve a statement of that mission. This 'should' be one that can enthuse employees. Creating a sense of mission also makes for better decision making, clearer communication and easier delegation, claims

Campbell (1989). Mission statements are also often used in an attempt to forge a link between different divisions or business units. In these instances their construction represents an attempt to provide some 'corporate glue' (see for example, Johnson, 1992).

A critical test of the use of mission statements would be the extent to which they are relevant to performance evaluation exercises in the companies which have them. An international comparative study of 15 multinationals (five German, five UK and five US) set out to explore this linkage (Coats et al., 1991). The cases revealed a fairly consistent use of missions/strategies in performance measures – though with some notable differences in emphasis. In particular, the German companies did not place the same stress on 'financial stability' as an objective as did the British and American companies.

There are a number of problems associated with mission statements which managers should note. Many statements are shaped around the idea of 'serving customers'. But, having a mission statement of this kind will not be enough if there are too few means to accomplish it (Brandt, 1989). Moreover, a 'market orientation' forced on a rigid organization, and an uncommitted or fearful workforce is unlikely to lead very far. Another problem revealed in our work is that 'enterprise' missions do not usually penetrate very deeply into organizations. Indeed, a significant proportion of executives themselves do not feel accountable for the missions which have been promulgated by their enterprises. All this points up the fact that the production of mission statements can all too easily be cynically viewed (even by those involved in devising them) as merely a formal exercise.

What evidence is there of the actual take-up and use of mission statements? There have been only a few attempts to research what is happening. In the United Kingdom there is some limited survey evidence and this tends to point towards an increasing use of mission statements (Klemm et al., 1991). In the USA, a survey and content analysis was made of mission statements across all *Business Week* top 1000 firms – i.e. large companies in both manufacturing and services (David, 1989). Of the 181 responses, 59 per cent stated that their firms had not developed a formal statement. From those which did supply a statement it was found that the typical component elements were: an orientation towards customers, products or services; concern for survival; or concern for public image. 83 per cent of manufacturing firms and 76 per cent of service companies included the 'concern for customers' element. Another mailed instrument study, this time of *Fortune 500* firms, tried to ascertain whether the mission statements of higher performing enterprises differed in any way from those of lower performers (Pearce and David, 1987). The analysis of statements supplied revealed that higher performers were more likely to have written statements for public distribution. The content of these was geared towards issues of corporate philosophy, self concept, and competitive strengths.

A well-constructed mission statement is expected to serve multiple management functions. Synthesizing the literature, a lengthy list could be constructed; a few examples will suffice here. They are expected to:

1  provide a sense of direction
2  augment job satisfaction
3  enthuse
4  indicate what is expected and why
5  encourage adaptability
6  encourage innovation
7  engender a team spirit
8  foster customer orientation

and to promote

1  higher profits
2  employee commitment
3  better decision making
4  clearer communication
5  easier delegation
6  consistency
7  common vision.

(Simpson and McConocha, 1991; Reyes and Kleiner, 1990; Campbell, 1989; Morrisey, 1988.)

Mission, vision and culture management have certain elements in common. The basic argument is that under the new competitive conditions senior management have to adopt new strategies and structures which 'empower' those individuals working closest to the product and the customer. From an IR/HR point of view what this means is the need for different forms of control. A good example of this is revealed in the renowned case of Levi Strauss & Co in the US. Its chief executive, Robert Haas, has emphasised the role of 'values' – these, he says, provide a 'common language for aligning a company's leadership and its people'. In a dynamic and empowered environment he suggests that management have to rely on controls which are 'conceptual'. It is management's job to 'set the parameters' which are expressed through these conceptual structures (Howard, 1990).

There has been growing recognition of the fact that customers actually learn about companies not from their formal statements but as a result of dealing with first line employees. Such encounters often fail, however, to reflect the sentiments found in the high-sounding mission statements. Drennan (1988) puts forward a set of actions to help ensure that the mission and strategy reach down to all levels in the organization. These include the recommendation that statements should be clear and simple (he cites Mariott Hotels' offer to deliver breakfast on time with a money back guarantee); a demonstrated commitment to the statement (he cites the SAS airline's approval of a $1.8 million programme to make itself the 'most punctual in Europe'); and consistency in objectives. Reflective of OD-style methods, Drennan also recommends taking 'dramatic action' to get employees' attention and the sending out of strong 'new era' signals, as well as the now very familiar idea of 'celebrating success'.

The construction of mission statements may be construed as an employment management device. Obviously there is also a degree to which they are used for external image building but a crucial aspect appears to be the way in which mission statements are used as a tool by managers to assert their objectives within the organization. The mission-drafting process is itself a way in which people are brought together to subscribe to 'agreed objectives'. The ensuing hierarchy of statements can subsequently be used to legitimize some behaviours and to render other behaviours illegitimate. We have numerous case examples of instances where the mission statement is used by management as the base-line from which to commence all wrangles with the trade unions. Notably, the declared primacy of 'customers' is usually interpreted to mean that managerial plans and proposals for labour flexibility are *ipso facto* legitimated. As we argue in the final section of the chapter, this apparent short-cut to negotiative success rarely succeeds and seems unlikely to do so.

In recognition of this fact, many managers have sought to go one (big) step further: their objective has been to 'engineer' a wide-ranging culture change. We will now examine what this means in practice.

## Managing corporate culture

Ever since the publication of Peters and Waterman's (1982) *In Search of Excellence*, the idea that 'corporate culture' can be a vital source of competitive advantage has increasingly enjoyed currency among British managers. The idea of 'organizational culture' had been around much longer but *In Search of Excellence* undoubtedly helped to popularize the notion. Nowadays, practically all senior managers can be heard talking quite freely about the need to 'manage a culture change'. But what *is* corporate culture and can it be 'managed'?

Culture has generated a great deal of excitement because it is perceived to offer a key to unlocking consensus, flexibility and commitment. These are three highly valued objectives. *Consensus* is assumed to express and rest upon a set of common values and beliefs. It is not hard to see why this is highly sought after. If agreement and concurrence of all employees with managerial goals (and perhaps methods) can be secured through investment in a 'culture programme' this would not only dispense with the tiresome process of securing (temporary) agreement with trade union representatives, it seems also to hold out the promise of a more deeply embedded and enduring compliance.

*Flexibility* is the second prize. If the 'culture' could be changed so as to eliminate restrictive practices and to improve upon work performance which merely aspires to rule-conformity, if bureaucratic buck-passing and job demarcation could be exchanged for spontaneous activity in pursuit of the (shared) end objective, then the problem of labour management would seemingly be practically solved at one fell swoop. (We say 'practically' because the issue of capability and training is a separate requirement.) *Commitment*, the third prize, would take labour performance to an even higher plane. Beyond a willingness to work flexibly as a matter of routine there would be a promise of endeavour which was powered by a motivation to succeed.

These three prizes are self-evidently highly desirable from an employer's perspective. But from the culture-change gurus and consultants comes the even better news: these ends can seemingly be attained at relatively little cost. Can all this be regarded as simply too good to be true? In order to evaluate the claims it is necessary to go back to basics and review the meaning of corporate culture and the precise methods by which it might be managed.

## *What is corporate culture?*

The simplest and arguably the best way to define culture is that it expresses 'the way things are routinely done around here'. A rather more elaborated definition is put forward by Edgar Schein (1984) who is one of the acknowledged experts in this field. He writes: 'Organization culture is the pattern of basic assumptions that a given group has invented, discovered or developed in learning to cope with its problems of external adaptation and internal integration.'

The key phrases here are the 'pattern of basic assumptions' and 'to cope with problems of external adaptation and internal integration'. Each of these raises vital issues related to our underlying theme of individualism and collectivism. *Whose* 'ways of doing' are being referred to? This question raises the issue of whether the organization is being conceived of as a unitary phenomenon (i.e. with essentially *one* set of legitimate goals and interests) or as a pluralistic phenomenon (i.e. with *multiple* and possibly competing goals and interests held by diverse parties). To point out these issues is also implicitly to draw attention to the distinction between the terms 'corporate culture' and 'organizational culture' – albeit these terms are typically used as if they were interchangeable. The former is suggestive of a top-down expression of 'the way to do things'. It may be seen as the 'official' version: the formal position.

By contrast, 'organizational culture' is suggestive of the way things are *actually* done. It is the informal and not necessarily approved reality of behaviour, beliefs and assumptions. The key point is that the culture of an organization (its values, norms and the artifacts that are created) is not to be viewed as something which is easily open to manipulation by management. 'Managing culture change' is perhaps best regarded as an *aspiration* rather than a straightforward rational project.

Contained within 'organizational culture' is likely to be a series of sub-cultures. These may be recognized among relatively distinct groups such as salespersons, IT specialists, warehouse staff, and executive board members. The source of these cultures may be traced to learned 'coping mechanisms' for dealing with typically encountered dilemmas. 'Culture' thus provides a ready-made formula for facing up to divergent expectations and multiple pressures (Hampden-Turner, 1990).

'Strong cultures' are extolled in the work of Peters and Waterman as associated with the excellent companies. Administrative systems and marketing strategies and other 'hard' business variables were found to have little consistency across their sample. In looking for a common thread they say they were driven to the 'softer' attributes most notable of which was the pervasiveness of a 'strong' culture – as found in Hewlett Packard, IBM and Proctor & Gamble:

> Without exception, the dominance and coherence of culture proved to be an essential quality of the excellent companies. Moreover, the *stronger* the culture and the more it was directed toward the marketplace, the less need was there for policy manuals, organization charts or detailed procedures and rules. (Peters and Waterman, 1982: 75, emphasis added)

Revealingly, Peters and Waterman also observe that poorer-performing companies can also have strong cultures but these are labelled as 'dysfunctional' cultures. Examples of such inappropriate strong cultures are those focused on internal politics or on numbers and procedures rather than the product and the people who make and sell the product. The epitome of success in culture terms and in business terms comes with no less than 'love of product' (p. 76).

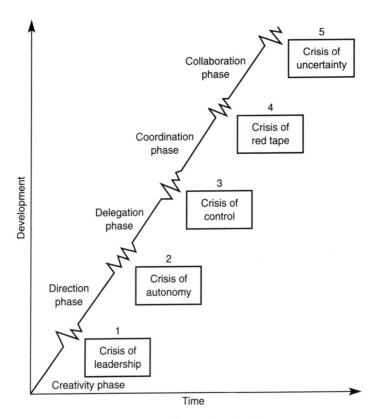

**Figure 8.1** Five points of crisis

## *How might culture be managed?*

There is in fact an array of techniques (or, as management consultants in the OD tradition prefer to call them, 'interventions') which can be brought to bear. In our experience with an extensive range of British employing organizations, senior managers who have bought-into culture change programmes have been fairly eclectic about which method they have been prepared to use. Some managers have been persuaded to adopt a particular package as put together by an influential consultant, but others have remained alert to new methods and 'collect' and experiment with any technique which comes their way which they think might be useful.

In the following pages we review some of the main methods currently in use in a range of British companies. The first set of techniques offers a set of tools or devices which help in raising awareness: they are in reality diagnostic instruments. These come in two sub-categories. The first sub-set helps in diagnosing the organizational situation while the second sub-set assists in individual self-awareness. An example of an organizational-level analytical tool is the model of typical 'stages' in business organization development. Figure 8.1 shows the four-phase/five crisis-point model.

The logic of this model might be illustrated with the medical analogy of different types of medicine and treatment for different stages of the human life cycle. It makes a difference to diagnosis and treatment, for example, to understand whether one is dealing with paediatrics or geriatrics.

At the level of *individual awareness* there are various techniques and models which are available. Numerous psychometric instruments are designed to illuminate an individual's readiness or resistance to change; to highlight preferred managerial style; and to uncover and bring into the open for discussion and analysis many other attributes which can be useful in preparing the ground for instigating a change in behaviour, attitudes and assumptions.

Another tool is the 'transition curve' as shown in Figure 8.2. This is based on the work of Adams, Hayes and Hopson (1976). This maps the expected phases of reaction to a change which has been instigated in the work organization. The $y$ axis records levels of performance and the $x$ axis denotes time. The model suggests that the change agent should be prepared for an initial *fall* in performance level as the shock of the change is felt. This is followed by a rise in performance as recipients of change rationalize the situation and persuade themselves that the change is not so drastic as they feared or will not have the consequences for themselves which they feared. However, this stage of 'defensive retreat' is a false dawn and a further decline in performance can be expected. This hits bottom at the 'acknowledge merit' stage when finally recipients make a realistic

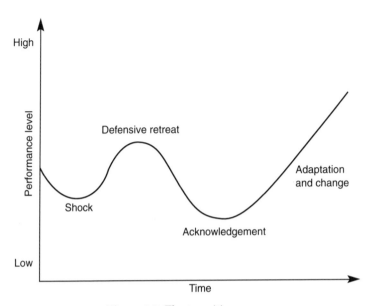

**Figure 8.2** The transition curve

assessment of the extent of the change. From here they can begin to climb up the curve through adaptation to the new circumstance and on to a higher level of performance. The model cannot be expected necessarily to be applicable to every change situation but its claimed utility is that by capturing common tendencies one can anticipate and plan appropriate management of change through its various phases rather than expecting a one-shot 'fix'.

Other tools of change are the numerous diagnostic instruments designed to collect relevant information about the current culture and to monitor progress following various interventions. 'Culture audits' are at the heart of these endeavours. As a result of collecting data from individuals the consultant is likely to provide a summary profile of the organization. Our own research in many large organizations which have been through this exercise revealed a remarkable common pattern in consultants' diagnoses. Typically, British organizations were depicted as in column one of Figure 8.3 and this state of affairs was contrasted with the 'recommended' culture as in column two.

| Current culture | Recommended culture |
|---|---|
| Rule-based | Flexible |
| Engineering-orientated | Market-led |
| Customer-avoidance | Customer-service |
| Procedure-focused | Results-focused |
| Centralized | Decentralized |
| Top-down | Bottom-up |

**Figure 8.3** Typical culture contrasts

A more detailed diagnostic plan would point to the appropriate focus for attention. This might, for example, be managerial style, or motivation in particular departments, or communication patterns. The plan would also identify suitable methods to tease-out the relevant data and would propose methods for re-shaping the revealed attitudes and behaviours.

A useful tool is available to analyse the phenomenon of 'culture lag'. Figure 8.4 shows how at time 'A' when an organization faces a set of environmental forces, various aspects of the organization – its strategy, structure, skills (but most of all its culture) are likely to be found 'lagging' behind the needs of that moment. The figure also indicates the potential advantages which could be accrued if, on the other hand, a cultural 'edge' could be gained. This would offer a source of innovation and competitive advantage: the organization would anticipate environmental change and would thus be ahead of the game.

Two other diagnostic tools are worthy of note: 'commitment mapping' and 'culture mapping'. The first of these lists the key players – i.e. those individuals whose behaviour is likely to be influential in determining the fate of the culture change attempt. Against each of these significant names is recorded an entry to show whether each individual is lacking in commitment to the change, is willing to acquiesce and let it happen, is more supportive and hence willing to help it happen or is fired-up and eager to make it happen. Figure 8.5 shows these various positions. On the figure, X indicates the level of commitment which a person is judged to have currently whereas O indicates the desired level. Typically, one would be seeking to notch-up

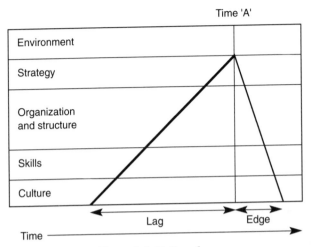

**Figure 8.4** Culture lag

commitment by moving individuals towards the right-side of this figure. However, this would not necessarily be so in every case. There could be instances where, perhaps for micro-political reasons, it is actually unhelpful to the cause to have a particular person openly championing the change. In such a case the diagnosis might lead one to seek to re-position such a person so he or she merely becomes willing to let it happen rather than be seen as promoting the change (see person number 7 on the example shown in Figure 8.5).

Another technique is 'culture mapping'. This juxtaposes the cultural values one is *seeking* to establish with the personnel and IR practices which actually *prevail*. For example, in Figure 8.6 the cultural values which are being sought are listed on the horizontal axis: innovation, openness, business awareness, teamwork, cost containment and flexibility. Key HR practices are listed along the vertical axis: recruitment and selection methods, the rewards system, appraisal criteria, training practices and so on. The culture map allows one systematically to evaluate the extent to which prevailing HR/IR practices actually support or militate against the proselytized culture.

The significance of the culture mapping device is that it draws attention to HR/IR and other organizational practices. Managing

| Key players | No commitment | Let it happen | Help it happen | Make it happen |
|---|---|---|---|---|
| 1. | | X——————— | | ➤O |
| 2. | | | XO | |
| 3. | X———➤O | | | |
| 4. | X———➤O | | | |
| 5. | | | | XO |
| 6. | X ———————➤O | | | |
| 7. | | O◄——————— | | X |
| 8. | | | | |
| 9. | | | | |

**Figure 8.5** Commitment mapping

a culture change is no longer merely seen as a question of attitudes and motivation. It is realized that the powerful messages about organizational priorities and realities derive from everyday concrete experience of appraisal, reward and promotion rather more than from senior management rhetoric.

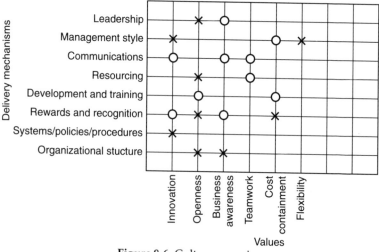

**Figure 8.6** Culture mapping

192

## Total quality management

The message from the total quality management (TQM) gurus can be readily seen as a sub-theme of the corporate culture movement. Deming (1986), Crosby (1979), Juran (1988) and Ishikawa (1985) all emphasize the vital importance of engineering a change in organizational culture which involves all levels and functions. As Hill (1991: 554) observes, 'quality' is much the same as 'excellence' in the current management jargon.

In broad terms the essential features of TQM can be summarized as follows. First, top management are the sponsors because quality is recognized as a strategic (i.e. competitive) issue. Top management is meant to lead by example; is responsible for setting up the machinery and procedures for ensuring quality; and oversees the whole quality process through an interlocking network of quality committees and coordinators which culminates in a top level steering committee or 'council' which may in fact be the executive management committee. Second, there are systematic techniques for problem solving and problem identification. All employees should be trained to use them. They include statistical process control, cause and effect analysis and decision-making methods. Third, quality operation is seen to require a break with traditional organizational structures and 'correct' procedures. Thus, interaction across departmental and functional boundaries is very much encouraged. In part, this is achieved through the concept of the 'internal customer' but in addition there is recognition of the value of individual employees making their operational needs known to colleagues in other departments and possibly in reaching joint solutions to problems. As for vertical hierarchy, the merit of cutting across these levels with the use of project teams and project management is recognized.

Fourth, the crucial role of management as people with the authority to make change and therefore to accept responsibility for quality is highlighted. Juran (1988) and others emphasize that responsibility can only be assigned to those who can actually make decisions. This implies a move to devolved authority and to greater participation. Deming in particular stresses the importance of involving people in decision-making and of 'empowering' in order to encourage and allow continuous improvement.

193

Every person should be involved: TQM applies *totally* throughout the firm. This in turn suggests the need for Western managers to change their styles of management fundamentally. Indeed, Deming (1986: 18) sets out the 'principles' for the transformation of Western management. The emphasis is upon *teamwork* and leadership of teams. The outlines of the transformation are captured in Deming's famous 14 points which he first enumerated in Japan in 1950. These are:

1 Create constancy of purpose towards improvement.
2 Adopt the new philosophy – take on leadership for change.
3 Cease dependence upon inspection, eliminate the need for inspection.
4 End the practice of awarding business on the basis of apparent price tag. Instead minimize total cost.
5 Constant improvement of the system of production and so decrease costs.
6 Institute training on the job.
7 Institute leadership (the job of management is not supervision but leadership).
8 Drive out fear so that everyone may work effectively.
9 Break down barriers between departments.
10 Eliminate slogans and exhortations.
11 Eliminate quotes and management by numbers.
12 Allow pride in workmanship.
13 Institute a vigorous programme of education and self improvement.
14 Put everyone to work in the company to accomplish transformation.

John Oakland (1989) has synthesized the ideas of all the main exponents including Deming, Juran and Crosby. He translates their ideas into key concepts such as the 'quality chain' in which each person in the organization is a supplier and customer to someone else in the same organization. If all these people consciously sought out their next customers and their precise requirements there would be scope for more accuracy in meeting these and for eliminating the waste which comes from inspection, rectification and rework. To aid this process a further range of tools which measure and record data on performance is available. These in-process techniques can, it is claimed, be applied to all operations including support services such as accounting, personnel and IT. The aim, additionally, is to pursue continual improvement and to get quality right first time every time.

So much for the principles. What information is available about their application in practice? Two recent pieces of empirical research give the flavour of the key considerations in the British context (Wilkinson et al., 1991; and Hill, 1991). The main finding from Hill's study of four companies was the seriousness and care with which TQM was introduced when compared with the launch of quality circles. On average, the companies spent about two years in preparatory work for TQM. Top management commitment was rarely questioned in the companies – mainly due to the level of resources involved. Middle managers were reported as generally supportive and to be delegating more. Involvement across all levels was seen as improved. Middle managers, it is claimed, appreciated the increased decentralization. TQM was thus seen as promoting middle management participation. Hill (1991: 561) takes a very optimistic view of this: 'TQM has the potential to align reality with rhetoric by means of participation.' By this he appears to mean that the talk of 'teamwork' can actually become reality with TQM.

Overall, Hill is impressed by TQM in his four cases. Quality improvement outcomes are described as 'significant' and line managers expressed satisfaction. Two of the companies had been working with TQM for more than four years and a third organization for more than three years. In consequence, Hill believes the measured success to be indicative of some change in substance and not merely a result of novelty. Notably, however, he observes that while there were definite signs of 'culture change' among management the picture was less clear for shopfloor and office employees. As with other studies the behavioural evidence is rather firmer than attitudinal change evidence. The overall judgement from Hill (1991) is that TQM can involve significant change over a broad front and that, in contrast with quality circles, TQM can be viewed as an 'influential and effective paradigm for flexible organizations' (p. 566). The main contrast is that TQM works from the top (not the bottom, as with quality circles) and is extensively resourced: 'The difference now is that the people who rule corporations appear far more determined to succeed with this latest development than they ever were in the past' (p. 566).

Despite the optimistic message from Stephen Hill's research there are plenty of salutary warnings that TQM programmes are prone to failure for a host of reasons (Dale, 1991; Dale and Cooper, 1992; James, 1992; Wilkinson et al., 1992; Witcher and Wilkinson, 1990). The sources of such failures are usually traced to lack of demonstrated commitment from management at all levels, lack of resources allocated to the change programme, deficiencies in managing the process side of change, and, especially critical in the context of our present discussion, a failure to motivate and involve employees.

These latter aspects point up the need for on-going attention to HR and IR practice. Collard (1989) has described many of the main elements and so too have Witcher and Wilkinson (1990) though the latter authors point to continuing deep-seated structural reasons such as short-termism, occupational specialization and industrial relations. These sorts of barriers can be readily seen as obstacles not only to TQM but to all other similar aspirations to 'transformative management'. It is therefore to the inter-link between culture change management and IR/HRM that we now turn.

## HR and IR aspects of vision, mission and culture management

There is now an extensive and ever increasing volume of literature on 'managing change'. Its most notable feature from our point of view is its almost total detachment from, and blithe disregard for, the grounded issues of personnel and industrial relations. The change prescriptions are seemingly located in some uncomplicated world where all that is required is 'top management commitment', 'clarity of vision' and of message and a series of relatively simplistic techniques for surmounting 'resistance to change'. Our objective in this section is to review the most useful aspects of the 'management of culture change' body of knowledge and to locate these to the HR and IR issues.

At bottom, the management of change, and especially the management of culture change literature, suggests that there are certain *conditions* which propel or impede managed organizational change and certain *stages* through which managed change has to progress. We refer here to the more thoughtful literature. There are many other contributions which merely in effect proffer shopping lists of prescriptions which are apparently based on no model at all. Using the concepts of 'conditions' and 'stages' it is possible to encompass most of the frameworks and models of change currently on offer (for example, Lewin, 1951, 1958; Lippitt et al., 1958; Bullock and Batten, 1985; Beckhard, 1989; Cummings and Huse, 1989). The skill or, as Buchanan and Boddy (1992) put it, the 'expertise of the change agent' then becomes the capacity to understand these factors and to be able to influence people and events through the competent handling of the manifest and latent agenda. Buchanan and Boddy refer to this latter aspect as the engagement with 'backstage' as well as 'frontstage' activity.

Managing, and achieving, a far-reaching culture change is not simply a matter of managerial will and good communication. As Richard Beckhard, one of the leading authorities on managed change has argued, there are certain structural features which must also be in place. Beckhard (1989) has elaborated upon these conditions or 'prerequisites' for successful change. These include a set of external conditions which makes the maintenance of the status quo unlikely or impossible; the need for a critical mass of support; an understanding that far-reaching change takes 'years not months' and a realization therefore, that the quick dramatic gesture although often helpful, should not be confused as the complete change effort. Executive management must also be willing to commit resources – technical, expert and consultative in support of the change programme.

Beckhard's model of change brings together these 'prerequisites' with an understanding of the various steps which a change process must go through. These steps or stages include a design of the desired future state; a diagnosis of the present state (generally the existing state is seen to contain a problem and the future state is the perceived solution). A third step involves identifying in detail what needs to be done and what is required (this is particularly where the prerequisites come in) to get from here to there. This includes identifying the resources that will need to be committed and the activities that need to be undertaken. This stage in particular highlights the importance of traditional HR and IR aspects. It involves clarifying, for example, the sorts of relationships which are to be encouraged, that organizational and management structure which must be in place, the evaluation and reward systems that will be needed.

A fourth step involves formulating a picture of how the organization will function during the transitional state. And each of the members of the critical mass can be analysed with regard to their readiness and capability to assist in the change process. The significance of this is that the change will entail modifications in the behaviour of those who hold key roles. Senior managers may need to switch from behaviour patterns which emphasize control to forms of behaviour which prioritize advice and facilitation. At this stage also, supportive mechanisms to ensure persistence of the new, preferred behaviours will need to be put in place. These can include HR and IR elements such as selection criteria, appraisal criteria, training and development, and rewards.

Where the 're-education' methods fail, culture change programmes may be driven through by substituting willing individuals for those continuing to resist. Redeployment and redundancy have been used in some cases. It is known for example that in the major change programmes at British Airways, Abbey National and British Telecom, significant numbers of managers (including senior figures) who found difficulty in accepting the new regime were 'separated' from these organizations. The pressure on 'traditionalists' (i.e. those associated with previously prevailing cultures) to leave may range from the subtle to the explicit. Rather less drastic as a means of substitution is the use of new appointments (at whatever level in the organization) in order to put in place persons who are supporters of the new order.

Clearly, the chances of success in managing a change in the organization's culture will be enhanced where the various methods are working in a synchronized way. Thus, where the mission and values statements are underpinned by, for example, new appraisal criteria which, in turn, are followed through in terms of new reward patterns and where those attaining senior positions are seen to be persons who have actually practised the promulgated way, then the messages will be mutually reinforcing and very powerful.

To a considerable extent the recent discussions of culture change and 'good' communications, team working and the like could be seen as a revisiting of what in industrial relations would be termed the 'unitary perspective'. Within this view of organizational life there is only room for one legitimate fountain of authority and one legitimate set of interests. Opposition, particularly organized trade union opposition expressed through industrial action, is viewed as illegitimate. As with the recent discussions of culture management it is difficult to know whether those who espouse unitarism fully subscribe to it or are merely using it as a persuasive technique.

Drawing attention to this comparison also raises the question of how the managerial drives towards vision, mission and culture management fit within a unionized setting and a pluralistic set of practices. It is notable that practically all discussions of managing culture change simply neglect this aspect of organizational life (for example, Carnall, 1990; Scott and Jaffe, 1989; Wilson, 1992) just to cite recent British texts. The American sources such as Kanter (1984), Schein (1986), Cummings and Huse (1989) are of course equally, though more predictably, neglectful of this theme.

## Conclusions

In this chapter we have shifted attention from the more traditional ingredients of HR and IR practice to the newer themes of vision, mission and culture management. From tentative beginnings in the British context these less mechanistic approaches have, in some organizations at least, come to assume a centre stage position. TQM can be regarded as but one, albeit major, manifestation of the coming into primacy of these concepts. To use Hill's (1991) terminology, there would appear to be some evidence of a new paradigm.

What is less clear at this stage is the extent to which this new paradigm can be embedded and sustained without calling upon the more traditional elements of HR and IR practice. Or will its success depend upon displacement of these former practices?

Vision, mission and culture management are aspects of the 'new management' which throw into particularly sharp relief the themes of individualism and collectivism which we have been discussing throughout this book. In many ways the new paradigm signals a decisive departure from the previously preferred mode of good personnel practice based on standardized procedures. In place of order based on rules is meant to be a new order based on common values and objectives. To this extent the paraphernalia of management control devices can be replaced or certainly drastically de-emphasized so as to make space for trust and commitment.

'Collectivism' in its traditional sense of dealing with labour through representatives of trade unions or staff associations in order to reach accommodations in the shape of agreed 'rules' would seem to be pushed aside by a new individualism. But in a different sense the new management could be said to be erecting an alternative form of collectivism. This new collectivism is based on strong culture, common assumptions and agreed ends and objectives. All that we know about the history of labour management tells us to be cautious about the exaggerated claims of a newly discovered resolution to long-standing problems. It is not without significance that even one of the founders of the TQM movement, Phillip Crosby, has observed that over 90 per cent of TQM programmes fail (Crosby, 1979). In tracing the sources of failure management consultants usually point to the need to follow certain techniques more carefully. But the roots of the problems experienced almost certainly go much deeper than that. As Deming has continually warned, the TQM message in its full-blown version entails nothing less than a *transformation* of Western management. Few, it seem to us have really fully listened to that part of the message. In the absence of 'transform-ation', traditional skills in HR and IR management will continue to be at a premium for a long while to come.

# 9

# MANAGING WITH TRADE UNIONS

---

This chapter deals with a number of strategic issues which managements have to face in dealing with trade unions. One is the decision about the nature and extent of the recognition of trade unions. A second (assuming the management concerned recognizes trade unions for the purposes of negotiating pay and conditions of employment) concerns the structure of collective bargaining. Key decisions here relate to the appropriate units and the levels of collective bargaining. Is management going to deal severally or collectively with trade unions? Is management going to deal with trade unions indirectly through the intermediary of an employers' organization or assume direct responsibility? Is the management in a multi-establishment organization going to deal with trade unions at the organization level or at the level of individual establishments? A third area is the choice of methods for resolving conflict. Here particular attention is given to two of the features which have figured prominently in the so-called 'new style' agreements pioneered by the electricians' union and some of the Japanese companies investing in the UK, namely 'strike free' provisions and pendulum arbitration. The fourth and final area is the nature of the collective bargaining relationship and the key distinction between joint regulation and joint consultation. These four arenas for managerial decision constitute the basis for the four-part structuring of this chapter.

## Recognition of trade unions

At first sight, the decision whether or not to recognize trade unions might appear to be a foregone conclusion. Surely, it might be thought, managements are unlikely to recognize trade unions unless they have to. Trade unions are concerned with representing the collective interests of employees, whereas management may want to place more importance on the individual. Trade unions represent an external influence – an alternative focus of loyalty which might be thought to disrupt the unitary approach of the company. Trade unions are interested in rules and regulations which impinge on management decision making and desire for flexibility. Trade unions sometimes use sanctions and take strike action in pursuit of their objectives. Moreover, even if trade unions were once necessary to offset the excessive power of employers, surely this is no longer the case? Managements, it is argued, have learnt the error of their ways and recognize the vital contribution that their employees make.

In the UK, it is important to stress, managements also do not have to recognize trade unions. Unlike in other countries, there has been no legal support for trade union recognition since the abolition of the relevant provisions of the 1975 Employment Protection Act. On the contrary, if anything, UK governments since 1979, have shown great hostility to trade unions, which has had a significant impact on the thinking of many managers; a welter of legislation has been introduced to curb trade union activities.

Against this backcloth it is interesting to consider the extent to which UK companies have taken the opportunity to withdraw recognition from trade unions in the 1980s and 1990s. The third in the series of workplace industrial relations surveys (Millward et al., 1992) offers the most reliable data on this issue. Actual de-recognition was, in fact, found to be limited between 1984 and 1990. Overall, only 3 per cent of all workplaces which had no recognized unions in 1990 had previously recognized unions at some stage since 1984. This amounted to only 1 per cent of all workplaces in 1990. There are two caveats. There is some data which suggests that the incidence of de-recognition was concentrated in the period since 1989 and this could conceivably therefore constitute a 'growing trend' (Millward et al., 1992: 74). The other caveat is that when the 'panel' of workplaces which were surveyed in both 1984 and 1990 are examined, the two snapshot pictures taken in those years reveal that nearly a fifth of those which recognized unions in 1984 no longer did so in 1990.

This data concerns actual de-recognition. The extent to which, overall, the pattern of recognition in 1990 compared with the pattern in 1984 is rather different. This latter pattern additionally takes into account industrial restructuring and the closure of workplaces. When this overall measure is taken there are grounds for talking about a 'substantial decline' in the extent of trade union recognition since 1984. It fell from 66 per cent of all workplaces in 1984 to 53 per cent in 1990 (Millward et al., 1992: 70).

On the other hand, the decline is very much concentrated in particular sectors and is very much influenced by establishment size. Thus, in manufacturing, the decline was especially marked in printing and publishing. The decline was notable also in establishments with fewer than 200 employees; above this size there was 'hardly any change' (Millward et al., 1992: 72). (In the light of this finding, the significance of the organizational re-structuring for the conduct of industrial relations as discussed in Chapter 4, becomes very evident.)

Here, it is the remarkable fact of 'hardly any change' in the mainstream workplaces with over 200 employees which we wish to examine in some depth. What does this lack of change in trade union recognition during a period of quite exceptional economic, legal and political transformation tell us about HR and IR management in practice? The reality is that many UK companies, whatever the senior managers may feel about trade unions, are in no position to withdraw recognition. It is not simply that they might face opposition from trade unions. They do not have an alternative set of HR/IR arrangements which they can realistically hope to put in place of those agreed with trade unions. Few have the managers with the relevant interpersonal skills to manage individually. Hardly any could afford the superior levels of pay and conditions which would almost certainly be necessary to persuade their employees to give up trade union membership.

Not only negative reasons are important, however. Trade unions also fulfil a number of important managerial functions which help to explain why a number of the foreign-owned companies coming into the UK have been willing to recognize them. One is the 'agency' function which is especially important where there are large numbers of employees enagaged in relatively homogenous activities: management escapes the time consuming and costly process of dealing with employees individually and also avoids inconsistencies which can be a major problem. A second is that trade unions 'voice' the grievances and complaints of employees (Freeman and Medoff, 1984). In the words of Henry Mond, who had a significant influence on ICI's early policy towards trade unions, 'the trade unions are extremely useful to us in bringing to our notice matters that we should not otherwise be aware of' (quoted in Reader, 1973: 66). A third, and in many respects the most important function that trade unions perform, is in helping to manage discontent by legitimating procedures and management prerogative.

This last point is perhaps best illustrated by drawing on US experience. As Kochan et al. (1986) show, throughout the 1970s a number of major US companies, including the car manufacturers Ford and General Motors, experimented with some aspects of HRM in much the same way as many UK managements have done in the 1980s. They found, however, that their pursuit of individualism at the expense of their relationship with trade unions was counter-productive; there was a great deal of mistrust on the shopfloor about management's motives and many of the individual initiatives did not have the hoped for benefits. It was only when management began to involve the trade unions in the programmes of change they wished to introduce that they began to achieve the breakthrough that they were looking for. Interestingly, this sort of experience has been replicated in certain sectors in Britain where the decision about union recognition suddenly became a real and pressing issue. For example, in the NHS the attainment of trust status permitted managers the freedom to take new employees out of the centrally determined Whitley terms and conditions. And for those long-serving staff who transferred their employment contracts across to the new trust there was the option for managers to refuse local recognition for trade unions. In a number of cases where this was in fact withheld, agreement with the unions concerned was eventually reached following the realization that failure to recognize was a source of widespread employee mistrust of management.

This serves as a reminder that recognition is not an open-and-shut issue: management also have to decide the nature and the extent of recognition. Typically, trade unions are recognized for the purpose of negotiating pay and conditions. Many variants of much narrower and much broader recognition are available, however. A company may, for example, simply recognize a trade union for the purposes of representing the individual grievances of employees such as is the case with the retail staff of Sainsbury. At the other extreme, trade unions may be involved in business and investment planning; the joint consultation process at ICI is a case in point.

One thing seems evident. Management needs to make a clear choice. If trade unions are not going to be recognized for the purposes of negotiating pay and conditions, then management needs to have a system of highly developed personnel and HR policies and practices in place. If it is going to recognize trade unions, it needs to remember that the relationship with trade unions has to be managed. In the case of a 'green-field' operation, for example, this means selecting a trade union to represent its employees. This can either be done unilaterally, possibly following the competitive consideration of a number of alternative union presentations (what has become known as the 'beauty contest') or in conjunction with the regional TUC. In the case of 'brownfield' sites, it means having clear views about the structure of collective bargaining or the relationship between joint regulation and joint consultation. There is a great deal in the adage that managements get the trade unions they deserve.

## The structure of collective bargaining

As well as the nature and extent of the recognition, managements have also to come to a view about the most appropriate structure of collective bargaining. This is above all true of the large multi-establishment organizations which dominate employment in the UK. Key issues are the units and the levels of collective bargaining.

## The unit

A great deal of attention has focused on the 'single union' arrangements associated with some of the Japanese companies such as Nissan and Toshiba (see, for example, Bassett, 1986; Wickens, 1987; Trevor, 1988; IRRR, 1989c). In practice, however, where a number of unions are already recognized, a single-union agreement is not normally a practicable proposition. The key issue is whether management is going to deal with the various trade unions it may recognize on a one to one basis or collectively around a so-called 'single table' (Marginson and Sisson, 1990). In practice, this latter means bringing manual and non-manual trade union representatives together, since many companies moved to 'single table' bargaining for their manual and non-manual employees respectively in the 1970s. As Table 9.1 shows, overall there was an average of two bargaining units for each workplace with recognised trade unions.

There were 43 per cent of establishments which had just one bargaining unit. This, as the table makes clear was, in fact, the predominant mode overall in both private manufacturing and services. The public sector was an exception: here, multiple bargaining units were more common.

At first sight the logic of 'single table' arrangements would appear to be irrefutable. Operating in this way saves managerial time and reduces the possibility of inconsistencies, anomalies and leap-frogging by one bargaining group over another. In addition, the single-table approach fits well with the trend towards harmonization and single-status workplaces. In general, it can be said to help establish and support a progressive organizational climate appropriate to a strategy which is respectful of joint regulation.

There are, however, some practical considerations to be taken into account. As has already been pointed out in Chapter 6, in the great majority of cases there continue to be substantial differ-

**Table 9.1**   Numbers of bargaining units, by broad sector, 1990

|  | All establishments % | Private manufacturing % | Private services % | Public sector % |
|---|---|---|---|---|
| Number of bargaining units |  |  |  |  |
| 1 | 43 | 63 | 58 | 26 |
| 2 | 32 | 22 | 25 | 41 |
| 3 | 13 | 11 | 13 | 15 |
| 4 or more | 12 | 4 | 5 | 19 |
| Mean | 2.0 | 1.6 | 1.7 | 2.5 |
| Base: establishments with recognized unions |  |  |  |  |
| Unweighted | 1417 | 450 | 373 | 594 |
| Weighted | 1058 | 189 | 349 | 519 |

*Source*: Millward et al. (1992: 86).

ences in the terms and conditions of employment between manual and non-manual employees. Many managements are afraid that putting the two groups together will mean levelling up more quickly than they can afford. In these circumstances, some managements may feel that they can gain some tactical advantage from playing off one group against another, although this hardly sits well with a desire to harmonize. Trade unions may also be opposed to the idea fearing that they will lose their individual identities.

Even when these considerations are not uppermost, there is a need to recognize that it will be necessary to have tiered arrangements. Otherwise there is a danger that groups will not feel their interests are properly being dealt with or the 'single table' becomes extremely over-loaded with issues which do not affect the majority of employees.

The other important issue in terms of bargaining 'units' relates to which groups of employees will actually be covered by collective agreements. Although as we noted earlier, the extent of overall de-recognition of trade unions has been small, there has, however, been a significant trend towards taking certain groups out of the collective arrangements. In fact, the fall in the proportion of the total workforce covered by collective agreements in the 1980s was substantial. In the words of Millward et al. (1992: 93) it was 'one of the most dramatic changes in the character of British industrial relations that our survey series has measured'. The aggregate proportion of employees covered by collective bargaining fell from 71 per cent to 54 per cent between 1984 and 1990. In private sector manufacturing there was a fall from 64 per cent to 51 per cent and from 41 per cent to 33 per cent in the service sector. As Millward and colleagues note (1992: 93–4) this means that in the private sector as a whole, coverage declined from a majority of employees (52 per cent) to a minority of employees (41 per cent).

Evidently, many employers have taken the view that they do want to take certain groups out of collectively agreed arrangements for pay and other terms and conditions. Prime targets for this have been successive levels of managerial employees. Other groups, such as sales and information technology staff, have been incorporated as union membership density has dwindled and as the opportunity has arisen.

## The level of bargaining

There have been major changes in the levels of collective bargaining in recent years. There is no dispute about the general trends. There have been:

1 a shift from multi-employer (national) to single-employer bargaining (for further details, see IRRR, 1989a and c); and
2 a shift from multi-establishment (company) to single-establishment bargaining especially in the large enterprises (for further details, see IRRR, 1989d; 1990).

In the case of the shift from multi-employer to single-employer bargaining, there was pressure from Conservative governments in the 1980s. But this was not the most important consideration. As one of us (Sisson, 1987) has argued in detail elsewhere, the decline in multi-employer bargaining in the UK is long-running. Multi-employer agreements in the UK, unlike those in other EC member countries, are not legally enforceable and the emphasis is on procedures rather than substantive terms. This means that multi-employer agreements have never had the authority of those in other countries.

In the case of the shift from multi-establishment to single establishment bargaining, the most important consideration has been the growth in the number of large multi-divisional organizations. This has meant the adoption of profit and cost centre management which puts pressure on 'bottom-line' responsibility for labour costs. Responsibility for pay determination, it is argued, should be given to the management with bottom-line responsibility for profit and costs. If there is a mis-match between levels and responsibilities, local management can shirk its responsibilities. Pay and conditions, it is also argued, need to be closely related to a) the profitability of individual businesses, b) differences in performance and skills and c) differences in local labour market conditions – the organization may be over-paying in some instances and under-paying in others. In some companies, for example GEC and Pilkington, this can even mean that the individual business unit on a multi-business site can become the level of bargaining. The consequence that will have to be lived with, however, is that people at the same location, possibly even doing very similar jobs, can be on different terms and conditions.

One point, however, must be made absolutely clear. Despite these trends, there is no consensus about what is the 'right level' of collective bargaining. This is above all true of the choice between multi-employer and single employer bargaining on which there has been an extremely vigorous debate. Certainly in industries such as clothing, construction and printing, managements as well as trade unions are committed to maintaining the system of multi-employer bargaining.

The case against multi-employer bargaining is broadly as follows. It is inflationary. Pay and conditions of employment need to be closely related to the profitability of individual companies and differences in performance and skills and related also to local labour market conditions. It is inflexible. Much-needed changes, for example in payment systems, working practices or training, are difficult to bring about and the industry tends to move at the pace of the slowest. It is an abdication of responsibility. If employees really are the most important asset, it is difficult to justify relinquishing the control of pay and conditions to an external body. It gives trade unions too much power: they can bring their relatively limited resources to bear on a single set of negotiations.

Conversely, the case *for* multi-employer bargaining goes something like this: it is neither inflationary nor inflexible – in most cases it sets minimum terms and conditions and allows considerable scope for local adaptation. It is relatively efficient. Managements in many companies, particularly small companies, do not have the time, let alone the expertise, to negotiate the total package of pay and conditions. It sets standards which help to ensure that companies are not undercut compared with others in the same industry. It usually provides a national disputes procedure which is a useful safety valve. It maximizes the bargaining power of managements: trade unions are less able to 'pick off' individual companies or engage in 'leap-frogging'. Supporters of national agreements can point to the dispute in engineering in 1989–90 to show what can happen in the absence of national agreements (for further details, see IRRR, 1989a and c).

Much depends on the specific circumstances of the industry or the individual organization – as will be argued in more detail below. Even more important, however, are the prevailing 'beliefs' of senior managers (and government ministers) about what is most appropriate. There is a widely held view, for example, that the decentralization of pay determination is an important instrument or lever in promoting the management of change. The important thing is not to be too easily swayed by the flavour of the month. Decentralized negotiations may be highly appropriate in some situations but equally highly inappropriate in others. This is why it is essential to study the circumstances before coming to a decision.

In making a choice between multi-employer and single-employer bargaining, three main sets of considerations need to be taken into account. The first relates to product market factors. Firms which operate in a highly competitive market where a large number of firms each has a small market share are likely to favour multi-employer bargaining. Labour market circumstances constitute a second set of factors to be considered. The more labour intensive the industry, the more likely it is that firms will want to stabilize wage costs by resorting to multi-employer bargaining. Third, this form of bargaining also tends to be favoured when the technology used by different firms is similar (ACAS, 1983). It is not difficult to understand therefore why multi-employer (national) agreements are popular in industries such as clothing, construction and printing. Each of them is composed of a large number of small and highly competitive firms, which employ very similar types of worker and which face large national trade unions.

Another choice facing managers in the unionised firm is whether to opt for company level or workplace level bargaining. Factors which need to be taken into account here include size of establishments, geographical dispersion of workplaces, diversity of product range and the degree of interdependence between sites. The larger the size of the separate establishments the more likely it is that management will favour decentralization. The more dispersed they are – especially if operating in markedly different labour markets – again the greater the likelihood that decentralized bargaining will be favoured. If the range of products is diverse and the process of production highly inter-dependent, then this will favour centralized bargaining (CIR, 1974; ACAS, 1983). It is not difficult to understand therefore why the car manufacturers, the clearing banks and the retailers prefer multi-establishment to single-establishment bargaining. In the case of the car manufacturers, interdependency is the critical factor; in the case of the banks and the retailers it is the size of establishment and similarity of services (and hence skills) which are important.

None the less, many managers now find themselves in a period of flux and some of these fundamentals are in danger of being forgotten in the headlong dash for decentralized bargaining. The current desire to relate terms and conditions to the fortunes of separate business units may push the above considerations to the sidelines. The extent to which this will present a serious problem to British managers will depend upon the level at which real decisions are in fact going to be made.

*Levels of management decision-making*

The research evidence – both from surveys (Marginson et al., 1988 and case studies Kinnie, 1985a and b) – is very clear. Although the level of bargaining has attracted most of the attention, it is not the only or, from the point of view of management, the most important issue to be considered. Far more important is the level of management decision-making. One might expect that with the tendency towards devolved financial responsibility to business units (see Chapter 4) company level managers would be involved less in workplace industrial relations. But the recent industrial relations survey (Millward et al., 1992: 209) shows that the reverse has been the case – in 1990 there was a greater propensity for senior corporate managers to be involved in establishment industrial relations matters. To put it bluntly, much of the decentralization that has taken place is an 'illusion'. Things may 'happen' at local level, but they are not 'decided' there. Many of the key issues of HR policy are likely to be determined at higher levels in the organization. Shifts towards harmonization or the introduction of quality circles or TQM are good examples. The same is true of specific conditions of employment. Most companies will have what might be described as a 'taboo' list – a list of the issues that managers must not make concessions on at local level. The working week is a good example: this is usually 'decided' at higher levels of the organiz-ation in most companies. Some companies even have seven-day 'approval' notices which require managers taking an initiative to circulate colleagues in other units for their views before going ahead.

As for pay determination, a range of possibilities can be found even in the most apparently decentralized of companies. Man-agement may dictate the increase or require local managers to justify their proposals in a mock 'negotiation' or they may leave local managers in no doubt of what they expect or they tackle the issue in the annual budgeting process. Local managers, for example, may be given complete freedom to pay what increases they think fit providing there is no increase in labour costs.

At first sight, it may appear to be contradictory to decentralize responsibility and yet to retain a significant degree of central control. It is perfectly sensible, however: senior managers are trying to get the best and to avoid the worst of both worlds. One important consideration is what might be described as the 'limited horizons' problem. It is all very well, in other words, making local managers 'operationally' responsible. They cannot, however, be expected to have the time or the expertise to do the long-term 'strategic' HR thinking that is going to be required. It is not very efficient to do so either – the organization is not getting the benefits of the synergies of the large organization. Simply bringing local managers together to discuss and debate the issues can be enormously beneficial in saving time and in arriving at solutions to common problems.

There is also the 'coercive comparision' problem. The theory of decentralization is fine: local managers are given responsibility to determine local issues in the light of local circumstances. The reality is very different. Individual units in the same organization are not, wisely, regarded as independent baronies especially if their employees are members of the same trade unions or professional organizations. It does not make sense to give local managers total autonomy – the price of one unit's freedom to do what it wants can be disastrous for other units. Concessions made in one unit can have extremely costly repercussions in others and the organization is left wide open to 'pattern bargaining' or 'leapfrogging' claims by trade unions.

'Pattern bargaining', it must be emphasized, is not simply an hypothetical possibility. A very recent and very successful example took place in the engineering industry in 1989–90. The breakdown of national negotiations over a reduction in the working week led to a classic case of the 'rolling strike'. The Confederation of Shipbuilding and Engineering Unions levied its members throughout the industry to set up a sizeable strike fund; it then targeted individual employers in a series of 'waves'; it conducted strike ballots in individual companies to conform to the relevant legislation – using the proceeds of the levy to pay substantial strike pay to the members voting to take industrial action in support of the claim.

The result was considerable success in achieving a reduction of the working week throughout large parts of the engineering industry and a considerable fillip for trade union morale. The irony is that it was the use of these very tactics – known also as 'whipsawing' in the USA – which led the engineering employers to introduce a national procedure agreement in the first place in the 1880s. Indeed, most advocates of decentralized bargaining often conveniently forget that it was managements who introduced centralized bargaining in many situations in order to stop unions engaging in 'pattern bargaining'.

A useful exercise for managers to undertake when contemplating decentralized bargaining is to list which terms and conditions will be handled in which way. Which, for example, will be subject to *instruction* from the centre (e.g. the basic length of the working week perhaps, or health and safety rules)? Which will be the subject of 'advice' or *guidelines* from the centre (perhaps, for example, a specific type of job evaluation will be recommended)? On other issues the units may have more autonomy though they may be expected to consult or even be *required to consult* before acting on changes, say, to the grading system. Or, at minimum, it may simply be that individual units are simply expected to provide the corporate centre with *information*.

The problem is that in practice, very few organizations go through this type of exercise before they decentralize. This is yet a further example of the lack of strategic thinking in HR/IR. Usually, arrangements are simply built up incrementally. In our experience, even where systematic analyses are conducted they are very rarely as formal as the exercise outlined above suggests they could be. However, such exercises are always highly confidential and so for this reason we are not at liberty to cite actual case examples.

## Choice of method for conflict resolution

How to resolve the conflicts that may arise between management and trade unions has been an especially prominent concern in collective bargaining in the UK. This is because there are two major differences between the UK and other countries in the contents and status of collective agreements. First, in the UK the relationship between management and trade unions has been built on procedural rules, whereas in other countries it has been built on a code of substantive rules in force for a specified period. Second, in the UK priority has been given to voluntary rather than compulsory collective bargaining; that is, the procedural rules are made by the parties themselves rather than imposed by government, and along with any substantive rules are deemed to be 'gentlemen's agreements' binding in honour rather than legally enforceable contracts.

The result is that in the UK the procedure agreements have to take the full strain of the relationship. They have had to deal with disputes over the making as well as the interpretation of agreements. This can also involve a variety of levels. In the case of the industries with multi-employer agreements, for example, this can mean the industry, the company and the workplace. Unlike in most other countries, where collective agreements are legally enforceable, there is also no closed season for collective bargaining; negotiation in the UK is highly informal and more or less continuous. Typically, then, procedure agreements in the UK have involved a hierarchy of levels usually ending in a form of conciliation involving a third party.

## How useful are strike-free clauses?

Much has been made of the clauses in 'new style' agreements which prohibit the taking of industrial action under any circumstances. In practice, however, the issue is largely symbolic. This is because the general rule in the UK is that collective agreements normally lack contractual status unless the parties decide otherwise. If the management and trade union do not sign a legally enforceable agreement, there is no redress against the union in the event of its members taking industrial action in breach of the agreement. Only if the union has not followed the provisions of the legislation in relation to balloting, picketing and secondary action, is it open to the management to seek legal redress. Management can seek redress against individual employees but, as the Royal Commission on Trades Unions recognized more than two decades ago (Donovan Report, 1968), this does not really amount to much. Individual members are unlikely to have the level of assets to make prosecution worthwhile and, in any event, are unlikely to return to work with enthusiasm if they are being sued by their management. The sanction of dismissal, which management is free to use under the law, is only viable if management is going to close down the unit or has an alternative workforce at its disposal.

In the circumstances, it might be wondered why management has not moved in the direction of making collective agreements legally enforceable especially as this is the norm in other countries. Trade union opposition is a consideration, but not the only one. British management has shown no great enthusiasm. Much as many managements would have liked procedural agreements to be legally enforceable, they have been much less enthusiastic about giving substantive agreements the same status. If collective agreements were legally enforceable, it would be more difficult for management to change the substantive terms to suit changing circumstances.

### Should reference to arbitration be included?

Along with the strike free provisions, a particular form of arbitration has been a key feature of many of the new style agreements. It is known as 'pendulum' or 'straight-choice' arbitration. Standard arbitration involves a third party making a judgement about the outcome of a dispute; in coming to this judgement, the arbitrator is free to suggest the most appropriate outcome he or she feels is appropriate. Under pendulum arbitration, the arbitrator has to make a 'straight choice' between the positions of one or other of the parties.

This form of arbitration was developed in the US in the public services where strikes are outlawed. The main theoretician of pendulum arbitration is Carl Stevens. In a celebrated article entitled 'Is compulsory arbitration compatible with bargaining' (Stevens, 1966), he argues that the threat of pendulum arbitration might stimulate compromise where there was no right to strike. In particular, pendulum arbitration might help to resolve some of the weaknesses of conventional arbitration: the 'chilling effect' – the reluctance to engage in realistic bargaining in the knowledge that there is another step; and the 'narcotic effect' – the tendency for compulsory arbitration to become habit-forming.

As with other features of the 'new style' agreements, it should not necessarily be assumed that managements will regard any form of arbitration as a good thing. Indeed, there are strong grounds for thinking the opposite. Resort to arbitration effectively means giving responsibility for making key management decisions to a third party. The point was put very succinctly in the Treasury's evidence to the Megaw Committee set up to look at pay determination in the public services: 'the only sure way for employers to avoid the risk of awards they cannot afford is refuse to go to arbitration. It follows that arbitration should not take place without their consent, but only on mutual agreement' (quoted in Bassett, 1986: 110).

As for pendulum arbitration, it is worth taking into account the comments of some of the key arbitrators. ACAS (1984) says the arrangements depend on a high degree of trust and may not be appropriate to every situation. Lewis (1988: 10) believes that 'the requirement to find entirely in favour of one side's final position makes the arbitration process more "adversarial" and less "inquisitorial"'. Kessler (1987) and Lewis (1988) both question whether or not it is appropriate to exclude provisions for conciliation and mediation. Arbitration, in other words, should only ever be the last resort. The most recent Workplace Industrial Relations Survey (WIRS) (Millward et al., 1992: 208) reveals that 68 per cent of managers with pay and conditions procedures in their establishments reported that they had provision for some kind of third party intervention to resolve disputes (this represented a decline from 79 per cent in 1984). The incidence of 'straight choice' arbitration, however, was low – it accounted for only 7 per cent of those establishments which had made arrangements for third-party arbitration.

## Joint regulation or joint consultation?

One of the features of the so-called 'new style' agreements which has received relatively little attention and yet which may turn out to be of most lasting importance, is the provision for a company consultative council. The general model has been set most notably perhaps by Toshiba. The Company Advisory Council (COAB) involves worker representatives meeting together with the chief executive and other senior managers and 'exists to advise the company on any issue it wishes to raise or on any issue which the company seeks advice' ('General Principles of the COAB System, 1981', quoted in Trevor, 1988: 256). The company also commits itself in the same document to supply 'regular accounts and meaningful information on the plans and performance of the company' (Trevor, 1988: 259). The COAB, which can include shop stewards, is also the forum where terms and conditions of employment are discussed in the first instance. The trade union becomes involved if any issue is not resolved in the council and represents individual members in the case of grievance, discipline and other individual matters.

Significantly, the Co-operative Bank plc which has long been organised by the Bank, Insurance and Finance Union (BIFU) was able to introduce just such a body in 1991. This was driven-through in the teeth of opposition from the union. The terms of reference of the new consultative council could be seen to throw into question many of the functions of BIFU in the future – albeit that nominally, at least, items for collective bargaining are not part of the council's remit.

To understand the potential significance of this type of development, the term 'collective bargaining' which has so far been used to describe relations between management and trade unions has to be unpicked. Collective bargaining embraces two processes. One is joint regulation. Here the implication is that the outcome of the process is an explicit agreement between the two parties. If the union withholds its agreement, management does not proceed. Or if it does, it recognizes that it may face industrial action. The other is joint consultation. Here the implication is that the management will seek the views of the union and take them into account in making its decision. It may go ahead with a decision, however, even if the union expresses its opposition.

In most other EC member states, the two processes are separate. The most obvious example of such a 'dual system' is to be found in Germany where it is enshrined in the legal framework. Joint regulation is largely the responsibility of the employers' organizations and trade unions and takes place outside the workplace at the level of the industry or the Land (region). Inside the workplace, the task of representing the interests of employees is taken over by the statutory works councils, which have limited rights of joint regulation but extensive powers of joint consultation as well as information, which means a much wider range of issues is discussed between management and employee representatives.

As Marchington (1993) describes, joint consultation in the UK has had something of a chequered history. Provisions for joint consultation were a key recommendation of the Whitley Committee at the end of the First World War and in some sectors, notably in parts of the public sector, the arrangements survive to this day. Joint consultation, in the form of production committees, was also very popular at the end of the Second World War. In the 1960s and 1970s, however, it came in for a great deal of criticism. The feeling seemed to be that if an issue was important enough, it should be the subject of joint regulation. Although the decline seems to have been arrested in the 1980s – and there is some evidence of growth – a joint consultation committee seems to exist in only a minority of cases. In a survey of 573 establishments in 1990, for example, ACAS (1991) found that less than half (40 per cent) had a joint consultative committee. Moreover, only about 19 per cent of the establishments which were part of multi-establishment companies (three-quarters of the sample) reported having a joint consultative committee above the level of the establishment, i.e. at divisional or headquarters level.

In our view there is a strong argument for managements and trade unions considering whether they should introduce joint consultation machinery covering a wider range of issues and at higher levels. There is an understandable reluctance on the part of management to make many of the issues which have been touched on throughout the book, such as changes in work organization, training, or future business plans, the subject of joint regulation. If everything has to be the subject of agreement, the process of decision-making can be slowed down. Yet there is a strong case for management to discuss them with trade union repesentatives: not only do these representatives have a contribution to make, but their involvement will add to the legitimacy of what management is seeking to do. Other things being equal, trade unions would prefer joint regulation on the grounds that this enables them to exercise a deeper influence on management decisions. Joint consultation, it can be argued, gives the semblance but not the substance of influence; there is also an understandable reluctance to accept that joint consultation may involve giving up the principle of 'single channel' representation, i.e. the insistence that the trade union is the only vehicle for representing workers' interests. The harsh reality, however, is that it is extremely unlikely that management is going to agree to extend the scope of joint regulation or that a UK government for the foreseeable future is going to force them to do so. If trade unions want to extend their influence, they will also certainly have to compromise in this regard.

## Key issues for the 1990s?

One of the key issues facing management and trade unions in the 1990s will centre on how they are going to adapt to the greater level of competition which will undoubtedly come as a result of the Single European Market. Whether or not Britain is in or out of the exchange rate mechanism (the ERM) there will be increasing pressure to ensure that UK unit labour costs do not grow faster or exceed those in other European countries.

A number of potential implications of this fundamental issue can be foreseen. There is likely to be more emphasis on forward projections of movements in unit labour costs throughout Europe and less on backward-looking measures of inflation or the 'going rate' in Britain. There will be a greater stress on the acquisition of new skills and less on those 'historically' acquired. There will be more emphasis on improvements in performance which come from new methods of working. And there may even possibly be attention paid to the coordination of pay bargaining within and between industries.

A second, and perhaps even more fundamental, issue is whether UK management and trade unions are going to be able to put their relationship on a more positive footing. The way that this might be done – by developing joint consultation over a much wider range of issues and at a higher level – is clear enough. The joint management–union initiative coordinated by the Involvement and Participation Association (IPA, 1992) is highly indicative of a possible way forward. The question is whether there is the will. Here it is going to be important to overcome the legacy of history. Managers may think they have little to gain; they may also fear that joint consultation will lead to joint regulation and so to rigidity. Trade unions may be concerned that developments in management practices are designed to undermine their position (see, for example, the discussion of different trade union positions in Martinez Lucio and Weston, 1992); they may also fear that they will compromise themselves if they become too deeply involved in key decisions without the power of veto. The experience of other countries, where there is also a history of 'confrontation' between management and trade unions, notably, Italy (see, for example, the discussion in Ferner and Hyman, 1992) and the USA (Kochan, Katz and McKersie, 1986), suggests that this is possible on the basis of distingushing between joint regulation and joint consultation. There are benefits to both parties if this can be done.

## Conclusions

The focus of this chapter has been upon a number of strategic issues which managers have to face when dealing with trade unions. Four areas were selected as being especially critical: decisions about the nature and extent of union recognition; the structural arrangements to be made for conducting collective relations; choices about methods for resolving conflicts; and the balance between joint regulation and joint consultation.

These four sets of decisions were grounded in an account of the changing contours of management–union relations. In particular, trends in the areas of recognition and de-recognition, shifts in bargaining levels and changes in the form and nature of management–union interactions were explained. The overriding message was that despite the fluidity of the institutional IR mechanisms (and there are suggestions in the recent WIRS data that the pace of change may be accelerating) certain fundamentals none the less remain and these require considered reflection.

Outright shifts away from trade union recognition and collective arrangements in favour of full-blown individualization of the employment relationship have been very rare – except in small organizations. In consequence, the need to understand the complex issues involved in managing IR and HR together have again been emphasized in this chapter as elsewhere in this book. The broader implications which this entails are picked-up and assessed in the final chapter.

# 10

# CONCLUSIONS: BALANCING INDIVIDUALISM AND COLLECTIVISM

We began the first chapter of this book with these two sentences: 'Just about every book on the subject of managing human resources and many a chairman's statement, makes the same point: it is people that make the difference. The workforce is the most vital asset.' In the intervening chapters we have endeavoured to track and explain potential and actual developments in the activation of this message. We have emphasized, like many others (see for example, Legge, forthcoming; Blyton and Turnbull 1992) that there is a considerable gap between rhetoric and reality. The much vaunted development-oriented, flexible, well-motivated, efficiently operating, highly skilled and well-paid economy is hardly in evidence. We have argued that this is not just because of many fundamental contradictions in HRM; but also because of a number of deep-seated structural conditions and, in particular, the tendency towards short-termism in management's approach.

We have also recognized that managers, and students of management, looking to analysts for guidelines concerning the way to proceed in employment management will not be satisfied or well-served merely by a critique of HRM. It is not enough to point out that the nostrums of Tom Peters and Moss Kanter are detached from the reality which most managers face. Most managers already know that. Similarly, a growing number of managers are only too aware of the problems which stem from the wider structures in which they have to work. Simply to go on multiplying the number of identified examples of contradictions in human resource management or reminding them of the implications of 'short-termism' is in danger of becoming counter-productive.

In this final chapter therefore we go further than either of us have done before in suggesting how those managers who are anxious to improve their approach to HR/IR might proceed. In the book as a whole we have not only focused on the most promising forms of intervention – planning, organizing for high performance, culture management, training and strategic management, we have also drawn attention to some of the basic problems that will need to be confronted and how these might begin to be addressed. We also, in the Appendix, discuss how managers might audit progress in developing a more strategic approach to managing HR and IR.

## Future imperfect?

If we had been writing this book in the late 1980s, we would certainly have noted the gap between rhetoric and reality and of the contradictions in the then emerging model. But we would also have been pointing to potential sources of optimism arising from the prospects of the Single European Market, and renewed investment in, and care of the employee resource in the face of the impending demographic time-bomb. We would probably also have reflected optimism arising from new evidence of greater attention to management education, training and development. The outlook then would have appeared reasonably encouraging.

Now it is rather less so. In place of the much-discussed 'Transformation' (Kochan et al., 1986) we have instead witnessed continued loss of competitiveness, job losses announced virtually every day, plant closures, and a continuing failure to rectify long-standing problems in the vocational education system. At that time there was a growing hope that economic management could be turned around and that new, effective, employment policies were being, at last, put in place.

We also have the evidence of the third Workplace Industrial Relations Survey (Millward et al., 1992) available to us. The most striking findings of WIRS 3, which have yet to be picked up in either the general or the specialist media, relate to the workplaces showing evidence of the fragments of HRM. Other things being equal, as the WIRS 3 team themselves point out (Millward et al., 1992: 363), one might have expected that the most likely work-places in which evidence of HRM would be found would be those that are union-free. This is where it is said many of the practices originated in the USA (Foulkes, 1980; Kochan et al., 1986). It is also where commentators have suggested HRM might be found in its most developed state in the UK (Sisson, 1989; Guest, 1989). In the event, the position is the exact opposite. It is the union rather than the non-union workplaces which exhibit the HRM initiatives that are to be found.

Thus, not only did a sizeable minority of non-union work-places have no procedures for raising grievances or health and safety issues, but informality characterized relations generally. It is worth quoting the WIRS 3 team in full on these points:

On a wide range of matters that could be expected to be of interest to employees, our results showed that managers in the non-union sector were much less likely to collect information on a regular basis, to review performance or policies. They were also far less likely to disseminate such information to employees or their representatives. Even on a matter of such broad interest as the financial position of their workplace, as many as half of managements gave their employees no regular information at all.

Methods of communication reflected the greater infor-mality. Managements in non-union workplaces were con-siderably less likely to use each of the main methods of communications covered by our questioning. A third of them used regular meetings between supervisors and all the employees they supervised. A similar number used an annual or more frequent meeting between senior managers and all sections of the workforce. Only half systematically used the management chain to communicate to all employees. Only a fifth had a consultative committee or similar body for consulting employees on general matters. Yet consultation with employees was one of the most important employee relations issues according to managers in the non-union sector, as important as in the union sector where the formalised methods and structures for consulting and informing employees were so much more common. (Millward et al., 1992: 364–5)

Another key finding on the same theme relates to (the lack of) employment security in the non-union sector. Workforce reductions were no more common in non-union than in union workplaces, but when they did occur they were much more likely to be achieved through compulsory redundancies. Non-union workplaces also made greater use of short-term, temporary contracts.

As for outcomes, industrial relations may have been perceived as being 'good' or 'very good' in union-free workplaces and strikes considered almost inconceivable, but forms of unorganized conflict were much in evidence. Turnover was as high as in union workplaces and safety, measured by a higher rate of accidents than in union workplaces, a major concern. Dismissals other than those arising from redundancy were nearly twice as frequent per employee as in the union sector. Claims to industrial tribunals for unfair dismissal and other alleged mistreatment were no less common than in union workplaces.

In the light of these findings it is now apparent that the general pattern in the non-union enterprise is far from the human resource management dream that the government hoped for in such published statements as *People, Jobs and Opportunity*.

So where does this leave the practitioner? The messages of the late 1980s – of flexibility, investment in training, more careful and systematic selection, more sophisticated human resource planning, and strategic integration of human resource policies and practices – have not entirely been discredited. On the contrary, many of these elements remain highly relevant and valid. The difficulty is that now, the nature of the overall problem is, to put it bluntly, worse than it was.

Not only is Britain vulnerable to frequent and prolonged recessions, but the real danger is that the economy could be caught in an overall downward spiral of cost cutting, lost manufacturing capacity and a deteriorating infrastructure. In place of 'excellence', 'transformation', 'commitment' or 'total quality' there is an all too well-grounded fear of a long-term swing towards a low investment, low skilled, poor quality, low wage economy. There will undoubtedly be an end to this particular recession and optimism will temporarily be rekindled. But the underlying problems are in danger of persisting.

In this context, our message is more basic and fundamental than that proselytized by the exponents of the formula at the 'high-tech' end of human resource management. For most of our managerial audience facing the sorts of conditions described in this book, the real issue is not how to finesse the performance management system or how to fine-tune the mission statement. In a context in which trade unions have been marginalized, where strikes are at their lowest level since records began, where collectively agreed terms and conditions now cover the minority of the total workforce, where a veritable welter of legislation has diluted the force of the unions – yet where, none the less, the economy has continued to deteriorate, there clearly has to be a fundamental re-think about what are the issues that need attending to most centrally.

The real issues, we suspect, go to the very heart of this book. There has been a widespread and understandable assumption that progress could be made by escaping from a collectivized, procedure-based and strife-ridden industrial relations model to an individualized, flexible and strife-free 'human resource' model. To this extent the non-union sector seemed to proffer a state of affairs with some attractions. Even as perceptive an analyst as David Guest (1989) appeared to be moving to a position which (a) saw HRM as a source of competitive advantage and yet (b) viewed it as hardly attainable in the unionized sector. In fact, as the most recent workplace industrial relations survey makes evident, the elements of HRM which have taken root in Britain (direct and extensive employee communications; participation and involvement and so on) ironically have done so largely within unionized firms. The union-free sector has, in large measure, failed to introduce the new initiatives. The real danger in Britain is that it will experience a backward slide to employment policies and practices which have all the starkness of the infamous Grunwick photo-processing company (details of this case can be found in Rogaly, 1977). If this were to happen, all the brave talk of 'winning commitment' and 'total quality' would become, in effect, irrelevant. Likewise, fine reticulations of the contradictions inherent in the full-blown HRM model would also badly miss the point.

That point is that for wide tranches of management the essential problem is to stem the back-tide. Faced with the kind of economic difficulties and the downward spiral described earlier, the real danger is that far too many British companies will be tempted by the simple cost-cutting option. Contracting-out, further marginalization of unions, peremptory or no appraisals, miserly training and development opportunities and a general lowering of standards and expectations: these are the imminent issues.

Of course, not all British managers face these stark conditions. There are many in union and non-union firms alike who are forging ahead with some or even all of the innovative policies and approaches described throughout this book. In recognition of this point we do not seek to suggest that there is one all-encompassing message for all sections of the managerial audience. Some of the readers of this book will, with justification, be able to claim that they are doing practically all of the leading-edge activities described here and elsewhere. But our experience suggests that for every one of these there are 10 other managers who are having to work very hard just to survive. For this latter group the need to be wary of becoming trapped in the downward spiral of low quality markets is the central message. Steps to stem the tide and then to begin to reverse it entail a fundamental rearrangement of relations with trade unions, a balance between individually targeted employment practices and collectively mediated policies, a recognition of the seriousness of the industrial relations issue, a focus on quality products and processes and an attendant set of policies to build a quality workforce.

Certainly there is an understandable temptation to 'move faster' by seeking to press ahead with human resource initiatives without any recourse at all to the union. But whether this will actually prove to be faster in the medium and longer term is a very moot point.

Attainment of a quality workforce capable of competing in world markets means paying attention to the fundamentals of devising and practising a mutually reinforcing set of employment practices which ensure that HR planning is actually done, that appropriate selection methods are used, that the performance management elements of goal-setting, communication, appraisal and reward are tackled in a way which fit the business needs. It means also that employee trust, commitment and capability are ratcheted upwards (rather than downwards) on a continual basis.

Who should be doing all this? Whose responsibility is it to take on board such prescriptions and to act upon them? At present a fundamental flaw in British HR/IR provision is the lack of a clear answer to these sorts of questions. There needs to be a sorting out of the respective responsibilities of headquarters, divisions and business units. In similar vein, the ambiguity of the respective roles of human resource/industrial relations specialists and line managers for HR/IR matters is a continuing source of weakness when it comes to stemming the backward slide discussed above. We are not referring here simply to the level of comfort or discomfort felt by personnel specialists and operational managers with their respective allotted roles. Rather, the issue is the extent to which the kind of forward-looking, mutually reinforcing initiatives discussed throughout this book are falling through the interstices.

## Individualism and collectivism: finding the balance

A distinctive feature of this book has been the attempt to break away from the conventional segmentation which results in books on 'personnel management' and separate books on 'industrial relations'. Our aim has been to reflect the trends in practice whereby initiatives engage with, and have implications for, both sets of activity. We now need to return centrally to this issue of the interplay between individualism and collectivism and then, from this, we want to focus debate upon a new agenda for the management of HR and IR.

Overall, there has been a secular drift towards 'individualistic' aspects in recent employer initiatives. These have included such elements as individual appraisal, individual goal-setting and individualized payment systems. At the same time there has been a movement away from previously prevailing 'collectivist' aspects such as extended collective bargaining, jointly agreed procedures and reliance upon communications through the trade union channel (Beaumont, 1991; Morris and Wood, 1991; Storey, 1992). As we saw in Chapter 9, instances of de-recognition, although growing, have been relatively rare. This generalization is especially true if one discounts small independent establishments. The current state of affairs therefore, entails the new individualistically oriented employer-led initiatives being pursued alongside a collectivist/procedure-based system inherited from previous decades. It seems to us that few employers have worked out an effective articulation between these two systems.

In the British context it appears unlikely that a wholesale adoption of a totally individual-based employment system is feasible for the main body of organizations. This is especially true in the public sector where requirements of comprehensive and universal coverage and of standardized levels of service obtain. But it is significantly true also for the larger private sector organizations which in the main do not have the wherewithal to emulate IBM or Marks and Spencer other than in a most superficial way. Marks and Spencer's sophisticated human relations policies cost a great deal of money. This company has positioned itself in the product market in such a way that it can afford to invest the required sums in employee services. It also has built up its managerial expertise over many years in a consistent way to ensure effective utilization of this investment. Few other firms are presently capable of following suit. On the contrary, there is even a distinct danger that standards of customer service will actually decline as large organizations abandon their consensual systems in favour of cut-down versions of certain well-publicized yet singular cases such as Disney. For example, the clearing banks have begun such a move. Despite all the talk of 'customer care', however, the levels of complaints continue to rise and banks have rarely been so unpopular. Similarly, health care institutions, electricity companies and others, have embarked on a headlong rush to disentangle themselves from their previous arrangements in favour of 'the new'. But the quality of analysis concerning what should appropriately constitute the 'new' often leaves much to be desired. One bank chief told us recently that he wanted to dispense with the long-standing collective 'cosy' arrangements in favour of the sorts of customer service 'built around lapel-badges and employee of the month awards which I believe works so well for McDonald's and Disney'.

But neither is there much scope for a return to a Donovan-style recipe. In the new competitive environment, the analyses and prescriptions advanced in the 1950s, 1960s and 1970s (see, for example, Clegg, 1970; Flanders, 1970a, b and c; McCarthy and Ellis, 1973; McCarthy, 1976), are also inappropriate. The insistence on the 'single channel' whereby negotiations, consultations, communication and participation would be handled through the medium of the trade union is unlikely to be viable. Under the new conditions, the requirements for adaptability, speed of response, and for direct effective communications mean that the traditional system will have to adapt.

Conformance to 'rules' (whether jointly agreed or otherwise) will no longer be sufficient for enterprise survival. Our bank chief was, to an extent, correct – individual commitment and effective performance at all levels are needed. It was his simplistic solutions which were poorly grounded.

So, what might be the way forward? This, we suggest, has to rest upon *both individualism and collectivism*. There is some truth in the message about empowerment, of the need to encourage individuals to identify opportunities and to pursue them; and there will be a need to build environments and cultures which encourage highly competent organizational members to excel above the norm. If there are a plethora of rules, procedures, customs and practices and accompanying attitudes which stymie productive behaviour and high performance, then the economy will be left behind. But there is an equal danger in taking all this too far without paying due regard to the abuses, cynicism and arbitrariness which can too easily emerge under such conditions unless checked by some regulative mechanism. The central issue then, is to find this balance.

While a definite prescriptive package is at this stage by no means easy to construct, the elements of one scenario might at least be identified. Three features seem to be critical and they each involve a clear acceptance of strategic responsibility at company level. They cover: a company-level commitment to relationship-building; a clarification of the nature of the relationship being worked towards; and a systematic identification of the actual mechanisms to be developed in order to conduct that relationship on an ongoing basis. These three elements together cover the who, what and how.

The first of these concerns the question of who is responsible and at what level for the HR and IR stance. As we have seen throughout this book, the British system is riven with ambiguity. Re-structuring often means that much responsibility is devolved to operating units. At the same time, the lateral responsibility between HR/IR specialists and line managers has become increasingly blurred. One consequence of this fluidity has been massive equivocation about fundamentals. Is there a corporate stance or philosophy on HR/IR or is this something to be determined severally by the business units? In the light of the analysis in previous chapters, our suggestion is that the company or organization should be the level at which HR/IR strategy ought to be developed. Managers from individual units need to be involved and they should have primary responsibility for operating decisions. It is too much, however, to expect them to be responsible for developing strategy on their own especially if, at the same time, the division or headquarters is going to impose financial targets on them that effectively crowd out attention to the medium and long term. It also does not maximize the advantages of belonging to a multi-unit organization in terms of experience and expertise. In many organizations making explicit what is already the reality – whatever the apparent 'de-centralization of bargaining' might imply – would be a bonus in itself: it would save a great deal of time and energy as well as removing much of the ambiguity about how much autonomy the individual unit really has.

Second, having resolved the equivocation about responsibilities, there is a need in many cases to reassess the relationship with trade unions at company and organization-level. We appreciate that in many organizations this is a taboo issue – trade unions are to be kept as far away as possible from the levels where the serious decisions are made. The experience of those managements that have maintained relationships with trade unions above the individual units, however, suggests that the advantages considerably outweigh any disadvantages. Trade union involvement in the general direction of HR/IR developments can smooth many of the wrinkles that might otherwise emerge in the individual units. It also does not necessarily follow either that a joint approach at the organization level means that the bargaining has to take place at this level as well. There is a tendency to forget that employees and their representatives value their autonomy as much as managers do.

The third element we identified concerns actual mechanisms. Here, we propose that the parties might place high on their agenda a review of the merits of separating-out joint regulation (collective bargaining) from the wider-frame 'jointism' which can occur by using a works council. Two models might be investigated as a starting point. One is the German, in which the works council is made up of employee representatives only. The other is the French, in which the works council is a joint management–employee representative body. Experience in both countries suggests that the separation of roles that such bodies involve can facilitate serious joint management–worker discussions of critical issues including product-markets, investment, and operational improvements. If they want proof, those UK managements working in international companies simply have to look to their German or French operations.

We recognize of course that, although the principles have a general application, the target group for this particular programme is mainly the large, multi-site already-unionized organizations. Our reason for focusing on them is that they set the tone for HR and IR in the UK. We appreciate too that many of these organizations have been equivocating for a decade or more about the future role of collectivism – and even about the future existence of unions. As the contents of this book have hopefully indicated, however, this kind of agenda is not entirely fanciful. The IPA initiative and the number of senior trade union figures and employers who were prepared publicly to register support for the principles of cooperation, illustrate the possibilities. At company level, the Rover 'New Deal' is significant. This includes a commitment to no compulsory redundancies, flexible working, and, as the personnel operations director put it, a new and increased role for shop stewards. In other words, the successful package comprises a mixture of individualistic and collectivistic elements.

Our main concern throughout the book has been with what UK managers can do for themselves to improve their management of human resources. But of course we recognise that many of the proposals and suggestions would have a much better chance of success if set within a suitable national HR/IR framework. Writing of the USA, which suffers from many of the structural impediments to investing in people that the UK does, Tom Kochan, the President of the International Industrial Relations Association (Kochan and Dyer, 1992) has recently argued that it is unrealistic to expect individual companies to make the kind of changes that are required on their own – the pressures to 'short-termism' are simply too great. What is needed, he suggests, is for a coalition of stakeholders, including management, trade unions and government, working together to bring about change.

Given the analysis in Chapter 2, the argument for a similar approach in the UK is as strong if not stronger than in the USA. Above all, it is time that the government radically reviewed its approach to the legal framework of HR/IR as it has done in the case of its economic policy since the withdrawal from the Exchange Rate Mechanism in September 1992. The evidence from WIRS seems to confirm that, if the aim is to achieve a 'high skill, high pay, high productivity' economy, the policy of deregulating the labour market is having the opposite effect. It has not only been sending the totally wrong signals; it has failed to take into account that, left to their own devices, many UK managements will take the 'low quality-low cost' route with damaging consequences for training, skills, and so on. By the same token, if the government believes that it is right and proper that management should communicate with employees and should encourage their participation and involvement, it should not be afraid to legislate to help bring about these practices. Otherwise, again, left to their own devices, many UK managements are likely to do little more than pay lip-service to the desired state. As well as doing what they can within their own organizations to bring about improvements then, those managers who are serious about change should be putting pressure on government to play its part. Finding the right balance between individualism and collectivism will require some action here too. The strategic vision required at this level is, however, an issue which would need full-length analysis in its own right.

None the less, as our analysis throughout the book suggests, the degree of urgency is now such that continued equivocation at the organizational level is a luxury that can no longer be afforded. The time to seek-out the appropriate balance between individualism and collectivism has now arrived. Further delay in evading this issue could in fact turn out to be the most costly choice of all.

# APPENDIX:
# AUDITING HR AND IR
# STRATEGIES

This appendix presents a framework which should be of practical use in reviewing and putting into practice the operation of many of the ideas which have appeared in the main body of the book. The focus is on the auditing of HR and IR activities. Auditing in this context is concerned with the gathering of information, analysing information, and then deciding what actions need to be taken to improve performance. Two main aspects are involved. One is the effectiveness of the organization's approach to HR and IR matters, i.e. the extent to which it is achieving the objectives it has set itself. The other is the efficiency of its approach, which involves some judgement about the relative costs and benefits of what it is doing.

We begin by discussing the reasons why the auditing of HR and IR activities is becoming important. In the next two sections we look at ways of assessing the effectiveness of the organization's approach to managing HR and IR and, much more controversially, of measuring the efficiency of HR and IR policies and practices. We go on to emphasize the increasing importance of benchmarking, using international comparisons, to judge the relative performance of HR and IR activities. In the final section we suggest an approach which organizations might use in auditing the specialist personnel department.

## Why auditing is important

Clearly, there is nothing new about senior managers wanting to know how well an organization is meeting its objectives and how efficient it is in the use of resources. This is plain common sense. The total quality management (TQM) movement sweeping the UK, coupled with the intense international pressure that many UK companies are under, has, however, given such activities a new urgency. Programmes in any area of management activity have to be justified. There is considerable pressure to seek continuous improvement at the same time as to reduce costs – or, as Kanter (1990) puts it, there is a drive for 'doing more with less'.

A particular reason for auditing in the case of functions such as HR and IR, which are regarded as staff or support activities, is that the organization is in a better position to know how to handle the activities involved. Two key questions are increasingly being asked. One is whether or not the organization should itself be undertaking the activity or whether it should externalize it – whether, to pick up the discussion in Chapter 4, it should handle it through 'hierarchy' or the 'market'. The second, even if the response is in the affirmative, is to ask about the basis on which the function is to be organized. This is especially true in the large multi-establishment organizations which are so dominant in the UK; the development of internal markets in which goods and services are traded between divisions as well as between head-quarters and divisions is giving rise to a variety of arrangements. We give examples of these, in the case of specialist HR and IR activities, in the final section.

One of the reasons why auditing is especially important in the case of HR and IR is that the expenditure on people is substantial. In the case of the National Health Service, for example, it amounts to between 75 per cent and 80 per cent of the total budget. Deciding between different policies and practices is therefore critical as is ensuring that the expenditure involved can be fully justified; which helps to explain why many of the recent initiatives in auditing on which this appendix draws come from the NHS and local government.

Another reason why auditing is especially important in HR and IR is that, for the reasons discussed in Chapter 2, there exists an enormous gap in many organizations between the rhetoric and the reality of top management commitment to the significance attached to the management of people. Thus, while it is increasingly accepted that the management of people is the key to competitive success, very often insufficient time and resources are devoted to HR and IR activities. Crucially, the financial pressures that many UK companies are under leads them to adopt the short-term perspective which is so inimical to serious investment in their human capital. In short, anything that helps to remind senior managers of the medium, let alone long-term damage that existing approaches are causing, has to be a good thing.

In the circumstances, auditing is not only a valuable tool for assessing effectiveness and measuring performance, it also provides an important opportunity to do the following: to get managers generally to develop a better understanding of IR/HR issues and, in particular, their importance and the contribution they make to the performance of the organization; to identify and decide priorities; to get a clearer understanding of roles and responsibilities in the area; and to help them make decisions about the best ways of delivering HR/IR activities. A final, and increasingly significant, reason for auditing IR and HR is public policy. Already in key areas, such as equal opportunities, organizations need to be able to demonstrate conformity to legislation in the event of their practices being challenged before industrial tribunals. In others, such as discipline and dismissal, they may also have to demonstrate that their actions are reasonable in the circumstances and therefore consistent with previous decisions. Many organizations, moreover, make a positive point of stressing their commitment to the principles enshrined in social legislation in their publicity material. This makes it especially important that they are able to demonstrate their systematic conformity to good practice.

## Assessing effectiveness

How might managers go about auditingtheir approach to HR and IR? The first of the two processes involved, the assessment of effectiveness, is largely subjective and involves judgements about the extent to which the organization is meeting the objectives it has set for itself. Most organizations typically have means to elicit the views of employees about the effectiveness of their policies and approaches to managing HR/IR. For example, a properly conducted appraisal of the kind discussed in Chapter 6 will reveal a great deal about these matters as will an effective two-way system of communication. Other sources of opinion about these matters are exit interviews and regular attitude surveys.

It is strongly recommended, however, for the reasons already given, that senior managers themselves, either individually or in teams, undertake a regular review across the full range of policies and practices to ensure that the reality matches up to the aspirations.

Two very practical guides will be used to show how this might be done. The first, *Strategic Planning for People*, was produced by a working party of the National Economic Development Office and the Manpower Services Commission as part of the 'People: the Key Success' initiative. The second, the *Human Resource Management Audit*, is published by the North Western and West Midlands Regional Health Authorities.

### *Strategic planning for people*

This is a simple diagnostic exercise to be carried out preferably by the chief executive and senior managers. It requires a response to four main questions:

1 What are our strategic objectives?
2 What strengths in our approach to people may help achievement?
3 What weaknesses in our approach to people may hinder achievement?
4 What action is indicated as a result of the above in order to build on strengths or to correct weaknesses in our approach to people?

A central tool is the questionnaire shown in Figure A.1.

Managing human resources and industrial relations

| Questionnaire | Yes | No |
|---|---|---|
| **1. Is there a clearly understood HRM strategy?** | ☐ | ☐ |
| 1.1 Is this strategy known and understood by all managers? | ☐ | ☐ |
| 1.2 Does this strategy support and fit in with the business strategy? | ☐ | ☐ |
| 1.3 Is the HRM strategy regularly reviewed? | ☐ | ☐ |
| 1.4 Is the strategy consistent with the organization mission? | ☐ | ☐ |
| 1.5 Are the values associated with the strategy consistent with the values of the organization's mission? | ☐ | ☐ |
| 1.6 Is the HRM strategy consistent with other functional strategies? | ☐ | ☐ |
| **2. Are people seen as a strategic resource by senior management?** | ☐ | ☐ |
| 2.1 Does the business plan demonstrate a belief that human resources are a valuable source of competitive advantage? | ☐ | ☐ |
| 2.2 Do managers at all levels manage their staff in a way that recognizes their role in strategy implementation? | ☐ | ☐ |
| 2.3 Do management training and development programmes take account of the need for all managers to think and behave strategically? | ☐ | ☐ |
| 2.4 Does senior management take a long-term view of human resource issues? | ☐ | ☐ |
| **3. Are there clearly understood strategies for the main elements of HRM?** | ☐ | ☐ |
| 3.1 Are these strategies integrated and mutually supportive? | ☐ | ☐ |
| 3.2 Do these strategies focus on improving individual and organizational performance? | ☐ | ☐ |
| 3.3 Have strategies been formulated for all the main elements of HRM? | ☐ | ☐ |

| Questionnaire | Yes | No |
|---|:---:|:---:|
| 3.4 Are the values of these strategies consistent with the values of the overall HRM strategy? | ☐ | ☐ |
| 3.5 Are these strategies tested by developing feasible implementation plans? | ☐ | ☐ |
| 3.6 Are these strategies consistent with other functional strategies? | ☐ | ☐ |
| **4. Does human resource planning (HRP) take account of internal and external environmental factors?** | ☐ | ☐ |
| 4.1 During the business planning process is a SWOT analysis carried out on human resources? | ☐ | ☐ |
| 4.2 Does HRP take account of long-term environmental trends? | ☐ | ☐ |
| 4.3 Are short- and medium-term HR plans consistent with longer term plans and forecasts? | ☐ | ☐ |
| 4.4 Are appropriate forecasting techniques used in HRP? | ☐ | ☐ |
| 4.5 Does HRP represent a proactive, as well as reactive, approach to the future? | ☐ | ☐ |
| **5. Does the personnel function have a strategic role in HRM?** | ☐ | ☐ |
| 5.1 Does the most senior personnel manager help formulate business strategy? | ☐ | ☐ |
| 5.2 Does the personnel department have a strategy for the delivery of its services? | ☐ | ☐ |
| 5.3 Is the strategic role of the personnel department understood by both personnel staff and the line managers? | ☐ | ☐ |
| 5.4 Does the personnel department's strategy focus on ensuring successful implementation of the organization's HRM strategies? | ☐ | ☐ |

**Figure A.1** Strategic human resource management audit

The exercise then involves the identification of the improvements needed under key areas of HR and IR such as leadership, involvement and communications, training and development, performance management, and pay and conditions. For each area, there is encouragement to spell out what improvements are required, by when and by whom.

### The Human Resource Management Audit

This second instrument is a much more detailed guide which is intended to provide managers with a framework to be adapted to suit their particular circumstances. The guide as a whole is strongly recommended reading for serious students of this subject, but two sections are especially relevant to the present discussion and these concern analysing strategy and assessing performance.

#### Analysing strategy

A first step is to assess the extent to which a strategic approach of the kind that has been advocated throughout this book is a reality. Put simply it involves the design of a questionnaire similar to that which is shown in Figure A.1.

Clearly, if there is a negative answer to any of the primary questions, there must be serious doubts about any claim to have a strategic approach. If any of the secondary questions elicits a negative answer, there will be a need to understand the reasons and to formulate an appropriate response, which might draw on one or all of the levers of change which have been discussed in earlier chapters. Those who have to draw up an HR and IR strategy from scratch are advised to consult the guide prepared by West Midlands Regional Health Authority (Collins, 1991).

It will be seen that the list of questions refers to one of the key issues touched on in Chapter 8, namely values. A section of the guide shows how to review the values which drive IR/HR strategy management. Figure A.2 suggests the main steps that managers need to go through. At each step, it is suggested, the following question should be asked: what assumptions can we make about our beliefs in how we should manage human resources and the way in which people should be treated?

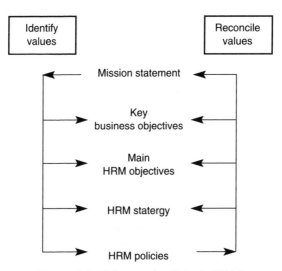

**Figure A.2** Values and policies in HRM

Managers are also advised to reconcile the values identified at any particular step to ensure that they are both integrated and complementary.

The guide also recommends that a key part of the strategy analysis should be a review of the environmental factors, external and internal, which will influence the management of IR/HR. This explains the reference to a SWOT analysis (strengths, weaknesses, opportunities and threats) in Figure A.1. The purpose of this analysis is to establish whether these factors represent strengths or weaknesses, if internal, and opportunities or threats, if external. Having compared the strengths and weaknesses, and the opportunities and the threats, it should then be possible to decide what, if any, changes need to be made and the priority with which they should be made.

*Assessing performance*
The analysis of strategy is only the starting point. The second step is to assess how the organization is managing IR/HR by comparing actual against desired standards across the full range of HR/IR activities. One way in which this can be done is also by

| The ability of managers to plan the current and future use of human resources is an integral part of their performance review | 1 2 3 4 5 6 7 | Little account is taken of human resource planning in performance review |
|---|---|---|

**Figure A.3** 'Human Resource Planning' – example question

questionnaire. In this case, however, it is suggested that, for each significant activity or process, paired statements are prepared which describe the potential extremes of a performance range. Performance is then rated by using a discrete numbered scale, with an odd number of intervals, so that an average standard of performance can be identified. Two examples, dealing with 'Human Resource Planning' and 'Employee Relations' respectively, are shown in Figures A.3 and A.4.

| The involvement of trade unions in improving productivity is encouraged on the basis of shared responsibility and shared rewards | 1 2 3 4 5 6 7 | Management considers action to improve productivity to be its sole responsibility |
|---|---|---|

**Figure A.4** 'Employee Relations' – example question

Clearly, such an exercise is very subjective. It does have value, however, in enabling the organization to gather and analyse information about the effectiveness of what it is doing in a systematic way. It is also a useful way of involving senior managers in getting a better understanding of the significance of IR and HR issues.

Another approach to assessing effectiveness is to set objectives in quantifiable terms and then to measure achievement against target. Below are examples of the measures suggested in the West Midlands Regional Health Authority guide with reference to what is generally regarded as the relatively 'soft' area of communications:

1 The timeliness of written reports following team briefings or surveys.
2 The quality of written reports measured by the number of employee complaints or queries per report.
3 The frequency of team briefings.
4 The level of employee understanding measured by the proportion of employees with the required level of understanding.
5 The level of employee satisfaction measured by the ratio of satisfactory to unsatisfactory employee evaluations.
6 The measurement of the level of feedback.
7 The investment in comunications measured, for example, by the proportion of staff hours devoted to communications. (Collins, 1991: 151–2)

Here there is an inevitable danger that the achievement of the targets becomes an end in itself – with little thought being given to the impact of what is going on. The value of the approach is that it underlines the importance of the activity. It also provides information which can be compared over time or between different departments.

## Costs and benefits

So far, the focus of attention has been on subjective judgements of *effectiveness*. A second concern has been the *efficiency* with which specialist HR/IR departments deliver their services. This latter raises the issue of the measurement of their costs and benefits.

Traditionally, little thought has been given to the costs of not making investments in human capital and personnel managers, for their part, have been reluctant to have their efficiency monitored with quantifiable measures.

Things are changing, however. There is increasing pressure to quantify the contributions in part due to the realization of the potential contribution of HR/IR to competitiveness and partly

| | |
|---|---|
| Leaving | Lost performance of job holder before replacement (measured by loss of revenue or extra costs incurred by others, e.g. overtime or contract labour); redundancy pay and other costs necessitated by legislation; ex-gratia payments; retirement payments; |
| Replacement | pre-recruitment preparation; advertising; candidate evaluation; induction; training; efficiency recovery (i.e. costs of lost performance before reaching standard or previous incumbent, including costs of machinery breakdowns due to inadequate skill, accidents, scrap and defective work); administration; |
| Prevention | 'financial handcuffs'; 'buying off'. |

**Figure A.5**  The costs of labour turnover
*Source*:  Cannon (1979: 100)

due to the devolution of decision-making which prompts the costing of personnel activities.

It is not too difficult to measure the costs of some aspects of HR/IR. For example, Figure A.5, gives the framework for calculating the costs of labour turnover.

But in other areas, especially those which might be described as 'discretionary' problems do arise. The organization does not have to have team briefing, for example. Justifying the time and expense involved in a quantitative way is not as easy as many of the standard textbooks assume. And when it comes to the measurement of the organization's overall IR and HR contribution the problem might be considered virtually insurmountable. This helps to explain why human asset accounting has never taken off despite considerable interest in the 1970s (see, for example, Giles and Robinson, 1972; Flamholz, 1974; Cannon, 1979).

246

However, there has recently been renewed interest in producing 'overall' performance ratings which compare, for example, HR/IR measures with industry averages and/or with set targets or previous performance ratings. It is, for example, eminently feasible to produce ratios of HR/IR specialist staff to total staff, or HR/IR total staff costs measured against total payroll, or even total HR/IR costs measured against profitability. A number of consultants are now very active in this field. It needs to be remembered though that the ratios should only be treated as indicative: the major difficulty remains of unravelling the impact of HR/IR policies from other management activities.

## Benchmarking: the value of international comparisons

In the circumstances, more and more organizations are looking at benchmarking as the best available guide. Benchmarking is simply the process of comparing an organization's performance with that of others to see how it can be improved (Zairi, 1992). The obvious points of comparison are close competitors, but some organizations recommend going beyond to identify best practice wherever it may be found. Thus, Xerox, where benchmarking is credited with being one of the main factors behind the revival in the 1980s, has evaluated organizations as various as railways, insurance and electricity generation (Holberton, 1991: 24). Typically, benchmarking has been used in such areas as new product development involving cross-functional teams. It has tended to exaggerate 'asset management' aspects and underplay or even totally neglect 'people management' aspects. But in principal there is no good reason why it could not become a valuable tool in the area of HR/IR.

It is here that international comparisons come into their own. Improved data about other countries' performance has already been an important catalyst in the thinking of policy-makers. In the case of post-compulsory education, for example, the relatively low staying-on rates for school leavers in Britain have come in for adverse comment (OECD, 1991). In addition, the generally low levels of attainment achieved in education and training in comparison with other countries has been an important factor in the changes in the government's approach to vocational education and training (see Prais, 1990). More generally, there is the data on labour costs and productivity. As the OECD data presented in Chapter 2 of this present book reveals, the UK is now a low wage and low productivity economy.

At company level, the most effective stimulus for auditing HR/IR so far has come from the arrival of Japanese companies in the UK. Their performance levels have helped to destroy some of the myths about the attitudes of British workers and to put the emphasis, more appropriately, on the policies and practices of management. The time spent on selection and on training has given critical food for thought for many UK managements. Similarly, the Japanese companies have shown that the time and effort put into direct participation can pay significant dividends in terms of cutting layers of managers and specialists which have traditionally been associated with the 'control management' approach of the typical UK-owned company.

We would also advise that the great majority of large British companies can look inside as well as outside for useful benchmarks. This is because they typically have operations of their own in other countries (see Sisson et al., 1992). This makes it possible to carry out inter-plant comparisons of their policies and practices. Significantly, many of these companies have plants in countries where there is a much higher degree of employment regulation than is the case in Britain. It would be extremely interesting to compare the practical impact. A good example would be the links between flexibility and employment security. Conventional wisdom in the UK has it that the less regulation, the more flexibility. But the experience of other countries, notably Germany and Japan, would suggest that the opposite may be the case: the greater employment security that employees enjoy, the more they may be willing to be flexible.

## Auditing the HR/IR department

Throughout this appendix, the emphasis has been on HR and IR as a set of activities. In this final section the focus shifts to the specialist department which is usually associated with these activities. The intention is to outline a possible approach to auditing the role and performance of the personnel department. A number of steps are involved:

*Step 1*:  Decide the composition of the audit team. Much depends on circumstances. Clearly there has to be representation from the personnel department and from among senior line managers if the exercise is to have any credibility. It may also help to involve an outside consultant or 'expert'. It is highly questionable, however, whether the audit team should be chaired by the senior personnel manager and be a 'family' affair of the personnel department as Humble (1988: 31) suggests.

*Step 2*: Identify the department's main customers. There are likely to be a number. The key decision, as Humble (1988: 32) points out, is to clarify 'who makes the final decision to buy our service?' In a decentralized multi-divisional organization it is likely to be the general managers of the strategic business units. But for headquarters personnel in 'critical function' organizations such as large retail chain stores and banks, it is likely to be the senior management team itself.

*Step 3*:  Review the HR department's mission. The West Midlands Regional Health Authority audit tool-kit will again be found useful here. It lists more than a dozen questions which are designed to arrive at a statement describing the 'reason for the personnel department's existence, its principal activities and its most important values' (Collins, 1991: 175–7).

*Step 4*:  Review the department's role in formulating the organization's strategy. The list of questions in Figure A.1 above are relevant here. This step will also be immensely valuable in establishing the links between HR and IR strategy, on the one hand, and the organization's overall strategy, on the other. If for example, the senior HR manager is not on the main board, and is not involved in formulating the organization's overall strategy, there must be a major question mark hanging over the status of any HR and IR strategy in which he or she is involved in drawing up.

*Step 5*:  Review the department role in developing key HR and IR policies and practices. Questions need to be asked here in relation to all of the main issues covered throughout this book including, for example, human resource planning, recruitment, selection and retention, training and development, performance management, and industrial relations. A particular point to note during this step is to ensure that HR and IR policies and practices are 'owned' by line managers as well as the personnel department.

*Step 6*: Review the delivery of personnel policies and practices: are there HR and IR activities currently being undertaken by personnel managers which could be done as well or better by line managers? Are there technically better ways of delivering HR and IR service currently being undertaken by personnel managers, e.g. computerized data bases which could be accessed by line managers? Are there HR and IR activities currently being undertaken by personnel managers which could be done better or more efficiently by external agencies? Are there superior ways of organizing the HR and IR activities for which the personnel department is going to be responsible, e.g. the 'in-house' agency, the 'internal consultancy', the 'business within a business'? Is the structure of the personnel department and the skills and experience of its staff appropriate to the service for which it is going to be directly responsible?

*Step 7*: Make external comparisons to establish 'best' practice. As Humble (1988: 33) points out, it does not require an 'espionage' system to get the data: articles in such publications as *Personnel Management*, *Personnel Today*, *Incomes Data Services* and *Industrial Relations Review and Report* carry a great deal of useful material as do job advertisements, recruitment brochures and annual reports. The comparator organizations do not only have to be sought among close competitors. Indeed, as the example of Xerox quoted in the previous section suggests, there are benefits in extending the analysis beyond such a group.

*Step 8*: Review the outcomes of the analysis and the policy implications with 'customers'.

*Step 9*: Implement agreed improvements.

One recent survey (Adams, 1991; RDR, 1991) identified four main ways in which the delivery of HR/IR activities could be conducted:

1 The 'in-house' agency, in which the personnel department or some of its activities – for example, graduate recruitment – is seen as a cost centre and its activities are cross-charged to other departments or divisions.
2 The 'internal consultancy' in which the personnel department sells its services to the parent organization or its units – the implication being that managers in the parent organization will enjoy some freedom in deciding to go elsewhere if they are not happy with the service that is being provided.
3 The 'business within a business' in which some of the activities of the function are formed into a quasi-independent organization which may trade not only with the parent organization and its units, but also externally.
4 The 'external consultancy' in which the organization and its units go outside to completely independent business for help and advice on IR and HR matters.

These four alternatives to the traditional IR and HR department can be seen as constituting a 'scale of increasing degrees of externalization, understood as the application of market forces to the delivery of personnel activities' (Adams, 1991: 44). Common to each of them, however, is some kind of service contract in which there is charging for the services delivered.

The local authorities have been especially active in the construction of so-called 'service level agreements' for personnel as well as other functions. Kent County Council has drawn a distinction between those centrally-provided personnel activities which support the provision of direct services, and those which serve corporate requirements. Individual service departments are taking responsibility for all the resources which contribute to running their departments and there is a process of negotiation and agreement with the 'provider' personnel department within the context of a medium term planning cycle. Only the resources associated with those activities primarily concerned with the strategic functions of the council remain with the corporate personnel department (Griffiths, 1989).

## Conclusion

Any serious consideration of the topic 'managing human resources and industrial relations' inevitably involves a critical
review of current practice. This has indeed been a feature
throughout the book. In this appendix we have sought to
continue this but, in addition, to switch the emphasis onto a
positive, practical, plane by showing how a practitioner, persuaded perhaps by the analysis in the main body of the book,
might set about the process of reform at the organizational level.
The practical steps outlined re-confirm one of the messages of the
book as a whole – there are no easy quick-fixes to be found for this
realm of management. None the less, the appendix does reveal
that there are a great many things that can be done to ensure that
the adage that 'people are our most important asset' becomes
something more than a shibboleth.

# BIBLIOGRAPHY

Adams, J., Hayes, J. and Hopson, B. (1976) *Transitions: Understanding and Managing Personal Change*. Oxford: Martin Robertson.

Adams, K. (1991) Externalisation vs specialisation, *Human Resource Management Journal*, 1(4), Summer 40–54.

Addams, H. L. and Embley, K. (1988) Performance management systems: from strategic planning to employee productivity, *Personnel*, 64(4), 55–60.

Advisory, Conciliation and Arbitration Service (ACAS) (1983) *Collective Bargaining in Britain: Its Extent and Level*. Discussion Paper No. 2. London: ACAS.

Advisory, Conciliation and Arbitration Service (ACAS) (1984) *Annual Report*. London: ACAS.

Advisory, Conciliation and Arbitration Service (ACAS) (1985) *Introduction to Payment Systems*. Advisory Booklet No. 2. London: ACAS.

Advisory, Conciliation and Arbitration Service (ACAS) (1987) *Annual Report*. London: HMSO.

Advisory, Conciliation and Arbitration Service (ACAS) (1988a) *Developments in Payment Systems*. Occasional Paper No. 45. London: ACAS.

Advisory, Conciliation and Arbitration Service (ACAS) (1988b) *Employee Appraisal*. Advisory Booklet No. 11. London: ACAS.

Advisory, Conciliation and Arbitration Service (ACAS) (1988c) *Appraisal Related Pay*. Advisory Booklet No. 14. London: ACAS.

Advisory, Conciliation and Arbitration Service (ACAS) (1988d) *Labour Flexibility in Britain*. Occasional Paper No. 41. London: ACAS.

Advisory, Conciliation and Arbitration Service (ACAS) (1991) *Consultation and Communication: The 1990 ACAS Survey*. Occasional Paper No. 49. London: ACAS.

Advisory, Conciliation and Arbitration Service (ACAS) (1992) *Annual Report*. London: ACAS.

Ahlstrand, B. and Purcell, J. (1988) Employee relations strategy in the multi-divisional company, *Personnel Review*, 17(3), 1–18.

Alexander, G. P. (1987) Establishing shared values through management training, *Training and Development Journal*, 41(2), 45–6.

Armstrong, M. (ed.) (1992a) *Strategies for Human Resource Management: A Total Business Approach*. London: Kogan Page.

Armstrong, M. (1992b) *Human Resource Management: Strategy and Action*. London: Kogan Page.

Armstrong, P. (1989) Limits and possibilities for HRM in an age of management accountancy, in J. Storey (ed.), *New Perspectives on Human Resource Management*. London: Routledge.

Atkinson, J. (1984) Manpower strategies for flexible organizations, *Personnel Management*, August, 28–31.

Atkinson, J. (1985) Flexibility: planning for an uncertain future, *Manpower Policy and Practice*, 1, Summer, 25–30.

Atkinson, J. (1989) Four stages of response to the demographic downturn, *Personnel Management*, August, 20–4.

Atkinson, J. and Meager, N. (1986) Is flexibility just a flash in the pan? *Personnel Management*, September, 3–6.

Baird, L. and Meshoulam, I. (1988) Managing two fits of strategic human resource management, *Academy of Management Review*, 13(1), 116–28.

Barbash, J. (1979) The American ideology of industrial relations, *Proceedings of Industrial Relations Research Association*, 30(8), 453–7.

Bassett, P. (1986) *Strike Free: New Industrial Relations in Britain*. London: Macmillan.

Bate, P. (1992) The impact of organizational culture on approaches to organizational problem-solving, in G. Salaman (ed.), *Human Resource Strategies*. London: Sage.

Beaumont, P. B. (1991) Trade unions and HRM, *Industrial Relations Journal*, 22(4), 300–8.

Beckhard, R. (1989) A model for the executive management of transformational change, in J. W. Pfeiffer (ed.), *The 1989 Annual: Developing Human Resources*.

Beer, M. and Spector, B. (eds) (1985) *Readings in Human Resource Management*. New York: Free Press.

Beer, M., Spector, B., Lawrence, P. R. et al. (1984) *Managing Human Assets*, New York: The Free Press.

# Bibliography

Beer, M., Spector, B., Lawrence, P. R. et al. (1985) *Human Resource Mangement: A General Manager's Perspective*. Glencoe IL: Free Press.

Bevan, S. and Thompson, M. (1991) Performance management at the crossroads, *Personnel Management*, November, 36–9.

Bevan, S. and Thompson, M. (1992) An overview of policy and practice, *Performance Management: An Analysis of the Issues*. London: Institute of Personnel Management.

Blissett, E. and Sisson, K. (1989) *Pay System Practices Labour Flexibility in the UK*. Paper presented for the International Labour Office, Coventry, University of Warwick, Industrial Relations Research Unit, mimeo.

Boxall, P. F. (1992) Strategic human resource management: beginnings of a new orthodoxy? *Human Resource Management Journal*, 2(3), 66–79.

Brading, E. and Wright, V. (1990) Performance-related pay, *Personnel Management Factsheets*, No. 30. London: Personnel Publications.

Brandt, S. (1989) When HMS Enterprise hits troubled waters, *Director*, 43(4), 141–5.

Brown, W. A. (1989) Managing remuneration, in K. Sisson (ed.), *Personnel Management in Britain*. Oxford: Blackwell.

BTEC (1992) General National Vocational Qualifications, a press release from the Business and Technical Education Council, London, 10 November.

Buchanan, D. (1992) High performance: new boundaries of acceptability in worker control, in G. Salaman (ed.), *Human Resource Strategies*. London: Sage.

Buchanan, D. (1993) Principles and practice in work design, in K. Sisson (ed.), *Personnel Management in Britain* (2nd edn). Oxford: Blackwell.

Buchanan, D. and McCalman, J. (1989) *High Performance Work Systems: The Digital Experience*. London: Routledge.

Buchanan, D. and Preston, D. (1992) Life in the cell: supervision and teamwork in a manufacturing systems engineering environment, *Human Resource Management Journal*, 2(4), 55–76.

Bullock, R. J. and Batten, D. (1985) It's just a phase we're going through: a review and synthesis of OD phase analysis, *Group and Organization Studies*, 10, 383–412.

Burns, T. and Stalker, G. M. (1961) *The Management of Innovation*, London: Tavistock.

*Business Week* (1989) Go team: the pay-off from teamwork, *Business Week*, 10 July, 35–8.

Butler, P. F. (1988) Successful partnerships: HR and strategic planning in eight top firms, *Organizational Dynamics*, Fall, 27–43.

Campbell, A. (1989) Does your organization need a mission? *Leadership and Organizational Development Journal*, 10(3), 3–9.

Campbell, A. and Yeung, S. (1991a) Brief case: mission, values and strategic intent, *Long Range Planning*, 24(4), 145–7.

Campbell, A. and Yeung, S. (1991b) Creating a sense of mission, *Long Range Planning*, 24, (1), 10–20.

Cannon, J. (1979) *Cost Effective Personnel Decisions*. London: Institute of Personnel Management.

Carnall, C. (1990) *Managing Change in Organizations*. Hemel Hempstead: Prentice Hall.

Carrington, L. (1991a) Investing in opinion, *Personnel Today*, 19 March, 30–2.

Carrington, L. (1991b) Working as a team member, *Personnel Today*, 22 January, 38–9.

Cassels, J. (1989) Facing the demographic challenge, *Personnel Management*, November, 6–7.

Chandler, A. D. (1962) *Strategy and Structure*. Cambridge, MA: MIT Press.

Channon, D. (1982) Industrial structure, *Long Range Planning*, 15(5), 2–20.

Clegg, H. A. (1970) *The System of Industrial Relations in Great Britain* (2nd edn 1972; 3rd edn 1976). Oxford: Blackwell.

Coates, J. (1991) Objectives, missions and performance measures in multinationals, *European Management Journal*, 9(4), 3–11.

Collard, R. (1989) *Total Quality: Success Through People*. London: Institute of Personnel Management.

Collard, R. and Dale, B. (1989) Quality circles, in K. Sisson (ed.), *Personnel Management*. Oxford: Blackwell.

Collins, J. and Porras, J. (1991) Organization, vision and visionary organization, *California Management Review*, 34(1), 40–9.

Collins, M. (1991) *Human Resource Management Audit*. Birmingham: North Western and West Midlands Regional Health Authorities.

Commission on Industrial Relations (CIR) (1974) *Industrial Relations in Multi-Plant Undertakings*, Report No. 85. London: HMSO.

Confederation of British Industry (1989a) *Towards a Skills Revolution*. London: CBI.

Confederation of British Industry (1989b) *A Europe of Opportunities for All*. London: CBI.

Confederation of British Industry (1990) *Involvement: Shaping the Future for Business*. London: CBI.

Confederation of British Industry (1991) *Competing with the World's Best – The Report of the CBI Manufacturing Advisory Group*. London: CBI.

Connock, S. (1991) *HR Vision*. London: Institute of Personnel Management.

Coopers and Lybrand Associates (1985) *A Challenge to Complacency:*

*Changing Attitudes to Training*. London: Manpower Services Commission.

Courtis, J. (1985) *The IPM Guide to Cost-Effective Recruitment* (2nd edn). London: Institute of Personnel Management.

Crosby, P. (1979) *Quality is Free*. New York: McGraw-Hill.

Cross, M. (1988) Changes in working practices in UK manufacturing, *Industrial Relations Review and Report*, No. 414, 2–10.

Cross, M. (1990) *Changing Job Structures*. Oxford: Heinemann.

Cummings, T. G. and Huse, E. F. (1989) *Organization Development and Change*. St Paul, MN: West Publishing.

Dale, B. G. (1991) Total quality management: what are the main difficulties? *The TQM Magazine*, 3(2), 6–8.

Dale, B. G. and Cooper, C. (1992) *Total Quality Management and Human Resources*. Oxford: Blackwell.

Dale, B. G. and Lees, J. (1986) *The Development of Quality Circles*. Sheffield: Manpower Services Commission.

Daniel, W. W. (1987) *Workplace Industrial Relations and Technical Change*. London: Francis Pinter/Policy Studies Institute.

David, F. R. (1989) How companies define their mission, *Long Range Planning*, 22(1), 90–7.

Deaton, D. (1985) Management style and large-scale survey evidence, *Industrial Relations Journal*, 16, Summer, 67–71.

Deci, E. L. (1975) *Intrinsic Motivation*. New York: Plenum Press.

Deming, W. E. (1986) *Out of the crisis: Quality, Production and Competitive Position*. Cambridge: Cambridge University Press.

Department of Employment (1968) *Company Manpower Planning*. London: HMSO.

Department of Employment (1989) *People and Companies: Employee Involvement in Britain*. London: HMSO.

Department of Employment (1990) *Training Statistics*. London: HMSO.

Department of Employment (1991) *Industrial Relations in the 1990s*. Proposals for further reform of industrial relations and trade union law, Cm 1602. London: HMSO.

Donovan Report (1968) *Royal Commission on Trade Unions and Employers' Associations*, Cmnd 3623. London: HMSO.

Drennan, D. (1988) Down the organization, *Management Today*, June, 129–37.

Dunlop, J. T. (1958) *Industrial Relations Systems*. New York: Holt.

Dyer, L. (1983) Bringing human resources into the strategy formulation process, *Human Resource Management*, 22(3), 257–71.

Dyer, L. (1985) Strategic human resource management and planning, in K. M. Rowland and G. R. Ferris (eds) *Research in Personnel and Human Resource Management*. Greenwich, CT: JAI Press.

Edwards, P., Hall, M., Hyman, R. et al. (1992) *Great Britain*, in A. Ferner and R. Hyman (eds), *Industrial Relations in the New Europe*. Oxford: Blackwell.

Elger, T. (1991) Task flexibility and the intensification of labour in UK manufacturing in the 1980s, *Farewell to Flexibility*, ed. A. Pollert. Oxford: Blackwell.

Feldman, S. P. (1988) Management in context: an essay on the relevance of culture to the understanding of organizational change, *Journal of Management Studies*, 23, 587–607.

Ferner, A. and Hyman, R. (1992) Industrial relations in the new Europe, in A. Ferner and R. Hyman (eds), *Industrial Relations in the New Europe*. Oxford: Blackwell.

Finegold, D. and Soskice, D. (1988) The failure of training in Britain: analysis and prescription, *Oxford Review of Economic Policy*, 4(3), 21–53.

Flamholz, E. (1974) *Human Resource Accounting*. Encino, CA: Dickenson.

Flanders, A. (1970a) *Management and Unions: The Theory and Reform of Industrial Relations*. London: Faber.

Flanders, A. (1970b) Industrial relations: what is wrong with the system? *Management and Unions*, 83–128.

Flanders, A. (1970c) Collective bargaining: prescription for change, *Management and Unions*, 155–211.

Fletcher, C. and Williams, R. (1992a) The route to performance management, *Personnel Management*, October, 42–7.

Fletcher, C. and Williams, R. (1992b) Organizational experience in Institute of Personnel Management. *Performance Management: An Analysis of the Issues*. London: Institute of Personnel Management.

Fombrun, C. J., Tichy, N. M. and Devanna, M. A. (1984) *Strategic Human Resource Management*. New York: Wiley.

Foulkes, F. K. (1980) *Personnel Policies in Large non-union Companies*. Englewood Cliffs, NJ: Prentice Hall.

Fowler, A. (1990) Performance management: the MBO of the '90s? *Personnel Management*, July, 47–51.

Fox, A. (1974) *Beyond Contract: Work, Power and Trust Relations*. London: Faber.

Freeman, R. B. and Medoff, J. L. (1984) *What Do Unions Do?* New York: Basic Books.

Galbraith, J. and Nathanson, D. (1978) *Strategic implementation: The Role of Structure and Process*. St Paul, MN: West Publishing.

Geary, J. (1993) Team working: employee participation enabled or constrained. *Personnel Management in Britain* (2nd edn, ed. K. Sisson). Oxford: Blackwell.

Giles, W. J. and Robinson, D. F. (1972) *Human Asset Accounting*.

London: Institute of Personnel Management and Institute of Cost and Management Accounting.

GMB/UCW (1991) *A New Agenda: Bargaining for Prosperity in the 1990s*, London: GMB and UCW.

Golden, K. and Ramanujam, V. (1985) Between a dream and a nightmare: on the integration of the human resource management and the strategic business planning process, *Human Resource Management*, 24, 429–52.

Goold, M. and Campbell, A. (1987) *Strategies and Styles: The Role of the Centre in Managing Diversified Corporations*. Oxford: Blackwell.

Griffiths, W. (1989) Fees for house work: the personnel department as consultancy, *Personnel Management*, January, 36–9.

Guest, D. (1987) Human resource management and industrial relations, *Journal of Management Studies*, 24(5), 503–21.

Guest, D. (1989) Human resource management: its implications for industrial relations and trade unions, in J. Storey (ed.), *New Perspectives on Human Resource Management*. London: Routledge.

Guest, D. (1990) Human resource management and the American Dream, *Journal of Management Studies*, 27(4), 377–97.

Guest, D. (1992) Right enough to be dangerously wrong: an analysis of the *In Search of Excellence* phenomenon, in G. Salaman (ed.), *Human Resource Strategies*. London: Sage.

Gunn, T. (1990) World class manufacturing, *Executive Excellence*, 7(3), 8–9.

Hackman, J. R., Oldham, G., Janson, R. and Purdy, K. (1975) A new strategy for job enrichment, *California Management Review*, 17(4), 57–71.

Hampden-Turner, C. (1990) *Corporate Culture: From Vicious to Virtuous Circles*. London: Hutchinson.

Hamper, B. (1992) *Rivethead: Tales from the Assembly Line*. New York: Fourth Estate.

Harris, P. R. and Harris, D. L. (1989) High performance team management, *Leadership and Development Journal*, 10(4), 28–33.

Helsby, G. (1989) Central control and grassroots creativity: the paradox at the heart of TVEI. *Education and Training UK*. Newbury: Policy Journals.

Hendry, C. (1990) The corporate management of human resources under conditions of decentralisation, *British Journal of Management*, 1(2), 91–103.

Herzberg, F. (1966) *Work and the Nature of Man*. Cleveland, OH: World Publishing.

Hill, C. and Pickering, J. (1986) Divisionalisation, decentralisation and performance of large UK companies, *Journal of Management Studies*, 23(1), 26–50.

Hill, S. (1991) Why quality circles failed but TQM might succeed, *British Journal of Industrial Relations*, 29(4), 541–69.

Holberton, S. (1991) How to help yourself to a competitor's best practices, *Financial Times*, 24 June 1992, 24.

Holden, L. and Livian, Y. (1992) Does strategic training policy exist? Some evidence from ten European countries, *Personnel Review*, 21(1), 12–23.

Holdsworth, R. (1992) Appraisal, in F. Neale (ed.), *The Handbook of Performance Management*. London: Institute of Personnel Management.

Hougham, J., Thomas, J. and Sisson, K. (1991) Ford's EDAP scheme, *Human Resource Management Journal*, 1(3) 77–91.

Howard, R. (1990) Values make the company: an interview with Robert Haas, *Harvard Business Review*, 68(5), 132–44.

Humble, J. (1988) How to improve the personnel service, *Personnel Management*, February, 30–3.

Hyman, J. (1992) *Training at Work*. London: Routledge.

IFF Research Ltd (1991) *Total Quality Management*. London: IFF.

Incomes Data Services (IDS) (1989) *Retraining*, Study No. 405. London: IDS.

Incomes Data Services (IDS) (1991) *Performance Pay*. London: IDS.

Industrial Relations Review and Report (IRRR) (1989a) *Developments in Multi-Employer Bargaining: 1*, Report 440, May, 6–11.

Industrial Relations Review and Report (IRRR) (1989b) *Single Union Deals*, Report 442, June, 5–11.

Industrial Relations Review and Report (IRRR) (1989c) *Decentralised Bargaining in Practice: 1*, Report 454, December.

Industrial Relations Review and Report (IRRR) (1989d) *Multi-Skilling – Linking Pay to Skill Acquisition*, November.

Industrial Relations Review and Report (IRRR) (1990) *Decentralised Bargaining in Practice: 2*, Report 457, February, 13–14.

Industrial Relations Review and Report (IRRR) (1991a) *Long-Term Earnings Trends (1971–91)*, Report 500, November.

Industrial Relations Review and Report (IRRR) (1991b) *Annualised Hours: The Concept of the Flexible Year*, Report No. 488, 4–8.

Institute of Personnel Management (IPM) (1992) *Performance Management in the UK: An Analysis of the Issues*. London: IPM.

Involvement and Participation Association (IPA) (1992) *Towards Industrial Partnership: A New Approach to Management Union Relations. A Consultative Document*. London: IPA.

Ishikawa, K. (1985) *What is Total Quality Control? The Japanese Way*. Englewood Cliffs, NJ: Prentice Hall.

James, G. (1992) Quality of working life and TQM, *International Journal of Manpower*, 13(1), 41–59.

Johnson, G. (1987) *Strategic Change and the Management Process*. Oxford: Blackwell.

Johnson, G. (1990) Managing strategic change: the role of symbolic action, *British Journal of Management*, 1(4), 30–42.

Johnson, J. (1992) New mission statement creates unity for health care system, *Trustee*, 45(2), 11–15.

Johnson, P. (1992) Population ageing and employment policies, in K. Bradley (ed.), *Human Resource Management: People and Performance*. Aldershot: Dartmouth.

Jones, B. (1991) Technological convergence and the limits to management control: flexible manufacturing systems in Britain, the USA and Japan, in S. Tolliday and J. Zeitlin (eds), *The Power to Manage: Employers and Industrial Relations in Comparative-Historical Perspective*. London: Routledge.

Juran, J. (1988) *Juran on Planning for Quality*. New York: Free Press.

Kanter, R. M. (1984) *The Change Masters*. London: Allen and Unwin.

Kanter, R. M. (1990) *When Giants Learn to Dance: Mastering the Challenges of Strategy, Management and Careers in the 1990s*. London: Unwin Paperbacks.

Keenoy, T. (1990) HRM: a case of the wolf in sheep's clothing? *Personnel Review*, 19(2), 3–9.

Keep, E. (1989) Corporate training strategies: the vital component? In J. Storey (ed.), *New Perspectives on Human Resource Management*. London: Routledge.

Keep, E. (1992) *Missing: Presumed Skilled – Training Policy in the UK*. Coventry: University of Warwick, Industrial Relations Research Unit, mimeo.

Kessler, I. (1993) Performance pay, in K. Sisson (ed.), *Personnel Management in Britain* (2nd edn, forthcoming). Oxford: Blackwell.

Kessler, I. and Purcell, J. (1992) Performance pay: objectives and application, *Human Resource Management Journal*, 2(3), Spring, 16–33.

Kessler, S. (1987) The swings and roundabouts of pendulum arbitration, *Personnel Management*, December, 38–42.

Kessler, S. and Bayliss, F. (1992) *Contemporary British Industrial Relations*. Basingstoke: Macmillan.

Kinnie, N. (1985a) Local managers control over industrial relations: myth and reality, *Personnel Review*, 14(4), 2–10.

Kinnie, N. (1985b) Changing management strategies in industrial relations. *Industrial Relations Journal*, 16(4), 17–24.

Kirrane, D. (1990) Managing values: a systematic approach to business ethics, *Training and Development Journal*, 44(11), 52–60.

Klemm, M., Sanderson, S. and Luffman, G. (1991) Mission statements: selling corporate values to employees, *Long Range Planning*, 24(3), 73–8.

Kochan, T. A. and Barocci, T. (1985) *Human Resource Management and Industrial Relations: Text, Readings and Cases*. Boston: Little Brown.

Kochan, T. and Barocci, T. (eds) (1985) *Human Resource Management and Industrial Relations* Boston: Little Brown.

Kochan, T. and Dyer, L. (1992) *Managing Transformational Change: The Role of Human Resource Professionals*. Paper for the Conference of the International Industrial Relations Association, Sydney.

Kochan, T. A., Katz, H. C. and McKersie, R. B. (1986) *The Transformation of American Industrial Relations*. New York: Basic Books.

Kochan, T. A., Katz, H. C. and McKersie, R. G. (1990) *Strategic Choice and Industrial Relations Theory: An Elaboration*. Paper presented to Second Bargaining Group Conference, Cornell University, 6–7 May.

Krafcik, J. (1990) *Training and the Automobile Industry: International Comparisons*. Washington, DC: Office of Technology Assessment.

Lammers, C. J. (1967) Power and participation in decision-making in formal organizations, *American Journal of Sociology*, 73(2), 200–24.

Lane, C. (1990) Vocational training, employment relations and new production concepts in Germany: some lessons for Britain, *Industrial Relations Journal*, 21(4), Winter, 247–59.

Lawler, E. E. and Mohrman, S. A. (1985) Quality circles after the fad, *Harvard Business Review*, January–February, 65–71.

Lawrence, P. R. and Lorsch, J. W. (1967) *Organization and Environment: Managing Differentiation and Integration*. Boston: Harvard University Press.

Leadbeater, C. (1989) Dilemma of giving teams their due, *Financial Times*, 5 June, 5.

Legge, K. (forthcoming) *From Personnel Management to Human Resource Management*. London: Macmillan.

Lengnick-Hall, C. A. and Lengnick-Hall, M. L. (1988) Strategic human resources management: a review of the literature and a proposed typology, *Academy of Management Review*, 13(3), 454–70.

Lewin, K. (1951) *Field Theory in Social Science*. New York: Harper and Row.

Lewin, K. (1958) Group decision and social change, in E. E. Maccoby et al. (eds), *Readings in Social Psychology*. New York: Holt, Rinehart and Winston.

Lewis, R. (1988) *Strike-free Procedures: Are They What They Seem?* Warwick Papers in Industrial Relations, No. 20. Coventry: Industrial Relations Research Unit.

Lippitt, R., Watson, J. and Westley, B. (1958) *The Dynamics of Planned Change*. New York: Harcourt Brace.

Liverpool, P. R. (1991) Employee participation in decision making, *Journal of Business and Psychology*, 4(4), 411–22.

# Bibliography

Long, P. (1986) *Performance Appraisal Revisited*. London: Institute of Personnel Management.

Lupton, T. and Gowler, D. (1969) *Selecting a Wage Payment System*, Research Paper 111. London: Engineering Employers' Federation.

MacInnes, J. (1987) *Thatcherism at Work*. Milton Keynes: Open University Press.

Manpower Services Commission/National Economic Development Office (1987) *People: The Key to Success*. London: NEDO.

Marchington, M. (1993) The dynamics of joint consultation, in K. Sisson (ed.), *Personnel Management in Britain* (2nd edn). Oxford: Blackwell.

Marchington, M., Goodman, J., Wilkinson, A. and Ackers, P. (1992) *New Developments in Employee Involvement*. Employment Department Research Series, No. 2.

Margerison, C. and Kakabadse, A. (1985) What management development means for CEOs, *Journal of Management Development*, 4(5), 11–19.

Marginson, P. and Sisson, K. (1990) Single table talk, *Personnel Management*, May, 46–9.

Marginson, P., Edwards, P. K., Martin, R. et al. (1988) *Beyond the Workplace: Managing Industrial Relations in Multi-Establishment Enterprises*. Oxford: Blackwell.

Marsden, D. and Thompson, M. (1990) Flexibility agreements and their significance in the increase in productivity in British manufacturing since 1980, *Work, Employment and Society*, 4(1), 83–104.

Martinez Lucio, M. and Weston, S. (1992) The politics and complexity of trade union responses to new management practices, *Human Resource Management Journal*, 2(4), Summer, 77–91.

Mayo, A. (1991) *Managing Careers: Strategies for Organisations*. London: Institute of Personnel Management.

McCarthy, W. E. J. (1976) *Making Whitley Work*. London: DHSS.

McCarthy, W. E. J. and Ellis, N. (1973) *Management by Agreement: An Alternative to the Industrial Relations Act*. London: Hutchinson.

McKinsey & Co/NEDO (1988) *Performance and Competitive Success: Strengthening Competitiveness in UK Electronics*. A report prepared by McKinsey & Co, London: National Economic Development Office.

Miles, R. and Snow, C. C. (1978) *Organizational Strategy, Structure and Process*. New York: McGraw-Hill.

Miles, R. and Snow, C. (1984) Designing strategic human resource systems, *Organizational Dynamics*, Summer, 36–52.

Miller, P. (1987) Strategic industrial relations and human resource management: distinction, definition and recognition, *Journal of Management Studies*, 24(4), 347–61.

Miller, P. (1989) Strategic HRM: what it is and what it is not, *Personnel Management*, February, 46–51.

263

Mills, D. Q. (1985) Planning with people in mind, *Harvard Business Review*, July–August, 97–105.

Millward, N. and Stevens, M. (1986) *British Workplace Industrial Relations*. Gower: Aldershot.

Millward, N., Stevens, M., Smart, D. and Hawes, W. R. (1992) *Workplace Industrial Relations in Transition*. Aldershot: Dartmouth.

Mintzberg, H. (1978) Patterns in strategy formation, *Management Science*, xxiv, 9, 934–48.

Mintzberg, H. (1979) *The Structuring of Organizations*. Englewood Cliffs, NJ: Prentice-Hall.

Mintzberg, H. (1987) The strategy concept – Parts I and II, *California Management Review*, 29(3) 1–22.

Mintzberg, H. (1988) Crafting strategy, *The McKinsey Quarterly*, Summer, 71–89.

Morris, T. and Wood, S. (1991) Testing the survey method: continuity and change in British industrial relations, *Work, Employment and Society*, 5(2), 259–82.

Morrisey, G. L. (1988) Who needs a mission statement? You do, *Training and Development Journal*, 42(3), 50–2.

Mortimer, K. (1990) EDAP at Ford: a research note, *Industrial Relations Journal*, 21(4), 309–14.

Müller, F. (1991) A new engine of change in personnel management, *Personnel Management*, July: 30–4.

Mumford, A., Honey, P. and Robinson, G. (1989) *A Guidebook: Developing Directors Using Experience*. London: Institute of Directors.

National Board for Prices and Incomes (NBPI) (1968a) *Payment By Results Systems*. Report No. 65. London: HMSO.

National Board for Prices and Incomes (1968b) *Job Evaluation*. Report No. 83. London: HMSO.

National Economic Development Office (NEDO) (1986) *Changing Working Patterns: How Companies Achieve Flexibility to Meet New Needs*. London: NEDO.

National Economic Development Office (NEDO) (1988) *Performance and competitive success*. A report prepared for the electronic industry sector committee by McKinsey and Co. Inc., London: NEDO.

Neale, F. (1991) *The Handbook of Performance Management*. London: Institute of Personnel Management.

Nolan, P. (1989) The productivity miracle? In F. Green (ed.), *The Restructuring of the UK Economy*. Hemel Hempstead: Harvester Wheatsheaf.

Oakland, J. (1989) *Total Quality Management*. London: Heinemann.

O'Connor, D. (1990) Trouble in the American workplace – the team player concept, *Records Management Quarterly*, 24(2), 12–16.

O'Dell, C. (1989) Team play, team pay, *Across the Board*, 26(11), 38–46.

# Bibliography

Organisation for Economic Cooperation and Development (OECD) (1990) *OECD Economic Surveys: United Kingdom*. Paris: OECD.

Pearce, J. and David, F. (1987) Corporate mission statements: the bottom line, *Academy of Management Executive*, 1(2), 109–15.

Pedler, J., Burgoyne, J. and Boydell, T. (1991) *The Learning Company*. London: McGraw-Hill.

Peters, T. J. and Waterman, R. H. (1983) *In Search of Excellence: Lessons from America's Best Run Companies*. New York: Harper and Row.

Pettigrew, A. (1977) Strategy formulation as a political process, *International Studies of Management and Organization*, vii(2), 78–87.

Pettigrew, A. (1985) *The Awakening Giant*. Oxford: Blackwell.

Pollert, A. (1988) The flexible firm: a model in search of reality or a policy in search of practice? *Warwick Papers in Industrial Relations*, No. 19. Coventry: University of Warwick.

Porter, M. (1980) *Competitive Strategy: Techniques for Analysing Industries and Competitors*. New York: Free Press.

Porter, M. (1985) *Competitive Advantage: Creating and Sustaining Superior Performance*. New York: Free Press.

Prais, S. (1990) *Productivity, Education and Training*. London: National Institute for Social and Economic Research.

Prais, S. J. and Wagner, K. (1988) Some practical aspects of human capital investment: training standards in five occupations in Britain and Germany, *National Institute Economic Review*, November.

Price, E. and Price, R. J. (1993) The decline and fall of the status divide, in K. Sisson (ed.), *Personnel Management in Britain* (2nd edn). Oxford: Blackwell.

Purcell, J. (1981) *Good Industrial Relations: Theory and Practice*. Macmillan: London.

Purcell, J. (1989) The impact of corporate strategy on human resource management, in J. Storey (ed.), *New Perspectives on Human Resource Management*. London: Routledge.

Purcell, J. and Ahlstrand, B. (1993) *Strategy and Style in Employee Relations*. Oxford: Oxford University Press.

Purcell, J. and Sisson, K. (1983) Strategies and practice in the management of industrial relations, in G. Bain (ed.), *Industrial Relations in Britain*. Oxford: Blackwell.

Quinn, J. B. (1980) *Strategies for Change: Logical Incrementalism*. Homewood, IL: Irwin.

Rainbird, H. (1993) Continuing training, in K. Sisson (ed.), *Personnel Management in Britain* (2nd edn). Oxford: Blackwell.

Ray, G. F. (1987) Labour costs in manufacturing, *National Institute Economic Review*, 120, May.

Ray, G. F. (1990) International labour costs in manufacturing 1960–88, *National Institute Economic Review*, 132, May.

Reader, W. J. (1973) *The First Quarter Century, 1926–1952. Imperial Chemical Industries: A History*, Vol. 2. Oxford: Oxford University Press.

Recruitment and Development Report (RDR) (1991) New ways of managing human resources, *Recruitment and Development Report*, 15, March, 6–16.

Reyes, J. R. and Kleiner, B. H. (1990) How to establish an organizational purpose, *Management Decision*, 28(7), 51–4.

Riley, T. (1992) *Motivating and Rewarding Employees: Some Aspects of Theory and Practice*. London: Work Research Unit, ACAS.

Rogaly, J. (1977) *Grunwick*. Harmondsworth: Penguin.

Rowland, K. M. and Summers, S. L. (1981) Human resource planning: a second look, *Personnel Administrator*, December, 73–80.

Sadler, P. (1989) Management development, in K. Sisson (ed.), *Personnel Management in Britain*. Oxford: Blackwell.

Schein, E. (1984) Coming to a new awareness of organizational culture, *Sloan Management Review*, 25(2), 3–16.

Schein, E. (1986) *Organizational Culture and Leadership*. San Francisco: Jossey Bass.

Schonberger, R. J. (1986) *World Class Manufacturing: The Lessons of Simplicity Applied*. Free Press: New York.

Schuler, R. S. (1988) Human resource management practice choices, in R. S. Schuler, S. A. Yaugblood and V. L. Huber (eds), *Readings in Management*, 3rd edn. St Paul, MN: West Publishing.

Schuler, R. S. and Jackson, S. (1987) Linking competitive strategies with human resource management practices, *Academy of Management Executive*, 1(3), 209–13.

Scott, C. D. and Jaffe, D. (1989) *Managing Organizational Change*. London: Kogan Page.

Sheard, A. (1992) Learning to improve performance, *Personnel Management*, November, 40–5.

Simpson, E. and McConocha, D. (1991) Making the organizational mission statement work for the supervisor, *Supervision*, 52(3), 9–11.

Sisson, K. (1987) *The Management of Collective Bargaining: An International Comparison*. Oxford: Blackwell.

Sisson, K. (1989) Personnel management in transition? In K. Sisson (ed.), *Personnel Management in Britain*. Oxford: Blackwell.

Sisson, K. and Scullion, H. (1985) Putting the corporate personnel department in its place, *Personnel Management*, December, 15–19.

Sisson, K., Waddington, J. and Whitston, C. (1992) *The Structure of Capital in the European Community: The Size of Companies and the*

*Implications for Industrial Relations*. Warwick Papers in Industrial Relations, No. 38. Coventry: Industrial Relations Research Unit.

Smith, D. (1986) Organizational culture and management development in building societies, *Personnel Review*, 15(3), 15–19.

Smith, D. (1987) Culture and management development in building societies, *Personnel Review*, UK, 15(3), 15.

Smith, P. E. (1986) Privatisation and cultural change, *The Journal of Management Development*, 5(2), 51–5.

Smythe Dorward Lambert (1991) *The Power of the Open Company*. London: Smythe Dorward Lambert.

Steedman, H. and Wagner, K. (1987) A second look at productivity, machinery and skills in Britain and Germany, *National Institute Economic Review*, November, 5–9.

Stemp, P. (1987) Improving management effectiveness, *Management Education and Development*, 18(3), 175–82.

Stevens, C. M. (1966) Is compulsory arbitration compatible with bargaining? *Industrial Relations*, 5(2), February.

Storey, J. (1987) *Developments in Human Resource Management: An Interim Report*. Warwick Papers in Industrial Relations, No. 17. Coventry: Industrial Relations Research Unit.

Storey, J. (1992) *Developments in the Management of Human Resources*. Oxford: Blackwell.

Storey, J. (1993) *The Take-Up of New Management Practices: A Leicestershire Survey*. Loughborough University Business School and Leicestershire Training and Enterprise Council.

Storey, J. and Sisson, K. (1989) Looking to the future, in J. Storey (ed.), *New Perspectives on Human Resource Management*. London: Routledge.

Storey, J. and Sisson, K. (1990) Limits to transformation: human resource management in the British context, *Industrial Relations Journal*, 21, Spring, 60–5.

Storey, J., Okazaki-Ward, L., Gow, I. et al. (1991) Managerial careers and management development: a comparative analysis of Britain and Japan, *Human Resource Management Journal*, 1(3), 33–58.

Streeck, W. (1985) Industrial relations and industrial change in the motor industry: an international view. Public Lecture. University of Warwick, Coventry: Industrial Relations Research Unit.

TGWU/GMB (1992) *Training for Britain's Economic Success*, a Joint statement of interest by Bill Morris and John Edmonds. London: Transport and General Workers Union and GMB.

Thackway, J. (1984) Educating for a commercial railway, *Management Education and Development*, 15(3), 10–14.

Thomas, M. (1990) What is a human resources strategy? *Employee Relations*, 12(3), 12–16.

Thompson, M. (1992) *Pay and Performance: The Employer Experience*. IMS Report 218. Falmer, Brighton: Institute of Manpower Studies.

Torrington, D. and Hall, L. (1991) *Personnel Management: A New Approach*. London: Prentice-Hall.

Training Agency (1989) *Training in Britain*. London: HMSO.

Trevor, M. (1988) *Toshiba's New British Company: Competitiveness Through Innovation in Industry*. London: Policy Studies Institute.

Walker, J. W. (1992) *Human Resource Strategy*. New York: McGraw-Hill.

Watson, T. (1989) Recruitment and selection, in K. Sisson (ed.), *Personnel Management in Britain*. Oxford: Blackwell.

Wellins, R. and George, J. (1991) The key to self-directed teams, *Training and Development Journal*, 45(4) 26–32.

West Midlands Regional Health Authority (1990) *Developing a Human Resource Strategy*. Birmingham: West Midlands Regional Health Authority.

Whittington, R. (1989) *Corporate Strategies in Recession and Recovery: Social Structure and Strategic Choice*. London: Unwin Hyman.

Whittington, R. (1993) *What is Strategy and Does it Matter?* London: Routledge.

Wickens, P. (1987) *The Road to Nissan: Flexibility, Quality, Teamwork*. London: Macmillan.

Wilkinson, A., Allen, P. and Snape, E. (1991) TQM and the management of labour, *Employee Relations*, 13(1), 24–31.

Wilkinson, A., Marchington, M., Goodman, J. and Ackers, P. (1992) Total quality management and employee involvement, *Human Resource Management Journal*, 2(4), 1–20.

Williams, A., Dobson, P. and Walters, W. (1990) *Changing Culture: New Organizational Approaches*. London: Institute of Personnel Management.

Williams, S. (1992) Strategy and objectives, in F. Neale (ed.), *The Handbook of Performance Management*. London: Institute of Personnel Management.

Wilson, D. C. (1992) *A Strategy of Change*. London: Routledge.

Witcher, B. and Wilkinson, A. (1990) *Total Quality Management in the United Kingdom*, Occasional Papers, No. 9072. Durham: Durham University Business School.

Zairi, M. (1992) *Competitive Benchmarking*. Bradford: Technical Communications Publishing.

# INDEX